"I've made a terrible mistake." So confessed Joy Sharp, a longtime budget director for the University of Arkansas. Trembling and unsteady, she informed her boss that she had lost control of their division's finances.

It was an understatement. University leaders would soon discover that Sharp had routinely spent millions of dollars beyond what was available, shifting money from one account to another in what the university's treasurer described as an attempt to "mask" her actions. In a private email, University Chancellor G. David Gearhart bemoaned that Sharp's actions had created "a colossal fiscal crisis." It was a hard admission; ten years earlier, Gearhart himself had promoted Sharp, his former aide, to the budget management position.

Most leaders would have responded to the disclosure by immediately commissioning a thorough audit and review of Sharp's actions. After all, it was possible that fraud occurred and that others were complicit. If nothing else, an audit would demonstrate the university's commitment to transparency and accountability, which happened to be the title of the school's strategic plan.

But instead, Gearhart and other university officials quietly engaged in a disturbing series of panic-fueled leadership decisions. The result was a slow-burning scandal, one that involved attempts to deceive investigators, hide and destroy records and silence witnesses. Those actions soon proved more costly to the university's reputation and credibility than the unchecked spending that created the deficit.

As the university's chief media relations officer, PLEASE DELETE author John Diamond was present when some of the most unsettling leadership decisions were made. After objecting to his bosses' actions, Diamond was abruptly fired—by text message. Weeks later, called to testify under oath at a state inquiry, he told of his superiors' release of a white-washed version of an internal review; their misleading responses to investigative auditors and news reporters; document shredding; and a pivotal meeting at which Gearhart angrily directed staffers to "get rid of" a troublesome budget document containing information reporters had sought under Arkansas's public records law.

PLEASE DELETE provides a case study of how a large institution, its powerful leaders and their well-placed allies responded to a crisis, and in the process, inflamed it. Diamond relies on thousands of pages of email, transcripts, financial records and first-hand accounts to complete a puzzle that investigative reporters, state auditors and prosecutors couldn't—or wouldn't—finish. PLEASE DELETE is a cautionary tale, one that reveals the damage, distrust and victimization that often result when public officials try to conceal their transgressions.

PLEASE DELETE

HOW LEADERSHIP HUBRIS IGNITED A SCANDAL AND TARNISHED A UNIVERSITY

JOHN DIAMOND

Publisher: John Diamond Books, Woolwich, ME
Cover and Interior Design: Presson Design Associates, Carrollton, TX
Publishing Consultant: Jane Friedman (Jane Friedman Media)
Senior Editor: Andrea Cumbo-Floyd
Editor: Jane D. Littlefield
Creative Consultants: Jimmy Gownley; Elizabeth Sutherland; Devon McNerney
Digital Media: Sutherland Weston Marketing Communications, Bangor, ME
Video Production: Ron Lisnet
Photography: Arkansas Democrat-Gazette, Little Rock, AR (reproduced with permission); Jeff Kirlin; Barbara Owen
Gratitude is offered and acknowledged to publishing advisers
Judith Briles (The Book Shepherd) and Joel Friedlander (The Book Designer).

ISBN: 978-0-9965531-0-0 (Hardcover)
978-0-9965531-2-4 (Softcover)
978-0-9965531-1-7 (Digital)

Library of Congress Control Number: 2015915671
1. Leadership 2. Public Relations 3. Journalism 4. Management
5. Higher Education 6. Ethics

First Edition

Diamond, John Nathan, 1954 –
1. PLEASE DELETE:
How Leadership Hubris Ignited a Scandal and Tarnished a University

www.JohnDiamondBooks.com

PLEASE DELETE

HOW LEADERSHIP HUBRIS IGNITED A SCANDAL AND TARNISHED A UNIVERSITY

JOHN DIAMOND

PLEASE DELETE

TABLE OF CONTENTS

AUTHOR'S NOTE

PLEASE DELETE: How Leadership Hubris Ignited a Scandal and Tarnished a University relies on a variety of sources to relate how and why the University of Arkansas scandal occurred. In writing the book, I depended on audio and video recordings of meetings and hearings, conversations with affected individuals with direct knowledge of relevant details, media reports and commentaries, and thousands of pages of email and documents that were provided to me or were obtained through Arkansas' Freedom of Information Act. Much of the dialogue is based on transcripts of events; as a result, statements and questions may not read as smoothly as they might have, had they been scripted. In other instances, dialogue is reconstructed based on my own recollection and notes as well as on conversations related to me by one or more participants or witnesses. When using transcripts and recordings to quote a character, I have not included that person's unrelated side comments unless they are necessary to convey the speaker's state of mind, reaction, or point of view. Similarly, I have included a character's pauses and fillers (e.g., "um" and "uh") only if they are important to understanding the person or the situation. In all cases, I have made every effort to replicate and represent events and dialogue in the most accurate manner and context possible.

John Diamond
June 1, 2015

To Marcia

PLEASE DELETE

Hubris (noun): *excessive self-confidence, exaggerated self-belief, and contempt for the advice and criticism of others.*

—Daedalus Trust

Prologue

LITTLE ROCK, SEPTEMBER 13, 2013

Chairman Hammer, Chairman King, and members of the committee, thank you for the request to join you today. My name is John Diamond, and I reside in Fayetteville.

Until recently, I was the University of Arkansas' associate vice chancellor for University Relations. In that role, I had responsibility for one of the three major units of the UA's Division of University Advancement. As associate vice chancellor, one of my duties was to be the principal coordinator of media requests for public documents, usually submitted in the form of a formal request under Arkansas' Freedom of Information Act, or FOIA. As I understand it, the committee's decision to ask me to testify was to get my perspective on the investigative audits before you today. I appreciate the opportunity to answer your questions and to offer these introductory remarks.

First, allow me to give credit to the state and university auditors for the work product they released earlier this week. You should know that in the months leading up to the audits' release, there was considerable skepticism within the Advancement division and on campus about what the audits would report. Many people suspected that the reports would whitewash the events and culpability that contributed to the Advancement division's overspending. Clearly, that was not the case.

However, the report does note elements of the auditors' work that could not be completed as thoroughly as investigators had hoped. That's in part because of the lack of documentation available to help complete the review. There are also questions regarding how the Advancement division operated and monitored and managed its finances.

I believe I can help address some of those gaps, based both on my role as an officer within the Division and on my familiarity with the way the university has handled documents of value or interest to auditors and to the media.

The issues I will address in my opening remarks focus on areas that are relevant to the audit investigation and reports. The points I will make can be corroborated by witnesses and/or documentation. I will address these topics briefly and will elaborate on them further during the question and answer session, should the committee so desire. The main points I have to share are these:

- A key document cited by the university and in the audit reports—the October 19, 2012 analysis of Advancement by University Treasurer Jean Schook—is of questionable credibility and value in that none of the associate vice chancellors or unit managers within the Division was ever interviewed as part of that review. When the existence of the Schook memo became known, members of the Division's leadership team questioned why we had not been interviewed, given our level of involvement with the programs, processes, and individuals being reviewed. These concerns grew as others outside of the Division publicly spoke of the thoroughness with which Ms. Schook reportedly conducted the review.
- The reports provide an incomplete depiction of the role played by Joy Sharp, the Advancement division's long-time budget director until September 2012. It assigns her the blame for the disappearance of certain valuable documents such as payment authorizations

related to Advancement's expenditures. However, many of those documents did indeed exist after Ms. Sharp left the Division and were in the Division's possession until immediately after the request for these audits was issued in February. The report also fails to address Ms. Sharp's role in co-managing, and apparently co-mingling, revenues and expenditures related to the vice chancellor for Advancement's Office and to discretionary accounts controlled by the chancellor. In other words, both Vice Chancellor Brad Choate and Chancellor G. David Gearhart had reasons—and the authority—to have Ms. Sharp make expenditures upon their requests. Those within the Division who understood this in retrospect view the expectations placed on Ms. Sharp, and co-mingling of funds, as a contributing factor to the Division's deficit.

- The auditors and members of the public would have had a more complete understanding of the Advancement situation had it not been for a culture of secrecy that developed and grew as the Advancement deficit was realized. In addition to diverging from what had been, until this year, a standard and effective practice of processing public document requests, members of the Advancement division leadership team and staff received directives from key individuals that resulted in the destruction of documents relevant to the audits and to FOIA requests. This occurred both before and after the February request for the audits. Those two reasons are, in part, why auditors could not find documents they sought, and that's why so few responsive documents were given to the media during the past several months.

As I stated at the beginning of these remarks, there are witnesses who can verify the information I share today, and there are documents available that shed light on the actions and behaviors I just described. Again, I thank you for the request to share my perspective on the audit reports. I will now respond to your questions and elaborate further on the abovementioned three points.

2012-13 ORGANIZATIONAL CHART (PARTIAL)

UA System Board of Trustees

UA System President
Don Bobbitt

UA (Fayetteville)
G. David Gearhart, Chancellor

Finance & Administration
Don Pederson, Vice Chancellor/CFO

Associate Vice Chancellor and Treasurer
Jean Schook

Director of Budget & Human Resources for Advancement
Denise Reynolds (beginning Sept. 2012)

Advancement
Brad Choate, Vice Chancellor (until Nov. 2012)

Chris Wyrick, Vice Chancellor (April 2013-present)

Associate Vice Chancellors
Bruce Pontious, Development (until Sept. 2013)
John Diamond, University Relations (until Sept. 2013)
Graham Stewart, Alumni Affairs (until Jan. 2014)

Director of Budget & Human Resources
Joy Sharp (until Sept. 2012)

Academic Affairs
Sharon Gaber, Provost & Vice Chancellor

Athletics
Jeff Long, Vice Chancellor/AD

Government Relations
Richard Hudson, Vice Chancellor

Chapter 1

FOREVER LINKED

Brad Choate and Joy Sharp were different in just about every way. Choate, the University of Arkansas' vice chancellor for University Advancement, was a sparkplug of a man. In his early fifties, his intensity for play belied his age. He was highly competitive, pursuing fundraising, SCUBA diving, and shoot-'em-up video games with equal passion. As a golfer with a single-digit handicap, he took no prisoners. He loved to entertain at his executive-style home on Fayetteville's east side. Unlike his wife Julie, for whom Sunday morning worship services were an important part of her week, Choate preferred the roar of his Harley-Davidson to that of a preacher.

"Work hard, play hard," he was fond of saying.

Choate knew he was good at his job and had the results to show it. He was nationally prominent in the field of university advancement, the sector of not-for-profit work that deals with fundraising ("development," in the vernacular) and other aspects of an organization's external relationships—activities such as alumni affairs, special events, communications and PR. He had spent 30 years in that field. Before moving to UA in 2008, he had been a senior fundraiser at

Ohio State, an associate vice president for Advancement at Penn State, president and CEO of the University of Minnesota Medical Foundation, and vice president for Advancement at the University of South Carolina.

By 2012, Choate was one of the most highly paid public university advancement leaders in the country. His compensation plan included a $348,000 salary as well as a leased car, country club membership, $50,000 annually in deferred compensation, and other health and retirement benefits. Considering he oversaw a fundraising operation that was bringing in more than $100 million a year, UA leaders viewed him as a good investment. He had a knack for putting together high-performing teams of professionals with complementary talents, and he delegated assignments effectively.

Joy Sharp operated in a much different world. She was Choate's director of Budget and Human Resources and a UA lifer; she joined the university's clerical staff right out of high school in 1973. Sharp earned her bachelor's and master's degrees at UA while simultaneously working full-time in a series of progressively responsible positions. In 2012, she was nearing 40 years of employment service to her *alma mater*. By all accounts, Sharp was as loyal to the university and as dedicated to her work as one possibly could be.

Hers was a big job, although in 2012 her $87,164 salary was below market compared to her responsibilities. Just about everything that occurred within Advancement reached Sharp at some point for review: job postings, personnel actions, purchasing requests, payment authorizations, meeting agendas, budget reports, and more. Of particular note was her work with the UA Foundation, a not-for-profit investment entity that existed to manage privately donated funds intended for the betterment of the university. Campus fundraisers often steered donations of money and property to the Foundation; in return, the Foundation provided millions of dollars each year to Advancement and other units of the university to help underwrite their operations and support their programs. Sharp served as the interface between Advancement and the Foundation, managing transactions and communications between the two.

Sharp was a devout Christian who maintained a modest lifestyle and a passion for NASCAR. She was a friendly woman with short brown hair, sparkly eyes, and a warm smile. Each day she commuted to the Fayetteville campus with her younger sister Betty, with whom she lived. Betty also worked in the Advancement division, serving as a mid-level manager in the fundraising office.

If colleagues had a criticism of Sharp, it was that she handled too many details herself. The Advancement division's day-to-day managers felt that the budget information she provided to them should be more detailed than what they actually received. Development officers—i.e., fundraisers who spend a lot of time on the road visiting donors and prospects—complained that it took much too long to get reimbursed for their out-of-pocket expenses. In response, Sharp apologetically blamed delays on the UA Foundation, which covered many of those reimbursements.

Choate and Sharp were brought together in 2008 by G. David Gearhart. At the time, Gearhart was making the transition from the role of UA's vice chancellor for University Advancement to chancellor—the institution's CEO. Choate had worked as a top deputy of Gearhart's when the latter was the fundraising vice president for Penn State during the early 1990s. Gearhart soon became Choate's mentor and *de facto* big brother. They and their wives became close friends and each other's extended family. Choate coached Gearhart's son in Little League baseball. The relationship continued after Gearhart left Penn State in 1995 for a consulting job and Choate left for the University of Minnesota position. After Gearhart returned to his native Fayetteville in 1998 to become UA's vice chancellor for Advancement, the Choates occasionally visited.

In 2008, UA System trustees named Gearhart their one and only candidate to succeed retiring Chancellor John A. White as head of the Fayetteville campus. Gearhart had become a folk hero on campus and in Arkansas. He had devised and led a phenomenally successful capital campaign, raising over $1 billion for the university. It was an unprecedented amount and, for a while, an unfathomable outcome. Now, as he prepared to assume UA's top leadership position, he wanted someone capable of similar performance to succeed him as vice chancellor. He recruited his protégé Choate—by then well situated as vice president for Advancement at the University of South Carolina. It would be a lateral move at best for Choate; within academic circles, South Carolina was considered a more prestigious university. But Gearhart was his friend and he relished the opportunity to reconnect and help him succeed. The university conducted a perfunctory search, consistent with its policies and practices. Choate was given the job, as he had expected. Reunited at UA, they soon created a remarkably strong and experienced fundraising team, one arguably as good as any other public university's. They began planning UA's next fundraising campaign, meeting regularly at the Gearhart family's Ozark Mountains getaway home, which friends referred to as "Camp David." The duo set a tentative goal: to raise at least another billion dollars and help elevate UA to elite status academically among the nation's public research universities.

Sharp was part of the team Choate inherited. Years earlier, Gearhart promoted Sharp, his assistant and former high school classmate, to be the Advancement division's budget director. It was an unconventional appointment, given her lack of formal training or education in financial management. But she was a quick study; Sharp learned on the job and had held the position ever since. In selling Choate on the idea of leaving his South Carolina position for UA, Gearhart praised Sharp as a tremendous resource. She understood the university's budget, knew how the division worked, had strong relationships on campus and with the UA Foundation, possessed a great institutional memory, and was tireless and loyal.

The university's chief financial officer, Don Pederson, echoed that assurance. When Choate told Pederson he wanted to relocate

Sharp's office from a building across the street to one adjacent to his own, Pederson praised the move as a smart idea.

Within two years, Choate augmented the Advancement team his predecessor left for him with a couple of key additions of his own. One was Bruce Pontious, an experienced higher education fundraising leader with a national reputation. Pontious, a longtime friend of Choate's, was a natural fit. One of his early successes was to repair a damaged relationship with a major donor whose interest in supporting UA had lessened because of a falling out with Gearhart. Pontious worked hard to mend fences, and it paid off: the donor regained his enthusiasm for helping UA financially and for advocating for it among his influential circle of friends.

I was Choate's other addition.

I never gave a thought to being a higher education leader until the day I was asked to be one. It was July 9, 1992, a few weeks away from the start of my fourth year on the University of Maine faculty.

"I'd like you to be my new public affairs director," Fred Hutchinson, the university's new president, told me. "Will you do it?"

As public affairs director, I would be the university's chief external relations officer. The job covered two areas I was experienced in: media relations and government relations. It also covered leadership and management of marketing, graphic design, the campus printing operation, and a couple of other administrative areas. Hutchinson said he would make me a member of his cabinet, the university's leadership team.

Initially, I said I wasn't interested; I liked teaching and wanted to complete my Ph.D. within a few years. But Hutchinson was persistent. He asked me to take a few days to think about it. Within a week, I accepted his offer.

I was diverting once again from my intended career path. I had always wanted to be a journalist. As a child in the early 1960s, that interest was fueled by my parents' passion for politics and current affairs. They were news junkies long before that condition and term came into vogue. It was something they passed along to me. I watched the evening news with them. I thumbed through *LIFE* and *LOOK* magazines each week when they arrived in the mail. I did my best to make sense of the headlines in the morning paper.

My parents, Nat and Eleanor, had been Big Band musicians; Mom was a singer and Dad a trumpet player. Both of them got their professional starts as teenagers. Even as the genre faded in mass popularity in favor of rock 'n' roll, they continued to perform together professionally into the mid-1960s. Through their musical careers, my parents gained a more informed perspective on discrimination and civil rights issues than what I would pick up by listening to other adults in my hometown of Bangor, Maine. To most of them, the societal events taking place in the Deep South were figuratively and literally far removed from what we in Maine experienced or could relate to.

During those formative years, 1963 stands out vividly. I was eight years old. I remember asking my parents why the policemen on the TV news were letting dogs bite the people standing around in Birmingham and why those people were being knocked down with fire hoses. I remember my mother explaining the reasons why the March on Washington was so important and necessary. I remember her tears as she tried to help me understand why someone had just killed the president, the man whose picture was taped up alongside those of John Glenn and Mickey Mantle on my bedroom wall.

Mom and Dad encouraged my interest in the news in other ways. Using my mother's typewriter and an old mimeograph machine that my father bought, I produced my own hometown newspaper, the "Bangor Bugle." As best as a kid could do, I wrote about important topics such as my friends' bicycles, the neighborhood dogs and cats, and sports. I also drew pictures to go along with my stories. One remaining copy depicts a sketch of Superman on the front page, speculating that he might someday visit Bangor. I was six years old when I produced that edition.

Fortunately, my writing and news judgment continued to mature as I did. I wrote for the school paper in junior high, high school, and college. I worked as a reporter and producer for the campus radio station while a student at the University of Maine. I also worked as a part-time reporter and announcer for Maine Public Radio, the state's NPR affiliate. A few weeks after graduating from college, I landed a job as a reporter for the morning newspaper in Maine's second-largest city, Lewiston.

In 1978 I took what I thought would be a short professional-development leave of absence to run a local politician's Congressional campaign. I thought the experience would prove helpful to my understanding of politics and government, the reporting beat I wanted to pursue. The day after my candidate lost in the Primary, U.S. Senator Bill Hathaway hired me to help with his fall reelection campaign. Fall he did; he lost to future Secretary of Defense Bill Cohen.

I quickly landed a job with the Democratic Party leaders in the Maine House of Representatives. Soon they encouraged me to run for the Legislature myself in the next election cycle, 1980. I did and I won, finally making it to the winning side of a campaign. Four years later, I was elected House Majority Leader. It was a fast ascension; I had just turned 30.

In October 1985, I started dating Marcia LaRochelle, a Maine native who was the deputy press secretary to U.S. Senator George Mitchell. We married a year later. Agreeing that political life was not conducive to our family plans, we set our exit strategy. We decided we would both return to our original career passions by the conclusion of my fourth term in December 1988. Marcia became a teacher and, later, a Catholic school principal. I reset my sights on journalism—not as a political reporter but as a college professor. I began the steps necessary to pursue a Ph.D., with the intent to teach somewhere in the Northeast so the kids we envisioned having would always be close to family.

I lucked out; a position opened at the University of Maine, and I was offered the job. I would be able to teach, conduct research, and work on my doctorate. I'd also be able to moonlight as a regular panelist on *MediaWatch*, a statewide television program that critiqued state and national news coverage of current events.

Then, on that July day in 1992, Fred Hutchinson called. Once I settled in to the job, I became active in several national higher education organizations, and gleaned "best practices" in my new profession from peers at universities much larger than UMaine. One tenet that my national colleagues stressed related to access: "Make sure you are at the university's leadership table when tough issues are discussed and when decisions are being made!" I heard plenty of horror stories about presidents, chancellors, and provosts making decisions without thinking through the potential political or PR consequences. My counterparts shared the same advice that was given to me early on by Alan Miller, one of my former journalism professors, who had been UMaine's public affairs director under a previous president. Miller explained that when at the leadership table, a public affairs (a.k.a. university relations) officer must consider and present issues and decisions from the perspectives of the institution's external stakeholders. Those viewpoints, he said, are easy to dismiss when leaders are fixated on answers that satisfy their own interests but not necessarily the university's. The university relations officer must protect the president or chancellor from making avoidable mistakes in judgment or action—mistakes that could erode the leader's credibility, damage the university's reputation, and destroy confidence and trust.

"Do the right thing and get caught doing it," Miller told me, a sound piece of advice that applied to much more in life than my new PR job.

I stayed in that position at UMaine for ten years. In 2002, I moved to a similar position with Maine's state university system office to help its CEO, Joseph W. Westphal, develop a new communications and marketing initiative. But seven years later, the Great Recession forced massive budget cuts throughout state government, including to public higher education. With a new System chancellor, staff positions eliminated, and the possibility of additional cuts and consolidation, I decided to look for a position outside of Maine. It was a disconcerting thought; Marcia and I were active in numerous civic and community organizations, holding leadership roles in several non-profit organizations in Maine. I also served on the Supreme Judicial Court's Committee on Judicial Responsibility and Disability, which was responsible for investigating complaints of judicial misconduct involving Maine judges and justices. Appointed by the state's chief justice, I was scheduled to assume the chairmanship of that committee in 2012.

Though we had previously talked about someday moving on to a larger university outside of Maine—ideally one with shorter winters—we had decided to hold off any such move until we were empty nesters.

Now, in 2010, the timing and conditions seemed right. Our youngest, Sarah, would be starting college in Florida in August. Son Johnny was finishing his bachelor's degree at UMaine. Daughter Heather was married and a mom. With the right position, Marcia and I could afford to shuttle to see the family and bring them to see us as well. We decided to focus on universities with stable finances and with leadership that understood and appreciated the role of strategic communications and advocacy—my specialties—to advancing its goals and political agenda.

We found what we thought was the perfect opportunity and location: the University of Arkansas in Fayetteville. Better known nationally for being the home of the Razorbacks, the university's powerful college athletics program, in recent years UA had made impressive strides in elevating its profile and reputation for academic quality. Unique opportunities and conditions for growth and private support existed, making UA the envy of many public universities.

First and foremost was the local presence of Wal-Mart, Inc., the world's largest and most economically influential retailer. In 1950, founder Sam Walton—still referred to as "Mister Sam" in some local circles 20 years after his death—opened his first retail store, Walton's 5&10, on the town square in Bentonville, Arkansas. Twelve years later, he opened a new type of retail store, the low-frills Wal-Mart, in Rogers, Arkansas, a community that abuts Bentonville and is located a few miles north of Fayetteville. The Walton family made a fortune as a result of Mister Sam's revolutionary business model: a customer-first emphasis on low prices, high-volume sales, "just-in-time" inventory control efficiencies, hardball price concessions from suppliers, and a counter-intuitive vision of doing business in rural locations, where Walton's "big box" department stores offered everything including the kitchen sink. According to *Forbes*, each of his three surviving children is now worth more than $3 billion and is among the world's wealthiest individuals.

Wal-Mart's corporate presence in Northwest Arkansas (NWA, as it's often called) transformed the region economically and culturally. Just about every corporation that influences the world's retail supply chain set up corporate headquarters in order to provide rapid response to Wal-Mart's needs and expectations. Thousands of well-educated, well-paid executives and sales representatives relocated to the region, increasing demands for housing, schools, entertainment options and other quality-of-life attractions. In addition to the family business, the Walton family fortune also has reshaped NWA. The most extraordinary example is Crystal Bridges Museum of American Art, which *Bloomberg Business* dubbed the "$1.2 billion castle" of founder Alice Walton, Mister Sam's daughter.

UA also has benefited from the Wal-Mart/Walton largess. Contributions to the university from family donors, the family's not-for-profit foundations, and Wal-Mart executives did more than any program or leader to reengineer UA from a sleepy Southern campus to a flourishing, albeit crowded, research institution with impressive academic and athletics facilities. The family name is conspicuous across campus. There's Bud Walton Arena, the 19,200-seat "Basketball Palace of Mid-America," named in honor of Mister Sam's brother and Wal-Mart co-founder. There's Walton Hall, a student housing facility, and Sam M. Walton College of Business, now one of the top B-schools in the U.S. There are programs, professorships, and scholarships with the Walton name associated with them. Walton Arts Center, a joint venture of UA and the Fayetteville community, hosts major performances that one might not expect to find in the region. There's even a mini-Wal-Mart—a small convenience store branded as "Wal-Mart on Campus"—adjacent to the UA's Maple Hill student housing complex.

The Tysons were another local family whose enormous entrepreneurial success helped transform UA and Northwest Arkansas. Three generations of the family—company founder John W. Tyson, son Donald J. Tyson and grandson John H. Tyson—built Tyson Foods into the world's largest meat producer. Tyson Foods was founded in Springdale, Arkansas, a city that neighbors Fayetteville. Its world headquarters remain there. The family name appears prominently on UA's campus, most conspicuously on the exterior of the John W. Tyson Building, located opposite the university's main administration building. The Jean Tyson Child Development Study Center, which opened in November 2012, was built in part with $2.5 million from the Tyson Family Foundation and the Tyson Foods Foundation.

Our own family had been part of the talent and labor in-migration to Northwest Arkansas. In 1999, our niece Karyn and her family moved to the region so that she could accept a position in Wal-Mart's corporate headquarters. Karyn and her husband Mike fell in love with NWA's beautiful hills, entrepreneurial nature, and its blend of Midwest and Southern culture and manners. Soon, she and Mike started a successful home design and construction business, capitalizing on the region's rapid economic growth. Karyn's youngest sister Ebony and her family moved to the area in early 2010, around the time that UA was beginning its search for a new associate vice chancellor for University Relations. Having seven family members living near campus put the UA opportunity on our list of relocation possibilities.

Another attraction at UA was the opportunity to work with Chancellor G. David Gearhart. Gearhart was an anomaly as a campus CEO: he had risen to UA's top leadership role after a career spent almost exclusively as a higher ed fundraiser. However, Gearhart was no academic lightweight. He held both a law degree and a doctorate in higher education administration. He had studied at Oxford University as a Fulbright Fellow. He also had authored a couple of books on the art and science of fundraising.

A native Arkansan, Gearhart was the son of a well-respected newspaper publisher and community leader. Gearhart's three brothers had also distinguished themselves professionally. Older brother Van was an Arkansas district court judge. Jeff was senior vice president and general counsel for Wal-Mart, a role that made him one of the global retail giant's most powerful figures. Doug was a vice president for fashion label Lida Baday in New York and the only non-lawyer of the four.

Gearhart's unique path to the top had been the cover story of a July 2010 edition of the weekly *Chronicle of Higher Education*, a must-read publication for those who work in or follow the politics and operation of universities and colleges. Gearhart became chancellor despite lacking the normally requisite classroom or lab experience that gives leaders *bona fides* with the faculty. It was equally remarkable that the trustees offered him the job of leading a public research university without conducting even the most superficial of national searches. Such was the reputation and influence that Gearhart possessed in Arkansas.

Much of that reputation was the result of what he had accomplished on his path to the top. Before becoming chancellor in 2008, Gearhart spent ten years as UA's vice chancellor for Advancement. He designed the game plan for the university's Campaign for the

Twenty-First Century, a fundraising effort that raised more than $1 billion—a remarkable amount, far greater than anyone thought possible in light of the state's socio-demographics. A key to the campaign's success was a $300 million gift from the Walton Family Charitable Support Foundation. Gearhart was a proven rainmaker, and in higher education as in politics, money is the "mother's milk" of success.

I liked the possibility of having a leadership role at a university whose CEO understood the interdependence of communications, external relations, and fundraising and was prepared to invest in those areas. Based on the presence of our family members and Gearhart's appeal as a leader, I applied for the job.

Marcia and I made our first visit to Arkansas on August 19, 2010. Joy Sharp made all the arrangements for us, ensuring that we got through our two days of interviews with no complications. I say "our" interviews because, though I was the one applying for a job, my would-be boss, Choate, wanted to informally evaluate both of us. He needed to make sure we both would like the region. He also wanted to make sure that we, as a pair, would be a good fit with his leadership team; a stable couple that would fit in at the numerous professional and social activities we'd be expected to take part in as a member of the university's senior leadership group. That was important to Choate; a mutual friend once told me that part of Brad's success and leadership style involved maintaining a sense of family among those who worked for him, and that involved making spouses and family members feel equally welcome. His practice also helped retain good talent. If anyone wanted to look elsewhere for a job, it would be emotionally difficult because Brad cultivated a positive camaraderie and sense of community that would be hard to give up.

Our visit to UA went well. Marcia and I started Thursday evening with a get-to-know-you dinner with Choate and his wife Julie. On our drive from our hotel south of campus to meet them, we were initially discouraged by what we saw: we rode through a run-down area of the city, not knowing whether or not it was illustrative of Fayetteville as a whole. (It wasn't.) We passed a business named Lowlife Tattoo, unsure of whether its title was a representative or derisive take on the citizenry. (It was neither.) We turned onto Dickson Street, which we later discovered was the heart of Fayetteville's entertainment district. We found it pleasantly hip and quirky. We had a nice evening with the Choates at Theo's, a trendy restaurant buzzing that night with young professionals. We left Theo's impressed with the meal and our new acquaintances.

The next day, Marcia met with UA's dean of the College of Education and Health Professions, the Fayetteville Public School's human resources director, and the principal of the local Catholic school. Joy Sharp had arranged those appointments for her. Meanwhile, I spent the day being quizzed in separate meetings with key campus stakeholders: the University Relations staff, whom I would lead if I got the job; Choate's Advancement leadership team, consisting of his executive assistant and the leaders of Development, Alumni Affairs, Constituent Relations, Budget and Human Resources, and Special Events; Gearhart's executive council, made up of UA's five vice chancellors and four senior advisors; and a handful of the university's deans.

My final meeting was with Gearhart and Choate. Seated at a small conference table in a corner of Gearhart's personal office, we talked about the relationship between a university's CEO and its chief external relations officer. I liked what I heard: Gearhart and Choate both said the person in the latter role had to be willing and able to raise or flag issues with campus leadership, even when the news or opinion might be contrary to the direction the university might be heading in.

"I agree," I told them. "Ultimately, the person in that job has to help keep the university out of trouble and in good favor with the public. 'Do the right thing and get caught doing it,'" I added, sharing Professor Miller's advice. Both men nodded their agreement. Gearhart assured me that if I got the job, I would always have unfiltered access to him, though technically I would report directly to Choate. Choate nodded again. I appreciated the reassurance.

Later that afternoon, Choate and I met in his office for my exit interview.

“I think it’s going to be unanimous,” he volunteered, speaking of the search committee. “It doesn’t really matter because at the end of the day it’s my decision. But that’s good.” On September 1st he called to formally offer the job and to arrange my start date. Though I had reservations about leaving our family and friends in Maine, I couldn’t wait to begin.

“It’s nothing like the stereotype of Arkansas,” our niece Karyn assured us. “You’ll love it here.”

Chapter 2

THE RAZORBACK WAY

The University of Arkansas shared a few similarities with the University of Maine, where I spent my first ten years as a higher ed administrator. Both schools were founded around the same time during the nineteenth century following passage of the federal Morrill Act of 1862, which gave each state land to use or sell off to create a state college dedicated to promoting "the liberal and practical education of the industrial classes in the several pursuits and professions in life." Creation of these so-called "land-grant colleges" is often cited as one of the most transformational initiatives Congress has ever produced. Today, both UA and UMaine are designated the "flagship" of their respective state's public university system. Each also performs the lion's share of university-based research conducted in its state.

But that's where the similarities end. When I joined Choate's team in the fall of 2010, UA's student population of 21,406 was almost double that of UMaine's. The cost of in-state student tuition at UA was lower, and financial aid amounts were higher. UA's facilities were newer, greater in number and in better condition than those of its

Maine counterpart. The dollar amount of federally and privately funded research conducted by Fayetteville faculty and students was larger and more diverse, too. The faculty pay differential between the two universities was great; the differential between the schools' senior administrators was even greater. Only UMaine's support staff—clerical workers, secretaries, custodians, etc.—received better pay and benefits than their Arkansas counterparts.

However, the biggest and most conspicuous difference involved the intercollegiate athletics facilities. UA, a member of the powerful Southeastern Conference, had a football stadium, baseball stadium, and basketball arena that rivaled many professional venues. Its track and field complexes looked Olympian to me, as they should; the Razorbacks had produced dozens of Olympians representing a number of countries besides the U.S. It had a new women's softball stadium with skyboxes, an impressive varsity tennis complex, and an older but venerable arena that housed the gymnastics and volleyball teams. Ticket sales and corporate sponsorships for the Razorback football, basketball, and baseball teams, along with the broadcasting contracts they commanded through its SEC membership, made the entire athletics program self-sustaining. Only about two dozen NCAA programs could boast of that distinction.

By contrast, UMaine depended on student fees and subsidies to maintain its Black Bear athletics programs. Except for the men's and women's ice hockey teams, they competed in what are known in college sports as mid-major conferences. The facilities were nice but nowhere near as large or as flashy as the Razorbacks'. The only aspect of the two universities' athletics facilities where I would give the edge to UMaine was the assortment of recreational and fitness facilities available to all students and to faculty and staff.

UA had aspirations to make its reputation for academics and research as strong as its reputation for athletic success. Gearhart and Choate were willing to invest in communications, marketing, and public relations, Choate commissioned GSD&M, a blue-chip advertising firm based in Austin, Texas, to research and produce themes and messaging that would help UA increase its enrollment even further. My job was to work with the agency and my own unit directors and staff to produce strategies and content that would grow undergraduate and graduate enrollment and build the University of Arkansas brand within the state as well as nationally. The challenge appealed to me.

Choate held weekly meetings with what he called his University Advancement Cabinet, or UAC, which consisted of the top leaders from each area within Choate's areas of responsibility: the associate vice chancellors of Alumni Affairs, Development (fundraising), and University Relations, the senior deputies within the division; the directors of Special Events and Constituent Services, the latter responsible for handling the needs of donors and VIPs; Choate's executive assistant; and Sharp, the Budget and Human Resources director.

We met most Monday afternoons at three-thirty. Choate set the priorities and Laura Villines, his executive assistant, prepared the weekly agenda. Each meeting included a budget status report. Except for Alumni Affairs, Sharp managed the individual finances of each unit within the division as well as the division as a whole. Most weeks she distributed one-page summaries showing the bottom lines as they currently stood. Before our meetings ended, Choate had each of us give a brief update on any news or topics that had not been part of the prepared agenda.

The meetings were productive and beneficial. They gave me and the rest of the division's leaders a more complete sense of the division's issues, operations and upcoming activities. I held a similar meeting with my own senior leadership team each Tuesday. I named my group RazorWorks, a play on Skunkworks, Lockheed's creative innovation project from World War II. Gradually, we made changes to our priorities and functions to better align with UA's goals and agenda. Our guide was the university's strategic plan, called "Transparency and Accountability for the People of Arkansas."

Internally, we referred to the plan as TAP. We adjusted the nature and delivery of the news and features that our writers, designers, video producers, and web personnel produced, measuring our productivity based on how much and how well our efforts moved the university closer to TAP's goals.

Over the course of two and a half years at UA, we launched several initiatives to support TAP: a TV and radio advertising campaign; sponsorship of National Public Radio's *Morning Edition*, the second-most listened to radio program in the U.S. (only Rush Limbaugh had a bigger audience); advertorials—i.e., feature stories that we produced and paid for—in in-flight airline magazines; high-profile special events on national topics; and a 90-second web-based video series called *Arkansas Short Takes*, which we distributed each week via email and social media to tens of thousands of alumni, donors, parents of students, policymakers, and opinion leaders in Arkansas as well as to the chancellors, presidents and provosts of universities and colleges across the country. We launched a marketing and PR campaign in north Texas to support our admissions office's tactical work there. We directed additional resources to support the Diversity Affairs office's efforts to recruit more students of color; UA was disproportionately white for a state with sizable African American and Hispanic populations.

We also put out a lot of fires. The most combustible and dangerous one involved Razorback athletics.

Around 6:45 Sunday afternoon, April 1, 2012, Bobby Petrino, the football team's feisty and successful head coach, lost control of his cherry red Harley-Davidson Road King on a back road east of Fayetteville. He and his motorcycle skidded to a stop in a roadside ditch, hitting a thicket of downed tree branches and severely injuring the 51-year-old coach. When Arkansas State Trooper Josh Arnold arrived at the crash scene, only the bike was there; a family had driven by, stopped to help and, following Petrino's appeal not to call 9-1-1, drove him back toward Fayetteville. Bleeding and in severe pain, Petrino called State Police Captain Lance King, his friend and the head of the coach's game-day security detail. Petrino asked him to meet him at a designated spot on Fayetteville's east side. King did so and transported him to a small 20-bed hospital, where the celebrity's presence would be less conspicuous.

"Because of sun & wind I could not manage the turn," Petrino later wrote in his statement for the trooper's accident report. "Drove off the road. Tryed [sic] to drop the bike down and the next thing I knew I was lying in a wood pile!!"

Remarkably, just two days after the crash, Petrino showed up at Donald W. Reynolds Razorback Stadium for spring football practice. Battered, red-faced with numerous abrasions, and sporting a stiff plastic neck brace, a smiling Petrino held a news conference, expressing his gratitude to be alive. National sports media ate it up. So did Razorback fans: *He's one tough guy. He's Bobby Petrino, dammit!*

The near-fatal crash would end his career in Fayetteville but not due to the serious physical injuries he suffered. Instead, it was the married father of four's attempt to cover up the presence of a young, newly hired female staff member, who was his passenger at the time of the accident.

On Thursday afternoon, April 5th, Petrino called his boss, UA Athletics Director Jeff Long, to fess up. He had misled Long, he admitted. Jessica Dorrell, a former Razorback volleyball player Petrino had just hired, was his passenger when he crashed. (She was not seriously injured.) Yes, he had told the investigating officer of her presence but had not told others. Dorrell's car was parked at the spot where Petrino had arranged to meet King; she got in her car and drove away as the officer ferried the coach to the hospital.

Petrino's admission at this particular time was driven by necessity. The State Police had given the coach a heads-up that it was going to publicly release the accident report, including reference to Dorrell's involvement. *Dammit, Bobby Petrino!*

I happened to be with Long when Petrino called. We, along

with Gearhart, Choate and about three dozen other university administrators, were returning to Fayetteville by bus following a two-day planning retreat at a conference center on Arkansas' Petit Jean Mountain. Petrino called around 3:10 p.m. About fifteen minutes later, Long walked over to where I was seated.

"Step into my office," he said, motioning me to join him a couple of rows back. He filled me in on what his football coach had just revealed to him.

We spent the remainder of our travel time—nearly two hours—talking together and at times with Gearhart and Choate about how to deal with the news. Clearly it was an embarrassment to Long; he had been deceived by the person who was arguably the most popular man in Arkansas—and, at more than $3.5 million per year, the state's highest-paid public employee. Something had to be done about it—and that something might cause harm to Long's own career in the process.

After arriving back on campus, Long asked me to meet him later in the evening at his office. Meanwhile, I connected with Kevin Trainor, Long's public relations director, to see what he had been hearing from staff and reporters. Kevin had already received a copy of the accident report and summarized it for me.

We all gathered shortly after seven o'clock: Long, his senior associate Jon Fagg, Gearhart, university attorney Scott Varady, and I. Trainor joined us at times; he was getting ready for a news conference Long would hold around 10 p.m. at which he would announce he was suspending Petrino pending an investigation into his conduct.

Long's personal office within Razorback Stadium was by far the largest and most spectacular of any on campus. Its extensive south side was a wall of glass and overlooked the football field from its north end. We met there several times over the next few days and nights. One such meeting lasted past one in the morning. As darkness set in, Long would lower the curtains so that no one from the outside could see who he was meeting with.

Sports media and fans in Arkansas and across the country immediately began speculating about Petrino's fate. He had become immensely successful during the previous two seasons. Some prognosticators were listing the Razorbacks as pre-season contenders for the national championship. Locally, fans held a rally to support Petrino, calling on Long and UA to forgive and forget Petrino's errant deeds. Gearhart told us that a couple of university trustees wanted Long to keep Petrino at the helm, possibly suspending him for one or more early-season games as punishment. Members of the powerful Razorback Foundation, the private fundraising body that helped pay Long's and Petrino's salaries, wanted the coach to stay as well.

Under all of that pressure, Long made his decision. He would immediately fire Petrino outright. Long and Fagg had interviewed Petrino, Dorrell, and other members of the athletics staff. They had learned that Petrino had been in a relationship with Dorrell prior to hiring her as a member of his football staff. He had recently given her $20,000 in cash. He hired the 25-year-old over 158 candidates for the job even though many other applicants had far more relevant and impressive professional credentials. They also determined that a few weeks earlier Petrino misled Long in order to get the athletics director's approval to fast-track hiring Dorrell. These facts certainly justified terminating the coach "for cause." Invoking that phrase would free the university from its contractual obligation to pay Petrino $18 million if it fired him for any other reasons.

At Long's direction, we began to plan. Long and Fagg would inform Petrino. Varady would talk with the coach's lawyers, who had flown in from Alabama and periodically had been waiting anxiously in Petrino's nearby office suite. I would work with Trainor and Zack Higbee, the director of football communications, to develop a statement that Long could present to the media and the public. Because the chancellor was the person to whom Petrino, under UA policies, could appeal Long's decision, Gearhart said he would stay out of the planning. He would not attend the news conference when Long made his announcement, either.

There was some discussion, though little disagreement, about how specific, in public, Long should be about the reasons for Petrino's termination. We considered what other universities and colleges had done when severing ties with presidents, coaches, and other high-profile members of the community. In many instances, they avoided getting into details; instead, they used euphemistic phrases like "going in a different direction," "time to make a change," and "best interests of everyone involved," even when the determining factors were widely known.

But circumstances discouraged that sort of response. At that time (and as now), the public and media were expressing lots of cynicism about college sports. The Penn State sexual abuse scandal was still fresh. So were NCAA sanctions recently levied against Ohio State and the University of North Carolina at Chapel Hill for rules violations. None of those schools received high marks for the way they handled their programs' misdeeds. They would not be good models for us to follow.

Furthermore, public sentiment in Arkansas seemed strongly tilted in Petrino's favor. Could UA communicate its decision in a way its stakeholders of students, employees, alumni, donors, fans, policy makers, and opinion leaders would understand and accept? We never discussed the possible consequences of Petrino's firing on Long's own career, though it likely was on everyone's mind. No doubt it was on his, too.

Ultimately, we decided that the best defense was a strong offense. After listening to Long think aloud about what Petrino had done, I began writing. I drafted a statement that went through Petrino's offending actions point by point, as would a lawyer presenting a closing statement to a jury. For the most part, that was exactly what Long needed to do: present a compelling and sincere argument in order to win his case in the Court of Public Opinion. After a couple of modifications by Trainor, Long okayed the remarks and began his preparation.

On Tuesday, April 10th, Long's deputy, Matt Trantham, hand-delivered a termination letter to Petrino's home. Shortly thereafter, Long scheduled a news conference to announce his decision. Reporters and satellite trucks gathered at Bud Walton Arena—home of the basketball teams, not the football program, in an effort to keep reporters away from Petrino's players and staff—where Long would make his statement. ESPN and other national media organizations covered it live.

Long began by reviewing what had occurred over the past ten days. Then, prefacing his announcement of Petrino's firing, he delved into what an Associated Press reporter later described as "a stunning laundry list of misdeeds against the man [Long had] hired away from the Atlanta Falcons four years ago."

Petrino "made the decision—a conscious decision—to mislead the public… and in doing so negatively and adversely affected the reputation of the University of Arkansas and our football program," Long stated. "Coach Petrino engaged in a pattern of misleading and manipulative behavior designed to deceive me and members of the athletics' staff both before and after the motorcycle accident… Coach Petrino's conduct was contrary to the qualities and responsibilities we demand of our head football coach."

"We have high standards," Long said, his voice breaking at times with emotion. "And a national reputation. Our expectations from our employees can be no less than what we expect of our students. No individual can be bigger than the team, the Razorback football program, or the University of Arkansas."

Long's principled decision to fire Petrino, despite the coach's success, shocked many college football fans as well as most Arkansans. It also earned Long and the university praise in the national media. Fox Sports commended Long's action as "correct and gutsy." Eric Adelson of Yahoo! Sports described Long's handling of Petrino as "a lesson for all other ADs." Perhaps the most gratifying response came from Matt Hayes of *Sporting News*: "Jeff Long showed what Mark Emmert and the rest of the NCAA hasn't been able to do in years: how to stand up and embrace accountability and responsibility."

Long's handling of the matter was lauded on campus as well. The governing senates of UA's faculty, staff, and students each passed resolutions praising the AD. Playing off his last name, student leaders worked with University Relations to distribute thousands of T-shirts that read "Integrity Goes a LONG Way." Meanwhile, the Donald W. Reynolds Foundation made a $1 million donation to Razorback athletics in Long's honor. In addition, that foundation's board chair made a personal donation of $250,000. Two weeks later, an independent statewide public opinion poll said 84 percent of Arkansans surveyed agreed with the university's action. Long's leadership gave a boost to UA's reputation on campus and off. He did the right thing and got caught doing it.

Chapter 3

JOY'S CONFESSION

Joy Sharp had a budget gap to close. It was the final week of June in 2012—the end of the fiscal year for the university. Year-end revenues had to match, if not exceed, the amount of money the Advancement division had spent over the preceding 12 months. It was Sharp's job to make sure everything aligned properly according to UA's policies and procedures.

UA's Advancement division was an essential part of the university's success and future. The division was responsible for cultivating relationships with donors, alumni, reporters, editorial writers, and other stakeholders whose opinions and actions influenced the university's relationships, reputation, and resources. That was why, outside of Razorback athletics, Advancement employed many of the university's highest paid non-academic employees.

In 2012, the Advancement division had 158 employees on its payroll. The largest percentage of them was associated with Advancement's Office of University Development: fundraisers, planners, records technicians, report writers, and support staff. Many members of the staff were assigned to work with the deans of

UA's colleges and schools—the administrative structures that housed all academic and most research programs. With few exceptions, this was the model used across campus. The dual reporting lines maintained the fundraisers' accountability and loyalty to both Choate and their respective deans and program directors.

As Advancement's budget director, Sharp managed funds that the division received from two primary sources: a yearly allocation from the university's central funds, which came mainly from the state legislature and from student tuition and fees; and monies from the nominally independent University of Arkansas Foundation, the private, not-for-profit organization whose mission was "advance higher education by securing private financial support for all units and activities of the University of Arkansas."

The UA Foundation depended heavily on Advancement's fundraising personnel (called "development officers"). They steered many types of donors' pledges and gifts to the Foundation, often to create endowed scholarships and professorships to support students and faculty. A small percentage of the interest on those gifts was shared with Advancement and other units to be reinvested in Advancement initiatives—primarily more fundraising. The arrangement provided an impressive return on investment: at least $10 in donations and pledges for every $1 the UA Foundation provided to Advancement.

Development officers also steered "unrestricted" gifts of cash, property, stocks, and other liquidable assets to the Foundation. The Foundation regularly dispersed unrestricted funds to certain designated campus leaders such as Gearhart, Choate, and the deans of UA's academic and administrative divisions to use at their discretion.

The Foundation was governed by a board of directors made up of current and former members of the UA System's board of trustees and other prominent Arkansans. The UA System's chief legal counsel, Fred Harrison, served as the Foundation board's secretary. In 2012, the Foundation had fewer than 10 people on its staff, led by Clay Davis, the organization's executive director and treasurer.

He and his team focused on managing money, not raising it. They counted on Gearhart, Choate, Development leader Bruce Pontious, and other university fundraisers to do that. Conversely, Advancement depended on the UA Foundation to provide about 40 percent of its annual revenue. Advancement used those funds to augment the state and tuition dollars it received—so-called "Educational and General" funds—to support its operation and to cover gifts, meals, entertainment and other purchases for which public or tuition funds could not be used. In many instances, the Foundation paid the bill directly, and because it was a private, not-for-profit entity, the Foundation did not have to publicly disclose the purposes or details of the expenditures—unlike the legal requirements placed on the university itself as a public institution. The same distinction and exemptions applied to the Razorback Foundation, another independent-on-paper entity created to raise and manage funds for UA's robust athletics operation.

As the Advancement division's budget director, Sharp was accustomed to asking the Foundation for fund transfers. She was also used to sending the Foundation items called "payment authorizations" to cover those expenses that needed to be paid (or would be less conspicuous if paid) by the private Foundation. Examples include expensive meals, liquor, and country club dues, which are staples of cultivating donors and prospects; types of employee travel costs; and gifts, furnishings, elaborate holiday decorations, and activities that are not illegal nor necessarily extravagant but whose cost or timing might prove embarrassing should reporters, legislators, or taxpayers learn about them.

On this day in late June, Sharp was taking advantage of the rare quiet that existed due to the seasonal nature of a university's operation. With the fiscal year ending on June 30th and the new one starting the following day, Sharp and other campus budget managers were busy making sure their respective units' revenues and expenses balanced. Their work would not be complete until the end of July, when the budget numbers for the just-completed fiscal year are finalized and in the hands of the university's chief financial officer, Don Pederson, and his top deputy, UA Treasurer Jean Schook. Those two positions are responsible for monitoring the flow of money in and out of the university's coffers. Their offices also exist to provide the checks and balances necessary to ensure that the university's finances are properly managed, intervening if and when they suspected things might be awry.

Aware that Advancement's expenses for the year had exceeded the revenues she had already received, Sharp initiated a process she had performed many, many times in her career. She prepared a series of disbursement requests—paper forms—instructing the UA Foundation to provide her, as Advancement's designee, with $500,000. Once received, she would book those dollars to cover payments due. One of those obligations involved a $225,000 deposit into Chancellor Gearhart's deferred compensation account, something he received annually as part of his agreement with the UA System's board of trustees.

Sharp completed the paperwork, sent it forward to CFO Pederson for his approval, and then waited for the Foundation to disburse the funds she needed to balance Advancement's budget. She had no reason to believe these requests would be denied. It had never happened before.

Friday, July 6th, was typical of the summer days Fayetteville was experiencing in 2012. It was hot. Temperatures had already surpassed 100 degrees several times so far that summer, and forecasters predicted there were more triple-digit days to come.

Choate was on campus that day, observing the lull in activity from his office on the top floor of the descriptive but unimaginatively named Administration Building. "Admin," as campus personnel referred to it, was an uninspiring concrete and glass structure built in the mid-1970s. Choate occupied one of Admin's four corner suites; Gearhart, Pederson, and UA's chief academic officer, Provost

Sharon Gaber, inhabited the others. The calm of Choate's day did not last long. Sharp entered his office from her own, shutting the door gently behind her. Head bowed, hands shaking, she spoke.

"I've made a terrible mistake."

And with that admission, Choate's long and successful career began its rapid disintegration.

"How can this be?!" an incredulous Choate asked.

Sharp didn't answer; she simply shook her head and looked away, distraught with the news she'd just shared. The UA Foundation had refused to provide the funds she requested to balance Advancement's budget for the recently ended fiscal year. Furthermore, the Foundation had frozen Advancement's access to any additional funds because the latter, at Sharp's request, had not only used up all of its FY2012 payout—over $4 million—but also had drawn on funds intended for disbursement to Advancement later in the new fiscal year.

Sharp found out about the Foundation's actions days earlier but had waited until now for something—anything—that would spare her from having to break the news to her boss. She knew the budget was in the red, she told Choate, but was not sure by how much. Sharp felt overworked, she confided, and lost track of Advancement's funds. There were vendors she hadn't paid. She didn't elaborate further, Choate later explained.

The normally unflappable Choate felt sick to his stomach. *It makes no sense!* he thought. He and Sharp had been meeting monthly about the budget for four years! They talked about finances almost daily. In fact, in June she had asked him to approve a new personnel line to help her with her human resources responsibilities. *I explicitly asked her if we had the funds to support that position!* he recalled.

"How, Joy?! Why?!" he asked, pleading for an acceptable rationale. She simply looked down and shook her head.

Once Sharp left his office, Choate called Clay Davis, the executive director and treasurer of the UA Foundation. Yes, it's true, Davis said. Advancement was severely overdrawn.

"You must not have been watching your spending, Brad," an irritated Gearhart responded after hearing the news.

"Dave, you know better than that," Choate countered. He reminded the chancellor that Sharp had been presenting weekly budget updates to Advancement's leadership cabinet. Sharp often, but not always, provided handouts depicting budget accounts and aggregate totals along with her oral report. She and Choate talked about the subject all the time.

"When I was vice chancellor, we had these big budget printouts that we went over together," Gearhart noted, referring to his own meetings with Sharp and other Advancement leaders. "We could account for every penny. Go tell Don and get him to help."

"We'll get to the bottom of this," Choate reassured him as he left to meet with the university's chief financial officer. He was unaware that his problems would become more complicated by some of the very people he would turn to for support.

Don Pederson already knew Advancement had a problem. Susan Slinkard, the person within Pederson's division who monitors the cash flow across UA's many accounts, had received word from the UA Foundation that it was freezing Advancement's access to funds. She in turn notified Pederson in an email.

The tall, lanky Pederson was a rarity among higher education CFOs. Unlike most of his peers at universities and colleges large and small, he had no formal education in business management, finance, or public administration. He was a physicist. Joining UA in 1972 as a faculty member in the College of Arts and Sciences, he eventually became the university's provost, the top academic position on campus and on paper the second-in-command to the chancellor. In 1998, Gearhart's predecessor as chancellor, John A. White, offered Pederson the CFO job. Had there been a conventional executive search, undoubtedly the vacant position would have attracted scores of candidates with considerable higher ed experience and advanced degrees in the field. But in this case, at White's request, Pederson slid over from the academic side to manage UA's finances and overall administration, gaining on-the-job training in the professional standards, practices, and nuances of managing university-wide revenues that in 2012 exceeded $705 million.

Advancement had borrowed on future payouts from the UA Foundation in the past with Pederson's knowledge and approval; as CFO, he had to sign the authorization forms before the Foundation would process the requests. However, this time the Foundation refused because the dollar amount Advancement had drawn on future payouts had grown so large. If the Foundation approved Sharp's June requests, Advancement would start the new fiscal year having already spent more than one million dollars—a quarter of what it was supposed to receive from the Foundation over the next twelve months. That amount was unacceptable to the Foundation's leadership.

After Choate's briefing, Pederson told him he would look into the cause and size of the problem. The next day, Pederson said Advancement appeared to finish the fiscal year $544,000 in the red. Without Foundation funds to close the gap, Advancement needed some other way to balance the budget. That action had to occur soon; end-of-year accounting for FY12 had to be completed by July 31.

For whatever reason, Pederson did not want to draw on the university's centrally held reserve accounts. UA had more than $30 million there; the university could have used some of those funds as a temporary or permanent patch for the Advancement shortfall. But instead, in an unusual move, Pederson asked the interim dean of the university's College of Engineering, Terry Martin, to loan Advancement $550,000 from Engineering's own UA Foundation accounts. Reimbursement, Pederson promised, would occur on or around the beginning of October, when the Foundation was scheduled to give Advancement its next quarterly payment.

Martin agreed, so long as he had Pederson's pledge in writing. He also would charge interest. The two leaders prepared and executed the loan agreement. Immediately after Advancement received the funds, it made initial payments to cover some of its many outstanding obligations to vendors and employees. It also made the $225,000 payment—nearly half of the money borrowed—to cover a payment to Gearhart's deferred compensation fund.

Only a few people on campus knew about the loan, even fewer than the number who knew about Advancement's deficit. In an email, Pederson told Choate that when he asked for the funds, "I presented it as a cash flow problem without attributing it to your office or the chancellor. I [sic] might be best to leave it that way. Coming from me it looks like a routine fiscal issue." Colleen Briney, Engineering's budget officer, knew something was up; she was the person who processed the transaction. In an email, she questioned whether Advancement was "broke." Choate heard about her email and complained about it. It wasn't true, he said, and he did not want rumors spreading. Things were already bad enough for him and his division, he told his friends.

Choate was understandably stressed. He had not yet told his wife Julie about what he was dealing with at work. In 30 years of fundraising and management, he had never exceeded his budget—until now. He was proud of his performance as a leader and knew that once the university's nascent $1 billion-plus capital campaign was finished, he could retire and look back with great pride on a lasting legacy of helping Gearhart fulfill his vision to transform the University of Arkansas into one of the nation's top public research universities.

But now, he was experiencing an intense period of self-examination. *What, if anything, could I have done to prevent or spot what happened?* he asked himself. He repeatedly talked it over with Development office leader Bruce Pontious, his close friend and the most senior of his three associate vice chancellors. Pontious himself had entertained questions about Sharp's performance. He had been concerned about the accuracy of what she provided for numbers. He had no reason to think she wasn't as competent as everyone on campus said; it was her rigid, centralized control of budget information that made him uncomfortable. It was something he had hoped Choate would correct. Too late now.

Choate and Sharp spent the rest of July trying to figure out just how much money Advancement had—or didn't have. It wasn't coming together; the piecemeal budget documentation Sharp provided did not reflect the existence of excessive spending on operations, which Choate and Pederson suspected was the deficit's cause.

On July 30th, Gearhart sent Choate an email saying that in the absence of understanding the size and cause of the shortfall, Choate immediately should start reducing his spending plans for the current budget year. Choate agreed; in fact, he had already given that instruction to me and the other members of his leadership team.

Around that same time, Choate decided it was time to remove Sharp from the process altogether. Choate first discussed his conclusion with Gearhart. He told his boss that he had consulted with the university's Human Resources director and did not think the facts gathered so far justified firing Sharp, at least at that point in his investigation. However, he was convinced he had to remove her from any further role in unraveling the financial mess. Though he hoped it wasn't the case, the possibility existed that Sharp was more aware of the division's financial problems than she had revealed so far. And there was an added possibility—unlikely, but conceivable—that she acted deliberately in ways that benefited her personally.

Gearhart left the decision up to Choate. The vice chancellor consulted with his Advancement Cabinet, which agreed that it would be best for her to go.

On August 24th Choate met with Sharp and told her she would no longer be responsible for Advancement's finances. Effective September 4th, Sharp would only handle the division's human resources activity. He also was reducing her annual pay by about one third to reflect fewer responsibilities. She would be moved back to an office in University House, the headquarters of the Development Office, where she had been posted when Gearhart ran the division.

Sharp took the news well. She anticipated a change and likely was relieved she still had a job.

At Choate's urging, and with Gearhart's patience wearing thin, Pederson agreed to provide staff assistance to help make sense of Advancement's finances. He assigned the task to Denise Reynolds, an accountant in Pederson's operation. Under the arrangement, Reynolds would remain as a member of Pederson's staff but would focus all of her work time on trying to reconcile Advancement's resources. She moved into Sharp's vacated office next to Choate's and delved into solving the deficit puzzle.

With Reynolds at his side, Choate felt confident about fixing the problem—or at least making sense of it. She was all business. Introverted and soft-spoken, Reynolds' facial expressions frequently telegraphed her feelings. Unlike Sharp, Reynolds kept her desk tidy, even well after the newness of her move to the vice chancellor's suite wore off. She maintained a stark office; it featured few personal photos or other items. It was as though she didn't expect to remain a part of the Advancement operation for very long. That would not be surprising: unlike her field of accounting, advancement work relies on the interplay of personalities and persuasion—i.e., politics—to get the job done. Not everyone is willing to make the adjustments and concessions it takes to stay happy in such a dynamic environment.

The new academic year started on August 20th. A week later Gearhart held a "back to school" news conference to update the public about the quality and size of UA's student body. Gearhart and others noted excitedly that enrollment continued to rise, a trend that had begun a few years earlier. The diversity of the student body had increased as a result of the university's strategic outreach efforts. Other metrics of growth and quality supported Gearhart's desire to solidify

UA's position and reputation as Arkansans' university of first choice.

Just a few weeks later, *U.S. News* issued its annual ranking of universities and colleges. Based on a survey of higher education leaders around the nation, the publication named UA as one of nine "up and coming" public universities. The distinction was in part a reflection of the concerted national rebranding campaign UA had undertaken at Choate's direction. It was a great bragging point to share with donors, alumni, and prospective students.

Things were indeed looking good on many fronts, not just enrollment. Federal research funding—an important but incomplete measure of academic quality—continued to increase modestly, as did the number of undergraduate students winning nationally competitive grants and scholarships. Fundraising was at an all-time high.

Furthermore, the Razorback football team—the one thing that seemed to unite all of Arkansas—was still considered a pre-season pick to contend for the NCAA national championship, despite Bobby Petrino's abrupt departure. It was a dizzying and fanciful status given what had occurred to the program earlier in the year.

While there was much for Razorback Nation to feel good about, it wouldn't last long. The football team played woefully all season. Though no announcement had been made about problems within Advancement—the scope and cause of the deficit were still unknown—suspicions were percolating. Staff within the division knew something was wrong when marketing funds were abruptly cut and pre-game receptions at University House were scaled back. Vacant positions within Advancement were frozen indefinitely while open positions elsewhere on campus were being filled.

Progress on untangling the mess was painfully slow for those aware of the problem. Choate had given those of us on his leadership team an overview but with the exception of his close friend Bruce Pontious, the head of Advancement's Development office, the rest of us did not realize just how serious Choate's problems were. During this period, several of us raised the obvious question:

Doesn't it make sense to seek an audit of Advancement's finances? All evidence pointed to its necessity. We thought we knew how and where it started—with Sharp—and we knew we *didn't* know where all the money went. No one could say with any certainly whether or not other financial or record-keeping mistakes existed, or whether anyone besides Sharp played a role, purposely or not.

Choate didn't need us to suggest the idea; he and Gearhart had discussed the possibility.

"Brad, an audit will make you look very bad," Gearhart warned him. Choate agreed but felt that a formal audit might be the only way to know for certain what happened—and who was to blame. That decision, of course, rested with Gearhart.

Back in Reynolds' office, Choate shared Gearhart's response. "Why do these guys not want an audit?" he wondered. Based on his own familiarity with his boss, he suspected it was because Gearhart did not want System President Don Bobbitt and the UA System Board of Trustees to find out that a huge deficit existed in one of the Fayetteville campus's highest-profile units. If they did know, word would likely leak out to the public. That would be bad for a number of reasons: in addition to the upcoming kickoff to the silent phase of UA's billion-dollar capital campaign, the state's 2012 legislative elections were a few weeks away. No one wanted to see UA's finances or management become a political issue, especially at a time when desperate candidates in close races look for something fresh and raw to rail against.

Choate later shared what he said was Reynolds' own speculation: An audit would reveal serious flaws in UA's financial management practices that reached far beyond the Advancement division. An audit is the last thing the university's financial management leaders wanted, Choate paraphrased.

Whether one or both of them were right didn't matter. They still had a problem to solve. They went back to work.

Chapter 4

PANIC

On September 28th, Gearhart phoned Choate. With Pederson at his side and Choate on speakerphone, Gearhart expressed continued frustration with the slow progress being made on figuring out Advancement's finances. The first quarter of the fiscal year was about to end; several essential fundraising and marketing activities remained on hold. People were asking questions. "What's the hold-up?!" Gearhart wanted to know.

"Dave, I'm more frustrated than anyone!" Choate bemoaned, explaining that every spreadsheet Reynolds prepared seemed to produce a different and larger deficit. The amount was now at least a couple million dollars, far greater than the $544,000 Pederson originally identified. Neither he nor Reynolds possessed the expertise to figure this out; they needed additional help from Pederson's finance experts, he said.

"I just don't have staff available to help you," Pederson responded during the call.

"Don, tell me a more pressing issue that your staff should be addressing," an exasperated Choate challenged. "Tell me a more pressing issue facing this university right now!"

The point was legitimate. It was now almost three months since Choate reported to Gearhart and Pederson about Sharp's "terrible mistake" and almost as long since Pederson quietly arranged for the short-term loan to cover Gearhart's deferred-compensation payment and some—not all—of the overdue vendor payments that Sharp had left behind. As a result of that day's conversation, Pederson's top deputy, UA Treasurer Jean Schook, became more actively involved. Schook was a licensed CPA as well as a certified fraud examiner. She had joined Pederson's staff in 2007 after a long career as an Arkansas state auditor. She had a positive reputation on campus and within her profession.

Choate was relieved to have Schook's help, especially given that she and Sharp had communicated about Advancement's finances on a regular basis. Of all people in Pederson's division, she possibly was in the best position to make sense of Sharp's actions.

On October 4, 2012, five days after the call with Gearhart and Pederson, Choate met in his office with Reynolds and Schook. The three reviewed everything they had compiled about the Advancement situation. Choate served as their scribe, typing on his keyboard as the three of them discussed their findings: Sharp had maintained shoddy and inaccurate recordkeeping. She had violated numerous university financial protocols and policies. She had approved and processed spending requests that far exceeded the division's annual revenues.

"There's no way you would have been able to realize what she was doing," Schook reassured a frustrated but relieved Choate. Reynolds reportedly agreed.

Wrapping up their work, they finished their draft. Choate saved the document on his computer and emailed it to Schook. She, in turn, would format the document and send it to the CFO.

At 5:45 p.m. that day, Schook emailed the trio's conclusions under her own name to Pederson, with copies to Reynolds and Choate. She labeled the message "Advancement Financial Position" and said it represented "a few initial thoughts."

1. I feel the problem is with unfunded personnel, not operational spending. Advancement had hired more people in recent years than it had funds to support.
2. This issue has been building for many years and is not a one-year problem.
3. It is clear the information provided to Dave Gearhart when he was [vice chancellor] and subsequently Brad Choate was inaccurate.
4. Funds from the foundation have been available over the years to 'mask' the deficits....In FY '12 sufficient foundation funds were no longer available to provide such masking and the problem was revealed.
5. There are significant inaccuracies in the system concerning staffing and budget units....These types of inaccuracies in the accounting system further confused salary and fringe requirements.

Choate was counting on a prompt response to the email from Pederson. Gearhart wanted to resolve the matter and put it behind him. Choate did as well. But unbeknownst to Choate, Schook had sent Pederson a second email forty-five minutes after her first one. The subject line read "Follow-up."

> Just wanted to let you know that the email I just sent was composed by Brad. He asked that I send it, though I can't understand what difference it makes. Didn't seem like something I wanted to challenge as I agree for the most part with the conclusions. I'm still not ready to conclusively say there are no other problems though.

The second email also made reference to an item not noted in earlier correspondence: a "deposit error."

"In my mind the $1.3M deposit error was an attempt to cover up the unpaid FY11 account receivable balance," Schook noted.

On October 8th, Choate briefed me and his other division leaders on what he, Schook, and Reynolds had concluded. We were surprised and disheartened. Each of us liked and had worked closely with Sharp. It was hard for any of us to accept that she would have—or could have—mismanaged the division's finances for years, and had done so in such a way that it escaped the university's system of financial controls and audits.

All of us waited anxiously for some kind of action or decision. Choate couldn't allow us to proceed with high-priority projects and activities until Pederson and Gearhart authorized funding, likely from university reserves. My office's marketing efforts, including a multi-faceted national branding campaign to boost enrollment and advance Gearhart's strategic plan, remained on hold.

Choate finally received Pederson's response on October 19th, fifteen days after Choate, Schook, and Reynolds had prepared their findings. Pederson handed him an envelope containing a revised version of the October 4th memo, which Pederson had received from Schook earlier that day. Its new title was "Re: Division of Advancement Financial Management Deficiencies." The four-page document bore a red CONFIDENTIAL stamp at the top of the first page. Along with the October 4th email's references to Sharp's culpability, this final version set the size of the overspending at an astounding $4.34 million—meaning that Advancement exceeded its annual allocated revenues by about 40 percent. The new memo also made allegations against Choate:

> Initial conclusions based on a review of both university and foundation accounting records and other supporting documentation, as well as interviews with key personnel, revealed the Vice Chancellor for Advancement, Brad Choate,...provided inadequate and essentially no oversight of the financial activities of the Division.

Schook detailed several findings critical of Choate: he gave Sharp his login-access credentials to the university's financial database, a violation of UA policies; he delegated too much of his financial review responsibilities to Sharp; he relied heavily on the accuracy of Sharp's word and reports with no attempt to verify their accuracy; and he failed to realize that Sharp's younger sister, Betty, often provided the required second authorization for transactions that the elder Sharp initiated. (Betty, an employee in the Development office, held the proper clearance to take such action but doing so in concert with her own sister was later deemed a violation of UA's conflict-of-interest policy.)

Schook's findings also faulted Choate for not maintaining his own copies of budget materials Sharp had provided to him at meetings; failing to ensure that his division's leaders had full and accurate knowledge of their units' revenues; and for hiring 20 additional staff positions in a four-year period without making sure he had, or asked for and received, sufficient funding.

Schook also blamed Choate for not realizing Sharp had reimbursed him twice for a $2,050 expense he had incurred in 2011 and for waiting more than three months after learning of the duplicate payment to compensate the university. (Choate was owed more than $7,000 in office reimbursements at the time, he quickly pointed out.) The memo also elaborated on Schook's October 4th email reference to Sharp's handling of a $1.3 million "deposit error."

> In what appeared to be an intentional effort to disguise a prior year account receivable balance that had not been cleared, the Budget Director deposited restricted funds—a gift for capital purposes—totaling $1.3 million dollars [sic], in May 2012, into the same unrestricted general operating account with the delinquent account receivable balance....The misdirection of funds occurred in spite of the purpose of the funds being clearly described on the face of the check.

Here Schook, the certified fraud examiner, was making a serious accusation. She continued:

> Because many fraud risks factors were identified, consideration was given of the need to request an internal audit examination. After careful consideration, the decision to request an internal audit examination should be left ultimately to the VCFA [Pederson] and the Chancellor.

In closing, she concluded that "an overwhelming amount of evidence…points to lack of management oversight, non-compliance with University policies and procedures and deliberate efforts to disguise poor financial management of the Division of Advancement resources." While there was "no evidence of intentional acts to misappropriate resources for personal gain," Schook pointed out that she had not looked at Advancement's books specifically for that purpose.

In other words, if Gearhart or Pederson wanted that question answered, they needed to instruct her to do so.

Choate finished reading the memo Pederson had just given him. In light of what he, Reynolds, and Schook had shared with Pederson in their October draft, Choate wondered why in the world these accusations were being made now.

"Well, you gave Joy your password," Pederson answered.

"That had nothing to do with any of this!" Choate responded, pointing out that Schook's revised memo did not suggest that Sharp's access to the login credentials played any role in Sharp's mismanagement or spending. He decided to prepare a response. But first, he was going to call his boss.

Gearhart didn't answer his phone. Choate left a voice mail message stressing urgency. The call was returned the following day. As the conversation progressed, Choate realized that the chancellor did not want to discuss the matter; instead he repeatedly urged Choate "to take responsibility" for what Schook had found.

"I certainly take responsibility for leading Advancement," he shot back, "but to blame me for this financial situation is not supported by the facts, nor does it help solve the problem."

Choate sent Gearhart and Pederson a 3,000-word response to Schook's memo, categorically denying accusations that he was not properly managing the budget or was negligent in his oversight duties. Gearhart was not persuaded. He wrote back:

> Brad: I will review this very closely and we can then discuss face to face, but a cursory read makes me very concerned that you are not taking responsibility for what happened.
> None of your senior staff had any involvement in the budget. They have admitted to me and to others that they would ask about their budgets, but would be given no information after multiple requests....I have to brief Dr. Bobbitt and the chairman of the board. I am very concerned about their reactions.
> Brad, you have been a friend and colleague for many years. I brought you here to help me. But your lack of oversight has created a colossal fiscal crisis....It breaks my heart. It truly does. I am terribly disappointed. But, ultimately, you have no one to blame but yourself. You need to take responsibility.

On Monday, October 22nd, Gearhart met with System President Bobbitt, according to a log of Gearhart's deficit-related activity that was compiled by his executive assistant. The log also shows that on October 24th, he held a meeting about Advancement's overspending with Pederson, UA Provost Sharon Gaber, Athletics Director Jeff Long, and Greg Lee, the retired chief administrative officer for Tyson Foods. A day previous, Gearhart had emailed the Schook memo to Lee—a UA donor and Gearhart friend—and sought feedback. In response, Lee provided a marked-up copy of the document with questions noted and sections underlined, apparently for discussion purposes only.

On October 25th, Pederson and Schook met with state auditors. The purpose was unrelated to Advancement; it dealt with the recently completed check on UA's finances. Each year state auditors sample aspects of an agency's total finances; they do not explore all areas in detail unless there's a concern spotted or raised. The process concludes with a formal "exit conference." During this meeting, the organization's chief financial officer is required to review and sign, if appropriate, a "management representation letter." The letter is the coda to the audit process; its language provides the audited agency one final chance to certify or clarify the accuracy of the materials and explanations it had provided. The management representation letter is considered an affidavit and can be used as evidence if the audit's accuracy were ever challenged.

Part of the management representation letter asks the CFO to attest to the following statement:

> We have no knowledge or any allegation of fraud or suspected fraud affecting the entity involving management, employees who have significant roles in internal control, or others where the fraud could have a material effect on the financial statements. We have no knowledge of any allegations of fraud or suspected fraud affecting the entity received in communications from employees, former employees, analysts, regulators, or others.

Pederson had received Schook's accusatory memo on Advancement's deficit six days earlier. He had delivered it to Choate and discussed it with him on the same day. He had met with Gearhart, Gaber, Long, and Lee the day before this exit conference. The memo included findings that there had been "misdirection of funds" and "an overwhelming amount of evidence that points to…deliberate efforts to disguise poor financial management of the Advancement division's resources." The memo's conclusions would soon be used as justification for terminating two employees.

But neither Pederson nor Schook mentioned the memo's existence or contents during the exit interview. Pederson simply took the letter from the auditors and signed it, affirming the declaration in the affidavit.

The ax fell on November 6th, though it didn't completely sever Choate from his employer.

Behind closed doors, Gearhart told Choate that a few days earlier he had briefed the trustees and UA System President Don Bobbitt on the Advancement deficit during an executive session of the board.

(This briefing was an apparent violation of Arkansas' open meetings law, which prohibits the discussion of such operational matters in closed session; Gearhart unwittingly confirmed the nature of the discussion in a media interview a few months later.) Gearhart said he shared Schook's October 19th memo with the board along with Choate's rebuttal. According to Gearhart, the board responded by telling him he should fire Choate.

"I couldn't save you," Gearhart offered regretfully.

But in a way he did—for the time being. Gearhart said the board and Bobbitt agreed to let Choate stay on so long as he was removed from any administrative responsibilities. Gearhart would make Choate a "generic" vice chancellor and would have him work at his, Gearhart's, direction. Choate would continue to receive his full salary and benefits until the following June unless he quit or found another job. In this new role, Choate would not be expected to attend any meetings unless Gearhart himself invited him. He would be allowed to keep his corner office and to receive whatever clerical support he needed. He could even search for a new job while at work and use university resources to do it.

Choate was stung by the news and immediately thought of how it would affect his reputation. *How will this play out? Will I be able to find another job?* It didn't cross his mind at the time that it was a sweet arrangement, considering the circumstances: full pay and perks with no day-to-day duties for eight months.

Believing he had no choice, he accepted the deal.

Over the next few days Gearhart held one-on-one meetings with me and the other members of the Advancement cabinet to explain his decisions. In addition to Choate's reassignment, he was removing Sharp from Advancement altogether; he had arranged for her to work in UA's Human Resources office, one of the campus units that reported to Pederson. However, unlike Choate, he left open the possibility that Sharp could remain employed by UA beyond June 30th.

He showed me, but did not let me keep, a copy of Schook's October 19th memo. He told me about his recent conversation with trustees and Bobbitt. He described Choate as a good man but a lousy manager.

"I couldn't save him," he lamented, using the same phraseology that I later learned he used with Choate.

"I understand you've never been given a budget," he continued.

"Actually, I was," I responded. "It wasn't in the same format that we used in Maine. Not categorical, not as much detail." I explained that my executive assistant, Dawn Mabry, and I met monthly with Sharp to confirm University Relations' budget numbers. This was important for two reasons: First, Joy had taken over the daily management of our office's budget after the death of our in-house budget manager, and second, we had a special marketing account that was funded through the money Advancement received from the UA Foundation. As our budget officer, Joy maintained our records. Mabry and I never encountered any discrepancies between our own monitoring of accounts and Sharp's until May of 2012. When we met with her that month, we told her the revenue totals she was sharing with us were about $90,000 lower than what Dawn and I had calculated. She said she'd look into it and within a day rectified the difference. We approached the final month of the fiscal year believing that University Relations' end-of-year totals would show a slight surplus.

With Choate gone, the division in a multi-million deficit, and the university's capital campaign underway in its initial "silent phase," there was a serious leadership gap. Consequently, Gearhart said he would assume Choate's leadership and management duties along with his chancellor's role. Understandably, Gearhart did not want to name any of the three associate vice chancellors as interim head of the division; each of us was too busy with the day-to-day work of our respective operations. His dual role would be temporary, he said, but would allow ample time to search for a permanent successor. For now, each of us would report directly to him. He and Judy Schwab, his chief of staff, would join us for our weekly Advancement Cabinet meetings.

"How do you want to announce this?" I asked. These developments would be major news well beyond campus. Choate was a prominent member of the UA administration and community; his absence from meetings and events would quickly be noticed. Word of Choate's demotion and Advancement's embarrassing shortfall would probably be reported in the *Chronicle of Higher Education*, the *Chronicle of Philanthropy*, and *Inside Higher Ed*, three prominent national news providers that report on education and fundraising. It was important to Gearhart's credibility that he show leadership and control of the situation by announcing the troublesome news proactively, on campus and off. Failure to do that would fuel speculation that the problem was worse—and perhaps even bigger than what Gearhart was sharing—whenever the first media query occurred, which was bound to happen. As with any potential PR crisis, we had to get in front of it with the facts, demonstrating accountability and transparency to our stakeholders.

To my surprise, Gearhart said he thought it was "premature" to announce anything about Choate or the Advancement deficit. We still didn't know how big the shortfall actually was, he explained. He thought we should wait until we were more certain.

"I'm not convinced we have that much time," I said. "Word is going to get out, for sure."

"I don't think so," he responded. It wasn't in Choate's interest or Sharp's nature for either to talk, he offered. Besides, there were others he needed to brief—key donors and alumni leaders, I presumed. He said he planned to take care of that over the next couple of weeks.

Gearhart decided to break the news on Monday, November 19th, at a regularly scheduled meeting of the university's deans and their top associates. Several attendees thought something out of the ordinary was up, given that Gearhart rarely attended their meetings.

They were run by Gaber, the university's chief academic officer. She was there, along with Pederson.

There were unfortunate and disconcerting problems in the Advancement division, Gearhart shared. He told them about Choate's and Sharp's reassignments and about his decision to manage his old division himself while Pederson and staff sought answers and remedies. He and Pederson distributed a short budget document so that each recipient could see Advancement's estimated deficit. It could be as high as $8 million once the current year's budget projections were factored in, they explained—about 80 percent above Advancement's total annual revenue. Gearhart assured the deans and others that neither their units nor other divisions within the university would have to cover Advancement's money problems; the division would have to do it itself, one way or another. Gearhart also said that while UA had plenty of reserves set aside for emergencies, he would not allow those to be tapped to cover the shortfall.

Before leaving the meeting, Gearhart and Pederson had attendees give back the budget handout. They did not want the details circulating on campus or ending up in the hands of an enterprising reporter. Of course, the news itself would be talked about; it was too stunning for the deans and assistants not to discuss afterward. Human behavior being what it is, it was also likely that at least a few present for Gearhart's pronouncement would share what they learned with trusted colleagues, staff, and friends. Some did.

Choate heard about Gearhart briefing the deans directly from a few of the attendees. Choate did not believe he was under any gag order—Gearhart had not instructed him not to talk—so he shared freely the assurances Schook and Reynolds had given him on October 4th: that he couldn't have known what Sharp had been doing with the budget; that UA's system of checks and balances had not caught her actions; and that the behavior dated back to Gearhart's days as head of Advancement.

PLEASE DELETE

The following day, November 20, Gearhart sent Choate a terse e-mail:

> Brad: I have had several folks tell me recently that you are blaming your situation on Don Pederson. That you are disparaging his name and using him as the reason for your demise. I have also been told that you are telling folks that you inherited this problem and the budget deficit existed before you arrived.
>
> Neither are [sic] accurate and in your heart you know that. All of the evidence supports otherwise.
>
> It is not doing you any good making remarks like this and in fact your comments are damaging you further. I'm asking you to stop the blame game. I assume you want me to give you a favorable recommendation when the time comes and you are making it difficult for me to do that.
>
> If I continue to hear these reports I will be forced to remove you from this building and assign you space elsewhere. The other alternative is to dismiss you immediately for cause. I have been very good to you allowing you to stay here while searching for a position, but I will not allow you to disparage my senior team or me. I hope I have made this clear to you.

Choate took it as a threat. He wrote back minutes later:

> I have not said one bad word about you and in fact have been explicit to say I don't want this to hurt you or the University. I have said that I think Don and the financial affairs system should have helped spot this issue before now.
>
> I'm sorry if those comments were misinterpreted and will be extra careful to make sure it doesn't happen again.

I heard about Gearhart's meeting with the deans from a few of the communications directors assigned to UA's colleges and schools. They assumed I knew that the presentation had taken place and thought I must have been part of its planning. I didn't and I wasn't. I quickly became concerned that the rumor mill would gin up the facts, producing false narratives that would put the university in a defensive, reactive mode—something people in my line of work always strive to avoid.

Fortunately for Gearhart, it was Thanksgiving week. Many students and employees had already headed off campus and out of town for the long holiday break, making it less likely that his talk with the deans would leak out. The silence, however, would prove to be the calm before the storm.

Chapter 5

INK BY THE BARREL

Dave Gearhart was a charismatic person. He dressed impeccably: sharp suits always ornamented with a pocket square, fine shirts and cufflinks, and power ties. He was fond of expensive wine and good cigars. Being chancellor of a Southern university often requires formal wear for events, and Dave looked impressive in a tux. His hair was always perfectly coiffed. He looked and acted the part of an influential and powerful man. And he was.

Donors liked and admired Gearhart. Many of them had known him for years, even before he returned to his hometown of Fayetteville in 1998 to become vice chancellor for Advancement. He successfully courted and cultivated wealthy Arkansans and UA alumni to create an enviable portfolio of donors, who helped Gearhart surpass the $1 billion mark in his first capital campaign as vice chancellor. He had a particularly intimate relationship with many key givers. Often, when exchanging emails with some of the older female donors, he would close with, "Love you, Dave." His sentiments were sincere and it seemed to me that his correspondents felt similar affection for him.

Marcia and I also liked Gearhart. Occasionally, following an event, we went for drinks with him, his wife Jane, and a few other mutual friends. One time, Marcia prepared a traditional lobster dinner for the Gearharts and the Choates, cooking up a dozen lobsters that one of her brothers back in Maine had shipped overnight to us. Dave and Jane entertained us with lines from some of their favorite *Saturday Night Live* routines. That evening, as on other occasions, the Gearharts engaged in playful repartee in which Dave would offer some profound observation to which Jane would respond with a dismissive put-down. He was a willing straight man, knowingly setting her up for some hilarious comebacks.

In most work and social situations that I observed, Gearhart could remain unflappable, even in the presence of critics and boors. Conversely, he could easily become enraged by any media coverage of himself or UA that he perceived as less than fully supportive. As good as he was at tolerating the demands and occasional bombast of legislators, donors, and alumni, he was far less obliging of members of the news media. He showed a remarkably thin skin when a story or editorial about him or UA was poorly researched, misinformed, or critical. His reaction may have been related to the job requirements of being a fundraiser: you are accustomed to conversations where you rarely challenge or question the opinions and decisions of your audience, and you avoid saying anything that might prompt disagreement. Compare his background to that of university presidents and chancellors who once spent formative years as faculty members and as deans: one can posit that they developed more tolerance of questioning and criticism as a result of having to defend their views and decisions to faculty, who are accustomed to having their opinions and research challenged by peers. When he didn't like the reaction or coverage he received, Gearhart in response often would offer *ad hominem* attacks on the particular individual responsible, such as trying to discredit one reporter's credibility by pointing out her presumed salary. ("What does she make? *Forty thousand dollars?!*") As is sometimes the case with certain types of well-entrenched leaders,

Gearhart was willing to engage the news media only to the point at which they failed to respond as he wished. It was a risky sensitivity for the head of an institution that was heavily dependent on public perceptions.

One constant irritant to Gearhart was Paul Greenberg, the *Arkansas Democrat-Gazette* newspaper's longtime editorial page editor and a nationally syndicated columnist. The *Democrat-Gazette* was a statewide, daily newspaper, by far the largest in circulation and influence. Greenberg, who decades earlier in his career won a Pulitzer Prize for editorial writing, was a champion of the liberal arts. When UA modified its core requirements in a manner that Greenberg thought weakened the university's commitment to classical education, he launched a series of nasty critiques that included labeling the university as the state's "sinking flagship." A pointed editorial cartoon underscored Greenberg's branding by depicting UA's iconic, twin-towered "Old Main" building as taking on water in Titanic-like fashion. Given competing world events and public sensibilities at the time, Greenberg's condemnation likely would have passed with little notice.

Stylistically, Greenberg personified muckraking-era writer F.P. Dunne's famous description of a newspaper's purpose: to "comfort the afflicted and afflict the comfortable." And on this occasion, Gearhart took the bait that Greenberg's editorial dangled. Dismissing another adage that Gearhart's own father, a newspaper publisher, might have offered ("Never pick a fight with someone who buys ink by the barrel"), Gearhart fired off an accusatory email response to Greenberg's characterization. He challenged several of the editorialist's assumptions and offered several compelling rejoinders. But, as was often his wont when he lost his cool, the chancellor also attacked the man himself as he tried to support his position. As I recall Gearhart's email (he shared it with me and others, but I did not save a copy), he told the 74-year-old Greenberg that he sounded like an angry old man or something similar. I suspect Greenberg still has the actual email.

Greenberg wrote back, asking Gearhart for permission to reproduce his email in the newspaper. Gearhart objected, saying his response wasn't intended for publication. Of course, Greenberg didn't need Gearhart's permission: with a few narrow exceptions—none of which pertained to this situation—the chancellor's emails and letters are considered public records under Arkansas law. Furthermore, Gearhart sent it to the newspaper without noting any conditions, therefore relinquishing any possible control he could have hoped to preserve.

To Gearhart's initial relief, Greenberg agreed to respect Gearhart's objection. Was he showing deference to the powerful leader of one of the state's most influential public institutions? Hardly. Greenberg surely recognized that by turning down his request, Gearhart was giving his adversary the opportunity to tell readers that UA's chancellor challenged, in writing, the editorial's merits but would not let the newspaper publish that critique. Consequently, Greenberg took advantage of his detractor's request: using Gearhart's undisclosed rebuttal as justification, Greenberg reiterated, in longer form and more conspicuous placement, his claim that UA had diluted the rigor of its academics without having to acknowledge the specifics that Gearhart had offered in UA's defense. Unwittingly, Gearhart had played into his critic's hands. Soon, he would do it again.

On November 26th, reporter Chris Bahn of the multimedia *Arkansas Business* news organization contacted me. A source had told him that a week earlier Gearhart, Provost Sharon Gaber, and CFO Pederson had met with the deans and told them there was an $8 million dollar deficit in Advancement. He had also been told about Choate's reassignment. Bahn asked me to provide details and, invoking Arkansas' public records law, asked for the document that Gearhart and Pederson had distributed, then reclaimed, at the deans' meeting. I told him I'd have to get back to him.

It was now too late for us to get out in front of this story with the facts. Anything we said or issued would be seen as reactive to a reporter's scoop. Worse, mild skeptics as well as hardened cynics would claim we were withholding important news or even trying to cover up what happened. The circumstances didn't support a cover-up; Gearhart had been gradually telling donors, alumni, and senior university leaders that Choate and Sharp had made a mess of Advancement's finances. Gearhart figured he had so far briefed around 150 people about the matter.

With a news story about to break, I advised Gearhart that we should prepare and issue a formal announcement and explanation. It needed to be shared as quickly as possible across campus as well as with alumni, donors, and the state's General Assembly, among other stakeholders. Nobody likes surprises, especially if they believe they should have been among the first to know. Gearhart agreed.

I produced the first draft of a statement and circulated it to Gearhart, his executive committee, and the university's lawyers for fact checking and word-smithing. With so many people weighing in, the process slowed down our ability to prepare something acceptable to release in advance of Bahn's story. Gearhart didn't sign off until Sunday, December 2nd. The following morning we posted a detailed 650-word statement on UA's website and its news feed, which reporters monitor. Presented in the first-person as a message from Gearhart himself, it included all of the details that I was aware of and assured the campus that no other division's budget would be touched to fix Advancement's deficit.

But Bahn's story was already out by the time the message was posted.

The front-page headline read "UA Works to Correct $4M Advancement 'Miscalculation.'"

> University of Arkansas officials confirmed last week that they are working to correct a multimillion-dollar deficit in the school's Division for University Advancement for the second consecutive year. Brad Choate, vice chancellor for Advancement, has been

> stripped of his day-to-day responsibilities and will lose his job at the end of the fiscal year, Chancellor G. David Gearhart told *Arkansas Business*….He wasn't fired, the chancellor said, because "there was nothing that showed that there was money misappropriated or misspent.
>
> "Brad was being told by his budget person that there were funds to cover it, when clearly there weren't," Gearhart said. "You could debate the issue of what his knowledge should have been. I think he would claim he was getting bad information from his budget person.
>
> "'As I said to the deans the other day, this doesn't mean that Brad's a bad person…but you really can't amass this kind of deficit and survive it," Gearhart said.

Predictably, Bahn's article and the university's statement prompted other Arkansas-based news media to jump on the story. Television stations in the state at first provided superficial coverage but did relatively little of their own investigation; unlike breaking news involving fires or car crashes, stories about financial mismanagement rarely provide the necessary visual elements that TV news depends on. However, print and online journalists aggressively pursued the story. In addition to Bahn, both the *Democrat-Gazette's* Tracie Dungan and *Arkansas Times'* Max Brantley submitted public records requests seeking financial documents, emails, and other papers related to the Advancement deficit and the decisions surrounding Choate's and Sharp's reassignments.

As associate vice chancellor for University Relations, I held primary responsibility for receiving and responding to public records requests that reporters submitted to UA under the Arkansas Freedom of Information Act (FOIA). It was a job I had performed for over 20 years, first in Maine and now in Arkansas, working almost daily with in-house attorneys to fulfill the university's legal obligations. Usually these FOIA requests would begin with a reporter's email. As confirmed to me by law professor Richard Peltz-Steele, co-author of the book *The Arkansas Freedom of Information Act* (considered the definitive text on Arkansas' FOIA law), reporters or citizens seeking public records are not required to explicitly invoke any specific phrase or "magic words"; they simply had to make the request for print or electronic records covering specific topics or individuals, and must be clear in their intent. The burden is on the public entity—in this case, the university—to comply. Once I received the FOIA request, I'd email it to Gearhart and to any other university officers whose duties related to the FOIA'd topic. I'd also share the records request with UA's legal counsel, attorneys Scott Varady and Bill Kincaid. Together, the lawyers and I would determine the types of documents and other records the FOIA request pertained to and which university employees we needed to consult. If a reporter's FOIA request was overly broad—meaning that it was too general in nature—I would tell the reporter so in writing. Usually, the reporter would then resubmit his or her FOIA with a narrower and more specific scope. We had to treat these requests as priorities; under Arkansas law, we had no more than three business days to respond, sometimes less, depending on the situation.

Arkansas law did not require us to create documents or compilations of data if they did not already exist. For that reason, we never asked employees to generate reports or documents that went beyond the law's requirements. In some circumstances, as part of responding to a FOIA request, I would give the reporter a layperson's explanation of the terminology, coding, or university policy that was cited in a particular document in an effort to minimize the possibility that a reporter would misunderstand or misrepresent the information he or she received. That safeguard is a standard practice in media relations, though it doesn't always prevent reporters' errors.

After collecting the various records, I would share them with Varady or Kincaid. We needed to determine if what we had received from employees was "responsive" to the request—that is, whether each document was, or contained, what the reporter asked for.

FOIA law protected employees from "clearly unwarranted invasion of personal privacy." However, aspects of an employee's personnel file must be made public if the state's attorney general or court finds that the public's need to know the information reasonably outweighs the employee's privacy protections. Arkansas' FOIA handbook says that state agencies should lean toward disclosing the information, emphasizing the public interest in transparency. In such a situation, the agency is instructed to redact (i.e., conceal) any information about an employee that falls within a list of 20 specific exemptions noted in Arkansas' FOIA—e.g., Social Security number, bank account numbers, choice of health insurance options, etc. If an employee objects to releasing the information, a process exists under the law that allows her or him to appeal the decision to the state attorney general for an opinion before the employer is permitted to make the information public. Conversely, employees may grant permission to their employer to release information that otherwise would be exempt from disclosure.

Once all of these concerns were taken into account, I would email the reviewed and approved material to the reporter who requested it. I'd also send a cover message confirming that the contents reflect all "responsive records" identified, qualifying that statement by adding that the university "retains the right to augment this response" in the event we unintentionally excluded something. I would then forward the response to Gearhart and the attorneys, just as I had copied them on the original FOIA request.

December was a chaotic month for me, given the volume of public records requests and related questions I fielded about the Advancement situation. We provided well over 100 pages of email exchanges and financial records to each of the reporters who submitted the first round of FOIA requests alone. Of particular note was a three-page timeline listing Gearhart's meetings and phone calls related to Advancement's deficit, covering July 13th through

November 19th. Gloria Sutherland, Gearhart's executive assistant, had begun to compile and maintain the timeline soon after it became apparent that one or more employees might have mismanaged funds. She wisely recognized that the timeline could be valuable should an employee challenge any disciplinary action against them.

With a few exceptions, the timeline identified participating individuals by their initials only. After receiving the timeline in response to her FOIA request, the *Democrat-Gazette's* Tracie Dungan wanted to know the actual names and titles that corresponded with those abbreviations. All of the initials belonged to university or UA Foundation employees except for one set: those of Greg Lee, the former Tyson Foods executive. According to the timeline, Gearhart and Pederson met with Lee on October 24th to discuss UA Treasurer Jean Schook's October 19th report entitled "Division of Advancement Financial Management Deficiencies."

"Why was Greg Lee involved?" Dungan asked me. I had no idea. I followed up with Gearhart, who became upset that Lee's name would be associated with the Advancement issue and that Sutherland had maintained a log without first being directed to. He justified involving Lee because he was a trusted advisor and a member of Gearhart's capital campaign steering team. He felt it was appropriate to involve him, given that the Advancement situation could affect the campaign. He authorized me to give reporters that answer.

In light of news coverage of Advancement's problems, legislators, reporters, and alumni leaders began asking Gearhart to meet with them to explain how the deficit occurred and what he was doing to remedy things. Based on their reactions after those meetings, editorial writers and commentators appeared to be as puzzled by Gearhart's decision not to immediately fire Sharp or Choate as they were with the overspending itself.

> In my world, I told Gearhart, one need not commit a felony to be judged so incompetent as to be fired on the spot....In the real world, people who are making a fraction of Choate's pay are routinely fired

> for performance failures much more minor than being so clueless as to accidentally overcommit to millions of dollars of perpetual spending. (Gwen Moritz, *Arkansas Business*)
>
> Gearhart justifies [keeping Choate] in part because of Choate's ongoing contacts with moneybags on whom the university depends in its fund-raising....It is not surprising that keeping them happy is cited as a reason for continuing the employment of a person who busted a budget in a way that wouldn't be tolerated in private business. (Max Brantley, *Arkansas Times*)

It was Gearhart's nemesis Paul Greenberg who offered the lengthiest, if not the most acerbic, editorial criticism in response to the Advancement story. On December 11th the *Democrat-Gazette* carried Greenberg's broad take on the newspaper's coverage of various administrative wrongdoing in higher education, now adding UA to his list. Most of his editorial's reference to "the sinking flagship" targeted and mocked Choate; he barely mentioned Gearhart and laid no blame at the chancellor's feet.

"Back in the real world, the sooner this scandal is explained, and responsibility for it properly assigned and accepted, the sooner the university can get on with restoring its good name," Greenberg concluded. "These things happen in the best university families; it's only the worst that try to dodge responsibility for them."

The editorial angered Gearhart, perhaps because Greenberg invoked the term "scandal" four times in the 1100-word commentary. Others were equally displeased. Gearhart received several emails from donors and alumni who took exception to the editorial's content and to the self-described "inky wretch" who composed it. One donor wrote, "I am so angry with Greenberg that I am frothing at the mouth."

In response, Gearhart turned to a tool he often employed when he was enraged: a keyboard. At 10:30 that morning—just a few hours after Greenberg's editorial was published—he fired off an email to UA System President Don Bobbitt and the ten members of the System's board of trustees. He also blind-copied me and an unknown number of UA officials, donors, and alumni:

> No doubt you have seen Mr. Greenberg's editorial attacks on me and the University which obfuscates the truth and I believe were vicious and hateful. I am reminded of the now famous line from the Joseph McCarthy hearings, 'Senator, you've done enough. Have you no sense of decency, sir? At long last, have you left no sense of decency?'
>
> Brad Choate and Joy Sharp made a mistake, plain and simple. They are paying the ultimate price in losing their positions.

Gearhart then described personal and professional characteristics that he admired and respected in Sharp and Choate before returning his attention to Greenberg.

> And what about the claim, by Mr. Greenberg, the University attempted a cover-up. That is total nonsense....I never asked anyone to cover up anything, ever. I know it is not necessary to send you this email, but my A-type [sic] personality beckoned it.

I winced when I read Gearhart's email. I thought he was overreacting—a likely reflection of the chancellor's ongoing exasperation with Greenberg. I didn't think the editorial's content rated a comparison to McCarthyism. Nor had the editorial claimed that Gearhart or UA "attempted a cover-up." I was concerned that those assertions wouldn't play well with the chancellor's boss or the UA System's governing board; they might conclude that the stress was getting to him. But apparently they didn't.

"Very well said, Dave. As always, you have my full support," wrote Jane Rogers, the vice-chair of the UA System Board of Trustees at the time.

"Very well done," System President Bobbitt emailed to Gearhart. "I hope I get FOIA'd today."

Gearhart also received support from another prominent public figure:

"I appreciated your well written and hard hitting editorial in todays [sic] paper," wrote Asa Hutchinson, a former U.S. Congressman who, in 2014, would be elected Arkansas' next governor. "You have handled the situation very professionally and held people accountable. There is no need to bury folks because a mistake was made.

"I have had my share of harsh criticism in life," Hutchinson continued, "and sometimes you just have to push back, so I am glad you did."

Emboldened by such responses, Gearhart contacted me with a request for help. He said he wanted to submit a response to the newspaper—this time for publication—and knew exactly what he wanted to say. I took notes as he shared his thoughts and, afterward, started drafting something for him to review. I sent him the first iteration early in the afternoon. He quickly wrote back.

"It is good, but not tough enough," he replied. "Can you put a little more of my 'stuff' in it? That would make me feel much better."

Gearhart's "stuff" included his belief that Greenberg's editorials substituted facts "with distortions and fabrications." It speculated that some of the editorial criticism stemmed from "perhaps Paul Greenberg's personal animus against me." It stated that "the editorials' verbal piling-on calls to mind the *ad hominem* attacks that Sen. Joseph McCarthy leveled to advance his own agenda, to which Army counsel Joseph Welch angrily replied, 'Have you no sense of decency, sir?'" Per his instructions, I added his language.

Gearhart's guest commentary appeared in the December 15th edition of the *Democrat-Gazette*. If readers had missed Greenberg's long, rambling criticism of Advancement and UA four days earlier, the chancellor's riposte gave them a fresh reason to go back and read it.

Despite the volume of emails and financial records we provided in response to FOIAs, reporters were not pleased that the university had refused to include one particular document referred to in the material we had provided. It was described two ways in the timeline that Gearhart's executive assistant, Gloria Sutherland, prepared:

first, as a "document explaining Advancement issue" and second, as "the treasurer's office findings." Reporters wanted to know what exactly those documents were and what they might reveal about how and why a multi-million-dollar deficit occurred.

Both references were to Jean Schook's October 19th memo to Pederson, the document that cited Choate and Sharp for numerous performance failures and identified the size of the deficit at $4.34 million. It was also the document that both accused Sharp of intentionally redirecting a $1.3 million donation to the wrong account to conceal a deficit there and that acknowledged that no review had yet been conducted to determine whether or not Advancement division resources had been misappropriated. It was in this document that Schook said she would leave it up to Gearhart and Pederson to decide if an audit should be conducted.

The university's position was that the document was exempt from disclosure under FOIA. University lawyers had labeled Schook's memo a "job performance record" of Choate and Sharp, and such records are exempt from release unless they form the basis for an employee's termination. Choate and Sharp were not *fired*, UA's lawyers explained to me; rather, they were *reassigned* for the remaining eight months of the fiscal year and would not be rehired. There's a difference, they and Gearhart stated. I repeated that distinction to disbelieving reporters and reiterated our attorneys' statement: "The university views any records regarding reassignment as job performance records and therefore exempt from release under Arkansas' Freedom of Information Act."

It was a specious argument. Arkansas' FOIA law defines such exempt documents as those that are created by an employer for the purpose of evaluating an employee. Though Schook's memo did provide information about employee performance, it was not commissioned for that purpose, as evidenced by Choate's own participation in preparing the first draft. Furthermore, it also included non-personnel content, specifically the first hard findings about the size of the deficit and future financial projections. Normally, the lawyers would simply block out any part of such a memo that clearly fell within FOIA's protected-from-disclosure provision. This redacted version containing non-exempt content would then be provided to the inquiring reporters or citizens.

However, our lawyers chose not to follow that statutory precept. Their rationale may have been influenced by an email Gearhart sent to them, Pederson, and me at three o'clock in the morning on November 29th. In response to learning that Bahn, the reporter who was about to break the Advancement story, had submitted a public records request for documents regarding the deficit, Gearhart wrote back:

> Anything that can be interpreted as protected due to personnel in nature should be given consideration. John, let me see what you ultimately plan to send.

The Schook memo was not included in the documents the lawyers approved for me to pass along to Bahn and the others who would soon file similar requests. I had never received a copy of Schook's report, though Gearhart had allowed me to skim it while meeting with him on November 8th. With little recollection of the specifics, I had no reason to question the attorneys' decision that the document was exempt from public disclosure.

Chapter 6

"GET RID OF IT"

Once again, a holiday break provided a brief respite from the Advancement problem. UA's fall commencement ceremonies took place on Saturday, December 15th, the same day that Gearhart's response to Greenberg appeared in the morning newspaper. Campus had already quieted considerably as most students had headed home or elsewhere. For those still working on a degree, classes would resume on Monday, January 14th. A small number of students remained at UA; mostly international students and student-athletes whose teams were still in season.

Many university employees also had plans for the winter break. UA closed for a thirteen-day period encompassing Christmas and New Year's Day, taking advantage of low levels of activity and the opportunity to save money. Most hourly employees were not paid during those shutdown days, and less fuel and electricity were consumed since most campus buildings were closed up.

But that did not mean that efforts to resolve Advancement's issues were put on hold. Gearhart and Pederson continued to talk about the division's financial problems. Meanwhile, reporters continued to ask questions and submit FOIA requests. However, the university's closure provided more breathing room, as under Arkansas law the FOIA clock ran only when the university was open for business, a fact which reporters understood. As a result, the break permitted those of us working on public records requests to squeeze in some personal time without the pressure of a three-day response deadline. I was reviewing and preparing FOIA'd material remotely, having gone back to Maine for Christmas. Denise Reynolds, Sharp's replacement as Advancement's budget director, was working from afar as well. She, Pederson, Schook, and I exchanged a series of emails as we readied responses to the outstanding FOIA requests and prepared to explain to puzzled reporters the esoteric terminology that financial documents often feature.

Reporters wanted to learn more about one topic in particular: Gearhart's idea of taking a small percentage of certain types of donations that UA received and using that money to pay down Advancement's shortfall. Choate had suggested the option before the chancellor reassigned him in November. Gearhart was familiar with this funding option. Though many other universities and colleges used some form of this so-called "gift tax" to underwrite their fundraising operations, UA had not done so. It didn't need to; the UA Foundation and the Razorback Foundation generated enough revenue to sufficiently augment the university's fundraising needs. Or so most everyone thought until news of the Advancement deficit broke on December 3rd.

Gearhart was still contemplating the gift tax plan as the new year began. Development head Bruce Pontious asked me and others in my office to come up with a more palatable moniker than "gift tax"; something with that particular name would be a hard sell, especially if its purpose was to use donor dollars to fix a deficit caused by apparent gross mismanagement.

The academic deans did not like the idea of a gift tax at all, no matter what it was called. Many contributions that UA received were given specifically to bolster endowments for scholarships, fellowships, faculty, and some types of facility upgrades within the university's colleges. By taking a percentage of those donations, Gearhart's plan would lower the dollar value that academic units received. No chancellor or president wants to upset his or her deans; when they are unhappy, the faculty become unhappy. And vice versa.

With reporters and editorial writers churning out stories and commentaries about the deficit and gift tax, Gearhart searched for answers and relief. He had developed a painful bout of shingles, possibly a manifestation of the stress he had been dealing with for the past few months. He, like the rest of us, was anxious to move on. In early January, Gearhart gathered CFO Pederson, Development's Pontious, and me to discuss what to do. The gift tax idea was gaining no traction among deans and fundraising staff, two groups with close relationships with donors. If they weren't willing or able to convince donors that a gift tax was a reasonable response, neither Gearhart nor Pontious could be expected to do so, either.

Losing control of the gift tax as an option, Gearhart expressed frustration about media leaks. Someone—possibly more than one person—was violating the confidentiality of those discussions to advance their own agenda. *Arkansas Business*' Chris Bahn was dogging the gift tax idea, and some aspects of Gearhart's discussions with deans and others were making their way into Bahn's reporting. Gearhart speculated that it could be someone close to Bahn's wife, who was an events coordinator for Razorback athletics. The chancellor turned to Pederson and asked an awkward question: Was it possible to check the phone records of the deans and their fundraising officers to determine who, if anyone, had had recent phone contact with reporter Bahn or his wife?

"I assume we can," a seemingly surprised Pederson answered cautiously. The telecommunications office was part of his division. As a former provost, Pederson understood the delicate relationship that deans and chancellors maintain. Deans need the chancellor's support and approval to keep their job and to move up (or elsewhere) in higher education. Chancellors need the confidence and backing of their deans in order to have clout with, and the trust of, the faculty. A campus-wide backlash could result if the deans were to learn that the chancellor had someone check their phone records.

Turning to me, Gearhart said, "Do you have Bahn's number?"

"I do at the office," I replied.

"Get it to Don, will you, please?"

I fulfilled the request. Sometime later, in Gearhart's office, I asked if he and Pederson had found any connection between Bahn's phone number and the deans or development officers. No, the chancellor replied. The brevity of his answer led me to believe they had tried but had no luck. Had they decided against cross-referencing phone numbers with one or both Bahns, I would have expected Gearhart to say so. (Later I read that Gearhart told a prosecutor that he "decided not to pull phone records," according to notes from a November 20, 2013 interview of the chancellor.)

On January 10th, I prepared a memo at Gearhart's request to send to the deans, the chancellor's executive committee, and Advancement division leaders. It explained that Gearhart had decided against imposing a gift tax—referred to as "a reinvestment fee"—until at least the next fiscal year. The email was sent out precisely at 2 p.m. Several of the deans responded with expressions of gratitude. One dean told Gearhart that the chancellor "may have just saved the [capital] campaign from going over a cliff before it ever got started."

Earlier in the day, Bahn sent me an email, wanting to meet to discuss the status and workings of the gift tax. I told him I was tied up until at least 2:30, and would contact him later to schedule a meeting. After the message to the deans was sent, I wrote back to Bahn and told him I would give him a call instead; I was just too busy to meet. Once I did call, I told him that Gearhart was dropping the gift tax plan. "He'll decide at some point in the future whether or not to adopt such a fee," I told him. "It will definitely not be for fiscal year 2013."

That same week, we remained busy responding to additional FOIAs from the *Democrat-Gazette* and *Arkansas Times*. One lengthy FOIA from reporter Tracie Dungan repeated her previous requests for Schook's October 19th memo, which was still known only as the "treasurer's office findings." She received the same response as before: "The university views any records regarding reassignment as job performance records and therefore exempt from release under Arkansas' Freedom of Information Act."

Dungan also asked for spreadsheets, email, employee headcounts, and much more. One of her requests was "for detailed, complete, line-by-line budgets for Advancement and its units—that go beyond the framework of total salaries, total wages, total fringes, total [maintenance and operating costs] and grand totals—for Fiscal Years 2011, 2012, and 2013 (as the latter stands now)." She wanted those requests updated, correctly believing that the university would provide updates only if asked.

Gearhart remained frustrated by the ongoing FOIAs and repetitious questions. On January 8th I had sent him an email on the most recent FOIA, seeking his review. He sent back a two-sentence response: "I leave it to you and Don [Pederson]. I simply won't spend another second on this."

Matters became even more time-consuming for Pederson, the lawyers, and me that week when the *Democrat-Gazette* added another reporter, Lisa Hammersly, to cover the Advancement story. Hammersly was based in the newspaper's bureau in Fort Smith, located on the Oklahoma border about an hour's drive south of Fayetteville. She was an experienced investigative reporter who had worked for the *Charlotte Observer* in North Carolina before moving to Arkansas. She also was a graduate of Columbia University's prestigious graduate school of journalism. Whereas her colleague Dungan had a slow, meandering interviewing style reminiscent of the detective on TV's *Columbo*, Hammersly's approach was more direct and polished; she approached interviews almost as if she were cross-examining a witness in court.

On Friday, January 11th, Hammersly sent Gearhart an email to introduce herself and to find out what UA "has done and where things stand on trying to balance the budget for the Advancement division for 2013." She appeared to be interested in constructing a broader overview of the deficit issue than Dungan, whose reporting was focusing on smaller, sometimes obscure, details. Hammersly also noted that she had contacted Pederson and me about interviews; neither one of us was available that day.

Hammersly also submitted a public records request for "documents indicating [w]here the Advancement division's budget stands, including for each of its arms, including Development." Separately, she also asked why UA had not commissioned an independent audit. Gearhart replied to her that afternoon in an email:

> I'm sorry I will not be able to respond. My daughter had a baby last night and I'm in Little Rock with my family. I know Mr. Diamond has been very patient in answering questions from the [*Democrat-Gazette*] as well as giving you reports, documents and materials as requested. No telling how many hours he has spent talking with Ms. Dungan, literally hours. I have also spent time with Ms. Dungan. Thank you for your understanding.

Monday, January 14th was the first day of UA's spring semester. The University Advancement Cabinet (UAC) was scheduled to gather at 3:30 that afternoon. We would be meeting in Heritage Room, the large conference room within the chancellor's office suite in the Admin Building. Gearhart, as acting head of Advancement, chaired the meeting. All members of the leadership team were present: besides me, it included the two other associate vice chancellors, Development's Pontious and Alumni Affairs' Graham Stewart; Pontious' assistant vice chancellor, Mark Power; budget director Denise Reynolds; Kris Macechko of Constituent Services; Melissa Banks from Special Events; and Laura Villines, the Advancement division's executive assistant. Judy Schwab, Gearhart's chief of staff, also attended.

The agenda included seven items. I was responsible for the fifth one: a briefing on a new video series called *Arkansas Short Takes*, which University Relations was preparing to produce as part of UA's national marketing campaign. These weekly meetings almost always lasted until 5 o'clock; rarely did they run long or end early.

The meeting opened with friendly banter about Gearhart's new grandchild. Following those informalities, Gearhart briefed us on the agenda's first topic: his weekly meeting with his executive committee. He noted that he and members of the executive committee had received universally positive reactions to his decision to abandon, for now, the gift tax idea. He said a few donors had complimented him on the decision as well. Macechko, a person deeply connected to donors and alumni through her work in Constituent Services, shared similar feedback.

Pontious and Power both said they, too, had found the response positive, without exception. One of them pointed out that, with the gift tax off the table, staff within the Development office now wanted to know how Advancement would fix the deficit.

"That's what reporters are asking me," I offered. "At some point soon we'll need to give them an answer. They're going to criticize us and call every day until we do."

That was the last comment I made during the meeting. Melissa Banks spoke after me, sharing the reactions to the announcement that she had heard. We then moved on the second item on the agenda: budget matters.

Reynolds was scheduled to give a status report on Advancement's finances and to explain the process that would soon begin to prepare next year's budget. Reynolds had finished compiling December's revenues and expenses data the previous week. It always a took a week or so to complete each month's report, allowing time to make sure that all documentation of money received and payments made during that period was properly accounted for. Reynolds had been giving us these monthly summaries since October. Her accounting was more detailed than anything we ever received from Joy Sharp—a refreshing change, but one that underscored how poorly we had been served in the past.

Gearhart was seated at the narrow end of the oval table—12 on a clock dial. Reynolds was seated a few chairs away from him, where the 4 would be on the clock's face. She took the budget documents, dated 12/31/2012, and started to distribute them. She passed a few copies to her right, a couple to her left, and skidded others across the table to where Judy Schwab and I were seated.

As she circulated the documents, Reynolds began to explain the status of her efforts to make sense of the financial mess she inherited. I don't recall the specifics of what she said; like everyone else at the table, we were looking at the report she had given us, curious to know whether the bottom line was any less in the red than it was in her November report. Suddenly, Gearhart interrupted her. "What is this?" he asked as he held the budget document in his hands. It was rhetorical. He recognized what it was and didn't like it. "Why are you creating these?" Gearhart continued, his voice quickly growing angry.

Reynolds, appearing startled by the question, began to respond. But Gearhart wasn't listening. Instead, he launched into an angry rant about FOIAs, his belief that the *Democrat-Gazette* was trying desperately to bring him down, and the failure of people around him to protect him.

"Brad fucked up!" he yelled, slapping the table with the flat of his hand. "He wasn't paying attention to his budget!"

"Get rid of it!" he ordered Reynolds moments later, as he shoved his copy of the budget document down the table to her. "And don't create any more!" The rest of us passed our copies back as well. As we did so, Gearhart abruptly rose from his chair, pivoted to his left, and stormed out of the meeting, exiting through the small pantry that separated the conference room from his private office. The episode might have carried on for three minutes, possibly a little longer.

None of us said a word. Schwab, his long-time aide, probably would have been the appropriate person to break the quiet. She had seen Gearhart angry before—had been the actual target of his anger—and had learned to let it roll over her. She had the kind of relationship with Gearhart and with each of us where she could have said something to defuse the situation. Maybe to remind us that Gearhart was under a lot of pressure and wasn't himself or to remind us that he wasn't feeling well. Having had previous conversations with Schwab about Gearhart's temperament, I expected her to say something to calm the waters.

But she didn't. She, too, seemed stunned by what we just witnessed. Finally, in the silent aftermath of Gearhart's angry departure, Schwab stood and left the room. Following her lead, the rest of us quietly exited as well.

Before leaving the Admin Building for our respective offices, Pontious, Stewart, Power, and I gathered in a separate conference room down the hall from Gearhart's office. Stewart had been with UA for just eight months. As the head of the university's alumni association, he had had a fair amount of contact with Gearhart in social settings and at athletic events. He was stunned by Gearhart's previously unseen behavior and particularly the singular blame he had laid on Choate, the person who hired Stewart to be an associate vice chancellor. Gearhart was a quintessential Southern gentleman; hearing him use the F-word in anger in front of subordinates was out of character for him.

For his part, Pontious said he had seen Gearhart lose his temper, though never in a work setting in mixed company. I noted that Macechko, who had been seated across the conference table from me, was visibly upset by Gearhart's anger. From my vantage point, it appeared that she had tears in her eyes. She and her husband Mike (Stewart's predecessor as Alumni's associate vice chancellor) had been personal friends with the Gearharts for decades, yet this incident truly shocked her. She later told me and others that as a result of Gearhart's outburst that day, she decided she no longer wanted to work at the university. She and Mike assessed their finances and agreed that she would quit. She submitted her resignation in mid-February, effective in June.

Meanwhile, Reynolds and Villines returned to the office suite they still shared with Choate, where they told him what they had just witnessed and experienced.

On January 15th, the day following his outburst at the UAC meeting, Gearhart met with university attorney Bill Kincaid and me in the chancellor's office. We were there to brief Gearhart on the outstanding FOIA requests. CFO Don Pederson joined us. Gearhart made no mention of the meeting the day before. Kincaid and I had spent a good part of the past weekend going through the scores of emails and documents we had received from UA's senior leaders and from staff in the Advancement division in response to the FOIAs. Bill had grouped them in three files: records that were definitely "responsive" to the FOIA request, those that might be considered responsive, and those that were unquestionably not responsive. At UA, responding to FOIAs was dependent on the honor system: employees were expected to turn over any documents that we said were covered in the FOIA requests, leaving it to us, as FOIA coordinators, to determine whether or not their submissions did indeed address the FOIAs. It was not uncommon for an email thread of exchanges to be turned over by one participant in the conversation but not the other or others. Individuals manage their email and other files differently, and the law does not require a person to save those items unless they have been, or are likely to be, sought as part of a FOIA request. Other documents, including certain types of budget records, are supposed to be maintained by each office's designated record keeper.

In addressing the recent flood of media FOIAs, Kincaid and I focused our attention only on the documents we had been given. I didn't think about the possibility that someone might have withheld documents that should have been turned over to us. The thick manila file folders Kincaid brought to the meeting contained everything we had. Sitting at the small conference table in Gearhart's office, Gearhart took the folders of apparently responsive documents and reviewed each item. Occasionally, he would comment on or question something he spotted in the file. In a few instances he disagreed with our conclusion that a document or email in the file was responsive to the FOIA. I left it to Kincaid to explain our reasoning.

Once we finished, Kincaid took the folders back to his office and had his assistant create a series of PDF files for me to email to the reporters. A media feeding frenzy was underway; pieces of the PDF files would be isolated, scrutinized, and turned into the latest news story, possibly taken out of context by one or more reporters who were not trained in forensic accounting. I prepared for a spate of calls and emails asking for more interviews, explanations, and documents.

On Tuesday morning, January 22nd, Hammersly sent me yet another email:

> I'm likely to write a story today for tomorrow about the FY 2012 deficit for Advancement and how it's being covered by being listed as a receivable. I will no doubt have some questions by early afternoon. Will Don Pederson or you or Dave Gearhart be available for any responses?

A few hours later, Hammersly sent a follow-up email.

> In light of the university's decision to write the Advancement division's FY 2012 deficit as an 'accounts receivable,' I request all documents and emails related to this decision and transaction, including any documents showing the money is owed or expected from the UA Foundation and when....I make the request under Arkansas public records law regarding freedom of information.

At the time I didn't recognize the significance of Hammersly's question about "receivables" and its influence on certain leadership actions and behaviors that would occur over the following days and months. (In fact, it wasn't until August that anyone connected the "receivables" topic to deliberate and unconventional accounting practices by UA officials outside of Advancement that allowed Joy Sharp's financial mismanagement to go undetected.) Per standard practice, I simply forwarded those emails to Gearhart, Pederson, and the UA attorneys. I didn't expect that the chancellor or CFO would want to respond directly; Pederson himself had turned down the *Democrat-Gazette's* last two queries, emailing reporters to "take your requests to John Diamond." However, I would need someone's help to explain decisions about "receivables" and other matters related to the division's accounting practices. I sought that advice from Pederson and from Clay Davis, the executive director of the UA Foundation. Following those conversations, I wrote back to Hammersly. My response included a particular point about "receivables" that Davis wanted Hammersly to understand:

> To be clear, this is not an obligation of the UA Foundation; it's an expectation that Advancement will repay the university from the funds it receives from the Foundation.

Hammersly quickly responded:

> It does not answer why the university decided to change the deficit to a receivable to balance the budget, and when that decision was made. Also, what I understand from talking to experts leaves questions about whether this fits the accounting definition of a receivable. I would like to talk more about that with Don Pederson or another financial expert.

I shared this second email with Gearhart and Pederson. The CFO responded the next morning: "We have already answered that this is a receivable." Twenty minutes later, he sent me another email:

> This is really getting to be harassment in my mind. I think we all feel, provost, chancellor, Dr. Bobbitt and me, that we need to end this dialogue. They are obviously trying to find something that damages the UA and the chancellor and there is nothing there, as you well know. I have spoken to the chancellor and legal counsel. Below is

what we believe should be the response to Lisa Hammersly. I do not plan on responding to any further inquiries. I have spent way too much time on this matter, as have you.

He then provided the message he wanted me to send:

Lisa: While I appreciate your continued questions, we believe we have answered your numerous inquiries multiple times, the same questions over and over again, and we have spent hours and hours trying to explain every aspect of this issue. We can continue to explain it to you, but we cannot understand it for you. Your questions as well as continued FOIA requests for the same information, to which we have previously responded, borders on the absurd and frankly, harassment. We have no further comment. You may feel free to quote me.

Red flags popped up as I read Pederson's message. I envisioned the headline possibilities that could appear: "UA Calls Public Records Requests 'Absurd' " or "UA Accuses Newspaper of Harassment." I sought input from a few members of my media relations staff before responding to Pederson a few hours later:

Don, thanks for your message. I understand. I have held off sharing your statement with the *Democrat-Gazette* until I had the opportunity to talk with you and express my concerns....Personally, I think it is unwise to issue a blanket refusal to respond further, as there will be occasions when we will WANT the opportunity to correct misinterpretations or misunderstandings. In addition, such a blanket response would inflame the situation, making our unwillingness to respond further yet another reason for the media to criticize us and to question the Advancement situation. An unfortunate consequence could be accusations (by media, legislators, alums, and/or others) to wrongly accuse the university of not being responsive or willing to be held accountable for what occurred and how it was handled.

Furthermore, it would be easy, though inaccurate, for media to

> generalize and position the university as not adequately responding to FOIA'd documents, putting us in the defensive position of saying we will only respond (and therefore be publicly accountable) if required to do so by law. Ultimately, the university would have to respond, this time under the real or perceived pressure of stakeholders....[I]t has helped that we have responded to questions and clarified misinformation; as a result, the story or stories that emerge tomorrow and/or Friday have a greater likelihood of accuracy because we responded—and that will convey a better sense of transparency than if we make a point of saying we will no longer respond except to FOIAs. Let me know whether or not you want me to proceed. Thanks.

Pederson responded that evening:

> We should probably get together with Dave tomorrow. I am not wedded to my earlier response so you should put it in your words and do what is required to shut this down. Most of your answers seem to be an effort to shut it down but you have to convince them that the questions that they have been asking are not meaningful in understanding anything. Every answer generates more questions because they do not know what they are doing and do not ask questions that make any sense.

First thing the next morning, Gearhart's assistant called me and said the chancellor wanted me to come over at 9 o'clock. I figured it was related to Pederson's suggestion that we all meet. It was a cold morning in Fayetteville, even by Maine standards, so I grabbed my coat and left Davis Hall to walk the half-block to the Admin Building. When I arrived at the chancellor's office suite, his assistant called into Gearhart's personal office to tell him I had arrived. I hung up my coat as she told me to go ahead in.

I opened the office door. As usual, Gearhart was seated behind his desk at the far end of the room, the computer monitor to his right and a small flat-screen TV next to it. One of the cable financial news channels was on. Normally when the two of us met in his office, he would stay at his desk and I would sit in a chair situated a few feet off to the side. This day would be different. He got up and motioned to me to join him at the two red leather chairs across the room. These were the same seats in which we sat in November when Gearhart informed me that he was reassigning Choate and Sharp. Since Pederson wasn't in the room, I suspected that today's topic was going to be about naming an interim vice chancellor to lead Advancement until a nationwide search for Choate's position could take place. It was logical that Gearhart would be ready to appoint someone; even under normal circumstances, the demands of doing double duty as chancellor and acting vice chancellor would be tremendous. Add to it a high-profile deficit and the rollout of a billion dollar capital campaign, and the stress could become paralyzing.

He didn't want to talk about relinquishing his Advancement role. Instead, he wanted to discuss my interaction with the news media. He said he was concerned about how "we" were interacting with reporters. He said I was too cordial in my email exchanges with the news media. Most of my emails would open with a courteous greeting—e.g., "Hi, Tracie. I hope you had a nice weekend."—and would close similarly. He felt I shouldn't engage reporters in such civilities. He seemed to believe that a less collegial attitude might quell the news media's demands.

I've never known that to be an effective strategy, I shared. Often it produced the opposite result.

Gearhart disagreed. He said I was fueling reporters' interest in the Advancement story by being needlessly accommodating. As a consequence, I was being overly demanding of Pederson's time by asking for his help in responding to media requests.

I was puzzled by that statement. Just a couple of weeks earlier, in his January 8th email, he had told me to work with Pederson on handling reporters' questions. I reminded him that I was following those instructions. I added that I had no alternative but to check with Pederson when a reporter asked for budget information or an actual interview with the CFO. It would be unwise for us to simply refuse to acknowledge those requests. I equated my approach to other aspects of external relations: I was doing my best to steward our media relations, just as our campus fundraising and alumni officers are expected to do with donors and graduates.

It's not at all the same, he responded. Donors and alumni aren't trying to "bring down" the university. In language that was remarkably (but unsurprisingly) similar to the message Pederson sent me the previous day, Gearhart told me to stop responding to media queries regarding Advancement.

"That's unrealistic, Chancellor," I said, believing I could help him recognize the unintended consequences. I reiterated the points I had shared with Pederson: in the absence of any input from us, reporters were bound to misinterpret the data that they could get through FOIA'd documents; they would turn to other sources whose knowledge and authority might be given more credibility and attention than they deserved; and by not responding at all to requests for information and clarification, we would be giving the public the impression we had something to hide. Maintaining a willingness to be responsive—to the extent we could, given the personnel issues related to Choate and Sharp—was the most prudent approach to take. It was basic PR 101, I said.

"I'm trying to help you," I added, trying to reassure him.

"Help me?!" he shot back, rising from his chair. "You think you're helping me?! Don Bobbitt and the trustees told me to shut John Diamond up!"

I was stunned, both by his physical reaction and by the thought that the university system's president and governing board had concluded that we—the university—should no longer respond to reporters about Advancement. If true, it was a politically dangerous posture for a group of public trustees to take.

"Wow," I said softly but audibly. I didn't know what else to say.

"From now on Bill Kincaid is going to handle media requests," Gearhart continued, still standing. "Tell reporters to talk to him."

At that point, Gearhart walked around and behind me toward the door. I stood and followed him. He opened the door, turned back around and headed to his desk without another glance or word. Our meeting—which Judy Schwab later told me lasted 42 minutes—was over.

I stepped out and closed the door behind me. I took my coat from the closet, walked out of the chancellor's suite, and headed toward Kincaid's office suite. His door was open; he greeted me from his desk.

"Have you talked with Dave lately?" I asked, my question being unintentionally ambiguous. Bill looked puzzled, not understanding what I was inquiring about.

"I'm not supposed to respond to any more media questions about Advancement," I told him. "I'm supposed to steer everyone to you."

Kincaid leaned far back in his chair as if the weight of this new responsibility physically landed on him. A quiet, soft-spoken man by nature, his facial expression telegraphed his reaction. He did not want the assignment.

By now, I was feeling a bit queasy, an aftershock from my conversation with Gearhart. Without anything more said, I left the General Counsel's office, put on my coat in the hallway, and headed back to Davis Hall. After taking care of a few immediate needs at the office, I decided I'd be better off working from home for the rest of the day.

The following morning, January 25th, Laura Villines sent an email on Gearhart's behalf to me and the other members of the University Advancement Cabinet:

> We will no longer be having UAC meetings. Dave has asked that if you have specific issues, you bring those to his attention individually. I have removed the UAC meetings from the calendar.

PLEASE DELETE

Despite Advancement's multi-million dollar deficit, the initial stages of a billion dollar fundraising campaign, and the beginning of the budget-development process for the next fiscal year, we would no longer be meeting as a group to discuss and brainstorm our work. We were left leaderless and rudderless.

Chapter 7

THE SECRET REVIEW

January had been a demanding month for me for reasons that went beyond FOIAs and meetings. About two months earlier, an executive recruiter for the University of Arizona contacted me. A college president he and I both knew told him I'd be a good fit for an open position at the university: a senior vice presidency to oversee communications, marketing, government affairs, and the university's public broadcasting stations. The recruiter wanted me to consider applying for the position.

At first, I had mixed feelings. On the positive side, the position was one of the top jobs in my field of expertise and would be an exciting challenge. The University of Arizona was one of the elite public research universities in the country. As sports junkies, Marcia and I liked the idea of following the Arizona Wildcats, a big-time college sports program like the Razorbacks. Furthermore, several Major League Baseball teams conducted Spring Training in the state, which was one of the reasons why Marcia and I had discussed Arizona as an eventual retirement getaway location: we could spend a couple of months of winter there and live in Maine the rest of the year. The senior vice presidency also offered an attractive salary, the recruiter said—about $100,000 more than what I earned annually at Arkansas. With our kids' college loans coming due soon and retirement seven or eight years away, the financial aspects of the job were appealing.

However, there were drawbacks. We loved Fayetteville and Northwest Arkansas. In addition to the presence of our nieces and their families, we had developed a large circle of friends through the university and because of our involvement with St. Joseph Catholic Church. Arkansas had a small Catholic population—a factor we weighed in 2010 when considering the pros and cons of me seeking the UA position. However, we had found a wonderful church community made up of native Arkansans, the region's fast-growing Hispanic community, and transplants like us from the North. We were comfortable and were content with the thought of staying at UA for the remainder of my career.

But the excitement of the Arizona challenge and the material benefits that accompanied the job carried the debate; I decided to apply. Just two weeks later, I received an invitation to travel to Tucson for an interview.

I had not yet told Gearhart or anyone else in Fayetteville about the Arizona possibility. My hesitancy related to Marcia's job. In 2011, she had become the principal of the Catholic elementary school in Fayetteville (also named St. Joseph), a role similar to the one she had held for many years in Maine. We were concerned about how news of her possible departure would affect the school's enrollment and fundraising. In addition, she had become involved in a re-energized effort to establish a Catholic high school in the region and was working with several major donors well-placed within Wal-Mart and Procter & Gamble to commission a feasibility study.

On January 3rd, I met with Gearhart for my regularly scheduled update. After we finished our regular business, I shared word of my Arizona candidacy. Afterward, I sent Marcia an email:

> Talked to Dave. He didn't act surprised and said, 'We'd hate to lose you.' He asked me to keep him posted and to let him know if it's offered. He asked how you feel about the possibility. I told him that we're both very happy here but that we've always looked at AZ as a place we'd like to end up. I asked him to keep this strictly between him and me, as we don't want to unnecessarily cause any concerns on campus or at St. Joe's.

My interview in Tucson went well. Two days after I returned to Fayetteville, the recruiter sent me a short email: "You are one of three advancing—very much on the merits." The university scheduled me for a return visit to Tucson on January 31st, at which time I'd meet with President Ann Weaver Hart, her cabinet, and with the heads of the various units I would oversee if I got the job. The recruiter's office said I should let my references know that they would be contacted soon.

Gearhart was one of those references. Following my January 24th trip to the chancellor's woodshed, I worried that having him as a reference might not be such a good idea. However, the next day he sent me a reassuring email: "John: I want you to know, despite our disagreements, I will give you a <u>very good</u> recommendation, which is deserved. Dave."

Though my second Tucson trip went well, I didn't get the job. It went to Teri Lucie Thompson, Purdue University's vice president of media and marketing and the American Marketing Association's 2012 "Higher Education Marketer of the Year." I was disappointed, but Teri was indeed the better candidate.

Meanwhile, back at UA, my relationship with Gearhart quickly returned to pre-woodshed normalcy. Media calls about Advancement were being referred back to me for handling. However, the chilling effect of the January 14th meeting on the division continued. Our weekly University Advancement Cabinet sessions were not restored, nor was distribution of Denise Reynolds' monthly breakdowns of revenues and expenditures. One untitled email Reynolds sent to Bruce Pontious and me in early February presaged the changes in the free flow of budget information that would occur:

> Please delete after reading...I feel like Bond, James Bond 007 after saying that. Anyway, have you had a chance to look at the 'calculated encumbrance' number that we discussed at the last UAC meeting? I would like to finalize my work on that this weekend, if at all possible. Thanks! Denise

Normally, the subject of "calculated encumbrances"—projections of the salary and wage totals Bruce and I would need her to protect in order to meet payroll for the remainder of the fiscal year—would be of little interest to anyone. But at the time, the *Democrat-Gazette* was trying to validate Gearhart's assertion that the deficit was the result of too much hiring, not overspending on operational costs. I don't know whether Reynolds had the newspaper's queries in mind; months later, Reynolds told a reporter she could not recall specifically why she predicated her message with "Please delete" and that her Bond reference was a simple attempt at humor. But Pontious and I interpreted those references in the context of Gearhart's January 14th directives. When the reporter asked Reynolds about what she herself had done with the email, Reynolds said she had deleted it.

Around the same time that Reynolds sent the "Please delete" email, Gearhart told me he might seek an independent audit of Advancement after all. I wondered whether his change of heart might be related to something said or heard a couple of days earlier. The UA System's board of trustees had met in Little Rock on January 31st and February 1st, the board's first assembly since Gearhart told members in executive session about the Advancement deficit. In light of the intense media and legislative interest in the Advancement story, I thought it was possible that someone at the board meeting had pulled Gearhart aside and advised or told him to seek an audit. (Advancement issues apparently did come up in sidebar discussions; a timeline Choate prepared indicated that on

February 4th, Gearhart told him that Bobbitt and trustees were uncomfortable with Choate's continued presence and wanted Gearhart to fire him.)

Even if conversations at the board meeting didn't motivate the requests for audits, Paul Greenberg's editorial following the trustees' meeting certainly did. In his February 5th commentary, Greenberg again challenged UA's repeated refusal to release its internal review of the causes of Advancement's overspending. He said it was time for answers.

> How could [it] happen? Inquiring minds—and the state's taxpayers—want to know, and have every right to know. But it won't be easy finding all the answers without access to the university's own review of the shortfall. And the university's nabobs refuse to release it—despite Freedom of Information requests from the *Democrat-Gazette*....[S]ecrecy reigns at the University of Arkansas' campus at Fayetteville where this financial review is concerned.

Citing recent criticism of UA's position from a FOIA expert, Greenberg continued:

> They've used what they contend is the letter of the law to violate its spirit, which is worse. They've given any benefit of the doubt not to the public interest but to their own in avoiding any further embarrassments this financial review might contain. The surest result of their little games will be to raise more suspicions (secrecy always does) and further erode the university's reputation.

I don't know at what time Gearhart read the editorial, but at 7:50 a.m., one of his assistants emailed Pederson, Schook, Varady, Kincaid, and me to schedule a meeting with the chancellor for later in the morning. Six minutes later, Gearhart himself sent a short email to System President Bobbitt: "Don: I would like to formally invite the system auditors to perform an audit of the Advancement overspending. Dave." A similar message was sent to Legislative Auditor Roger Norman, asking his office to conduct an audit as well. The brevity of both messages and the short acknowledgments that quickly followed suggested that Gearhart (or someone on his behalf) had recently conversed with one or both individuals to let them know that the request was coming.

We gathered at 9:30 a.m. in Gearhart's office to discuss how to announce his decision. Someone noted that Schook's October 19th memo would, of course, be among the documents turned over to auditors. The memo would now be part of an ongoing investigation, another factor that UA could cite to justify not releasing the report to the media or the public.

Later that morning, we issued a short news release that announced Gearhart's requests and reflected his confidence in the process he had followed to date. "The university has been transparent and accountable about this situation," Gearhart said in the statement. "I believe these audits will demonstrate that performance while still reflecting the legal protections afforded public employees under Arkansas law."

Three days later, Gearhart granted an interview to the *Democrat-Gazette's* Lisa Hammersly—his first interview with anyone about the deficit in weeks. She was accompanied by Jennifer Cook, the newspaper's managing editor in charge of its coverage of the Advancement matter. A story about the interview appeared the next day on the newspaper's front page:

> The University of Arkansas at Fayetteville's chancellor said Friday that he doesn't expect state auditors to learn anything more than has already been disclosed when they look into $3.37 million in overspending last year by the university's Advancement Division...."We think we know what happened. We feel pretty confident."

Deeper in the story, Gearhart defended his handling of the Advancement situation. "I think we've been pretty transparent," Gearhart said. "The bottom line is [Choate and Sharp] overspent their budget." He then offered an acerbic observation to the reporters: "You keep asking questions. I keep trying to explain it for you."

Hammersly and Cook asked Gearhart why he changed his mind

about the need for an audit:

> Frankly, I woke up one morning after one of Mr. Greenberg's editorials...and I thought "What the heck, let them come in and look at everything.... Let's let the auditors come in." Gearhart added that he had considered seeking an audit in November but "[i]n discussing it with Dr. Bobbitt and members of the board, they didn't feel it was necessary to do it."

What about the internal review that UA refuses to release? the reporters asked.

> "We're not going to give it to you because we don't believe we legally should and can. I would suggest to you, if you disagree with that, the appropriate thing to do would be to file a lawsuit against us."

And on Monday, their newspaper did so. In its filing, lawyers for the *Democrat-Gazette* argued that the report was "created to explain the budget shortfall, not specific conduct by the two employees."

> The University of Arkansas cannot hide embarrassing documents by claiming they were later used to evaluate and discipline employees. Even if the records in question were exempt as employee evaluations – which [we] do not concede – they must be disclosed regardless because both Mr. Choate and Ms. Sharp have already been suspended from their jobs.

If UA's lawyers truly believed that Schook's October 19th report was exempt under FOIA, they quickly gave up the fight. Varady contacted Choate, Sharp, and Sharp's sister Betty—cited briefly in the report—to obtain their permission to release Schook's memo. All agreed. Choate also signed an agreement not to say anything that might be interpreted as disparaging of the UA unless ordered to participate in a government investigation or audit.

Avoiding an appearance in court, UA gave the *Democrat-Gazette* the Schook document and other records that had been FOIA'd two months earlier. (Though I had briefly seen Schook's memo on November 8th, this was the first time I was given my own copy.) The materials provided that day totaled 88 pages. It was captivating reading. Reporters and the public learned for the first time about Joy Sharp's "intentional effort to disguise a prior year account receivable balance that had not been cleared" and "deliberate efforts to disguise poor financial management of the Division of Advancement resources." They read that Schook found "many fraud risk factors" and contemplated the need to call for an audit, choosing instead to defer to Gearhart and Pederson's judgment on that. Readers also saw Schook's acknowledgment that she had not conducted a forensic review of Advancement's books to determine whether any funds were misused or misappropriated, even though Gearhart later categorically assured trustees and the public that no funds had been affected in such ways.

Along with those revelations, the documents contained numerous email exchanges that previously had not been made public, ostensibly because they pertained to Choate's and Sharp's job performance. Jennifer Cook, the *Democrat-Gazette's* editor overseeing coverage of Advancement, now had four reporters working on the story, all combing through details for inconsistencies. For the next couple of weeks, the newspaper's front page kept the public mindful of the university controversy with a steady drip-drip-drip of headlines:

"UA Releases Deficit Report; Unit Slammed"

"UA Deficit Brewed for Years, Report Says"

"UA Board Satisfied on Deficit's Handling"

"Law Professor: UA Deficit Report Always a Public Record"

"E-mails Show Gearhart Had Audit in Mind"

"Gearhart Sent Files on Choate to Adviser"

"UA Files: Hiring Not All of Deficit"

Paul Greenberg also weighed in. Following up an earlier opinion piece called "The Fayetteville Follies," he wrote two more biting editorials after the Schook report became public: "The Games UA-F Plays" and "The Secret Review." The news coverage and editorial criticism seemed inescapable. The "scandal" label was gaining public credibility as the university's defense was losing its.

On February 15th—the same day that UA released the Schook memo—UA System officials learned that John H. Tyson, the third generation of his family to lead Tyson Foods, had resigned from the university system's board of trustees. What made it awkward for System officials was that they found out about Tyson's decision from a reporter, not from Tyson himself: according to the date on the letter, Tyson had actually submitted his written resignation to Arkansas Governor Mike Beebe a full ten days earlier. UA System spokesperson Ben Beaumont was caught off-guard when *Arkansas Business* asked for comment on Tyson's resignation; Beaumont said that he and his office colleagues were not aware that it had occurred. Beebe's own spokesperson, Matt DeCample, told the newspaper that the Governor had learned of Tyson's plans "a few days" prior to receiving the resignation letter. No one from the Governor's office discussed it with the trustees or others at the UA System because, as DeCample reportedly explained, it was the governor's practice to find a trustee's replacement before informing the UA System or other trustees of a member's resignation. If true, such a procedure would be pointless and impractical. What value or concern would justify keeping secret a public appointee's resignation from the public governing board and organization he had been serving? The phrasing of DeCample's response also suggested that Beebe knew Tyson was not intending to share his decision with the System office; that "detail" was provided days later, compliments of someone's leak to a reporter.

Tyson's letter to Beebe was dated February 5th, the same day that Gearhart announced his request for audits. Someone tipped off *Arkansas Business* about the existence of Tyson's resignation letter on or around February 15th; that was the day UA released the Schook memo and related records, which included the conclusions about Joy Sharp's "intentional effort" to cover a budget shortfall with $1.3 million in "misdirected" funds. Further reading of those documents would reveal the source of those funds: Tyson and his family foundation. They had given the $1.3 million to UA as part of a larger donation to fund a child development study center to be named in honor of Tyson's mother, Jean.

After the fact, a couple of trustees told the newspaper that they knew Tyson's resignation was coming. But why would Tyson not communicate his intention directly to his fellow board members and to UA System officials? In his resignation letter to Beebe, Tyson cited his busy schedule and "the fact that I have become increasingly frustrated with the board's inability to make meaningful change in the structure and delivery of higher education in Arkansas" as his reasons for stepping down. Some media reports suggested that his reasoning might have been tied to the Advancement situation. Others speculated that it was prompted by Tyson's disappointment in UA Athletics Director Jeff Long's choice of Bret Bielema, not Tyson's purported favorite Butch Davis, as the new Razorbacks' head football coach. When Tyson himself was unavailable to answer questions, a reporter turned to Archie Schaffer, Tyson Foods' recently retired executive vice president and a close advisor to Tyson. "I think he would say the letter speaks for itself," Schaffer said.

Only Tyson knows for certain whether or not his resignation was related to Sharp's mishandling of his family's donation. But eight months later, a conversation took place that suggested it might have been a factor. On October 30, 2013, Schaffer contacted one of Marcia's school employees to find out how to reach me. His query followed recent media reports that local prosecutors were interviewing me regarding the Advancement deficit. Archie reached me at home and arranged to meet me that afternoon at the Village Inn, a restaurant in Fayetteville.

I didn't know Schaffer very well; we had seen each other at various events and had a few mutual friends in Maine, dating back to his days as a senior political advisor to his uncle, former Arkansas U.S. Senator Dale Bumpers. But we had never met one-on-one. Amid Diet Cokes and small talk about work and elver fishing, we discussed the controversy surrounding Gearhart and UA. At one point I asked him when Gearhart had informed Tyson that his family's money had been misdirected as part of the Advancement scandal.

"He didn't," he said with a sardonic chuckle. "He [Tyson] learned about it the way everyone else did!"

Through news reports, I first assumed. If true, it was an astonishing example of UA's disrespect for one of its most generous and influential benefactors. Later, I checked the chronology of events. It's conceivable that the resignation letter had been backdated, especially in light of the fact that no one seemed to know anything about it until the day the Schook memo was made public. Another possibility is that someone with inside knowledge of Sharp's misdirection of Tyson's donation—System President Bobbitt or a member of the UA Board's audit committee, perhaps—alerted Tyson to the linkage, as a result of offline discussions of the Advancement mess during the trustees' two-day meeting in Little Rock on January 31st and February 1st. According to System records, Tyson did not attend the board's formal business meeting on February 1st.

Understandably, Tyson would be angry to find out that his family's donation had been redirected from its intended purpose. It would be even worse to learn that UA's chancellor and the System president withheld the news after discovering the violation. A private man, Tyson was not the kind to complain publicly if he felt he had been slighted. If what Schaffer told me on October 30th was true, the information was particularly timely, as Gearhart was now under even heavier scrutiny based on recent revelations.

The next day I sent Schaffer a short email, thanking him for the invitation to get together. He responded, closing his email with, "Hang in there with all your current 'opportunities'." As I had told him the previous day, I had no "current 'opportunities" at the time—other than invitations from legislators, prosecutors, and reporters to share what I knew about the Advancement scandal.

Chapter 8

"BROTHER HONKY"

Gearhart had a secret. It had been almost a month since January 14th, the day he stormed out of what would be his final Advancement Cabinet meeting as acting vice chancellor. During that time he had identified who he wanted to take over as Choate's replacement as vice chancellor. Gearhart planned to announce his pick on Wednesday, February 13th and contacted me to arrange for media coverage. However, because he said he feared that his selection's name would leak out before the announcement, he didn't want to tell me his choice so that I could maintain "plausible deniability" if anyone asked me. (I don't know why he was concerned. Had anyone asked, I'd simply say, "That's the chancellor's announcement to make," as I had in previous situations.) The new vice chancellor would be a "permanent" replacement, not an interim, he said. Gearhart said he would tell me and the rest of the Advancement division's leadership team who our new leader was on Tuesday afternoon. He planned to tell the rest of the division's staff at a short meeting on Wednesday morning, just before the news conference.

I was pleased we would be getting a new leader but surprised he hadn't asked Pontious, Stewart, or me for any input before making a choice. If for no other reason than a show of respect or courtesy, effective leaders seek the input of key stakeholders in decision-making processes as a way to cultivate acceptance and support. The leader doesn't have to accept the views or suggestions offered, even if they have merit. But stakeholders are much more likely to be supportive if they feel their opinions were sought before the decision was made.

The day before the announcement, Gearhart sent the Advancement leadership cabinet the name of his choice. It was someone we all knew: Chris Wyrick. A North Carolina native, he joined UA in 2008 as a senior fundraiser for Razorback athletics after holding similar positions at Vanderbilt and the University of South Carolina. But in September of 2012, he had left UA to become executive director of the Razorback Foundation, a private, not-for-profit organization whose sole mission was to help fund and support Razorback athletics. However, he didn't keep the job for long: after six months in that position, he accepted Gearhart's offer to return to UA, this time as a vice chancellor. The two jobs were different in size and scope: The Razorback Foundation had fewer than ten staff members; Advancement had more than 150. The Foundation focused on the insular world of college athletics; the vice chancellor for Advancement was involved in all aspects of UA's academic, research, outreach, and administrative operations. Athletics is a heavily top-down organizational structure; universities are decentralized with shared-governance policies, endless committee meetings, and high-intensity, low-stakes internal politics.

Like Gearhart himself six years earlier, Wyrick was selected without going through the rigors of a search process, not even one that ostensibly attempted to attract other applicants. He was not vetted by a search committee. He did not have to meet with groups of administrators, faculty members, staff, students, donors, and alumni to answer questions about his management style, vision, or priorities—all steps that candidates for much lower-ranking positions experience as part of the screening process. He did not have to explain why his lack of a graduate degree—an accomplishment nearly all of his would-be national peers had achieved—would not undermine his credibility with deans, faculty, researchers, and other constituencies when he was making decisions about their programs, priorities, and funding requests.

Those considerations may have been in the minds of his new staff when, on the morning of February 13th, Wyrick walked into the events room at University House to be introduced to the Advancement staff as the new division head. Most everyone was speechless. For several reasons—his recent move to the Razorback Foundation being one—his name hadn't been part of the internal speculation about Choate's replacement. Many thought Gearhart would pick Sandy Edwards, a former senior Development leader for UA now working at nearby Crystal Bridges Museum of American Art. The conventional wisdom was that Edwards would return to the university while Gearhart conducted a national search; after all, the UA vice chancellorship was a plumb job that would attract an abundance of experienced applicants. But the speculation was well off the mark.

Wyrick noticed the subdued reaction to his introduction and made mention of it during his brief remarks. He was in an uncomfortable spot: suddenly elevated to a new and unfamiliar role, asked to resolve major financial and management challenges related to the deficit, and lacking the comparable education, background, and breadth of experience of his predecessors and peers. He knew it and would acknowledge it. So did, and would, his new staff.

Following the Advancement meeting, Gearhart and Wyrick walked over to the Admin Building, where the chancellor formally announced Wyrick's appointment at a news conference. About 100 people attended, mostly UA administrators and Advancement division employees. A few major donors were also in the room, including billionaire Johnelle Hunt; she was the co-founder of J.B. Hunt Transport Services, another locally founded enterprise that, along with Wal-Mart and Tyson Foods, had risen to global economic influence. Hunt and Gearhart both delivered prepared remarks, speaking enthusiastically about Wyrick's suitability for the job. Gearhart elaborated on that point in response to a question.

"Relationship building is what it's all about," Gearhart told *Arkansas Business* reporter Chris Bahn. "He's an expert at that. I think it requires somebody in this job that has good administrative skills. And he's been proven to have those with the work he did with the Razorback Foundation."

Gearhart's prepared comments included multiple references to the appointment as a "promotion." It wasn't. Wyrick left UA's employment after he became executive director of the Razorback Foundation, which, like the UA Foundation, was a separate, private entity and immune to the personnel policies and public disclosure laws that covered the university itself. The semantics of the term *promotion* mattered, though no one made an issue of it. For a senior leadership position like this one, UA could rationalize waiving the search process (though not the university's equal opportunity policies and practices) by saying it was promoting from within. That was how both Gearhart and CFO Don Pederson had attained their current positions. However, it was harder to justify the action if the person being appointed was not already on the payroll, and Wyrick wasn't. For anyone concerned about respecting a process, the Wyrick appointment was a conscious bending—if not breaking—of the rules, something that soon would occur again and again under this new leader.

Gearhart had not yet established the actual start date for Wyrick to assume his new job; UA trustees were reluctant to have both Wyrick and Choate on the payroll at the same time. That would be resolved later, when in mid-March Gearhart announced that Wyrick would join the university on April 1st, and that the last three months of Choate's salary would be paid through private funds—presumably provided by the UA Foundation.

A few days after his appointment, Wyrick invited me to meet with him at his office at Razorback Foundation headquarters. Except for occasionally running into Wyrick at Razorback events, I had had little contact with him during my two-plus years at UA. I had met him for the first time in late 2010, when Choate invited Wyrick and me to stop by his house after work for a beer. Brad knew Chris from their days together at the University of South Carolina, where Brad was vice president of Advancement and Chris worked as a fundraiser for Gamecock athletics. That evening, with the three of us sitting on Choate's back patio, I found Chris to be an entertaining character. I told Marcia that physically Wyrick reminded me of Eric Stonestreet, the comedic actor who plays Cameron Tucker on the TV program *Modern Family*. At the time Choate thought that Wyrick might be a fun guy for me to get to know.

It was a damp, overcast day when I visited Wyrick at the Razorback Foundation offices following his appointment. I waited for him in the reception area, where a large trophy was on display. It was a tribute in honor of Chris's predecessor as the head of the Foundation, the recently retired Harold Horton. Horton was one of several legendary figures associated with Razorback football: a former player, coach, fundraiser, and networker. He and the most esteemed Razorback of all time, former coach and athletics director Frank Broyles, had led the efforts to build in Fayetteville some of America's finest college sports facilities. For a few short months, it had looked like Chris Wyrick would have the daunting challenge of continuing the expansion of world-class facilities, student-athlete scholarships, and coaching endowments that Horton, Broyles, and others had created. But instead, after just six months on the job, Wyrick was abandoning a chance at Razorback immortality to take on the much more complicated—and better-compensated—role of leading Advancement as a member of "Team Gearhart," as he called it.

Wyrick soon greeted me in the lobby. He pointed out the Horton trophy and made small talk about finishing up his work with the

Foundation while simultaneously trying to absorb all he could about Advancement and UA. He led me to the large board room where the Foundation's directors—many of them Razorback athletes from days gone by—met periodically to manage the organization's affairs and discuss the past, present, and future of "The Hogs." He offered me coffee, which I accepted. The room had a small table upon which sugar and a bowl of small plastic containers of half & half creamers sat. He handed me the Styrofoam cup of coffee into which I poured the contents of one of the little plastic tubs. The cream rose in the black coffee in disaggregated white speckles; it was spoiled. Wyrick noticed me looking at the cup and asked if anything was wrong. When I mentioned that the cream was spoiled, he acted frustrated and went to the door. "The cream's bad!" he yelled into the hallway to no one in particular. A young male staff member came from around the corner. Chris said something to the effect, "This man needs fresh cream!" When the staffer returned to deliver it, Wyrick sternly said, "Thanks. Don't let it happen again."

Was this reprimand serious? I hoped not! But neither person smiled, winked, or gave a laugh. I was embarrassed for the young guy. It was an odd and disrespectful way for a leader to treat a subordinate in front of a stranger.

Wyrick might have learned this behavior from working around college athletics, where many coaches employ passive-aggressive tactics as motivational tools. Often, I would learn, in group settings, Wyrick singled out a person and performed a three-step approach: first, he would caustically tease or criticize the person; second, he would retreat from his remark non-verbally by flashing a disarming smile; and third, he would quickly reinforce the original crack with one of his most frequently-invoked expressions: "Many a truth is spoken in jest."

Over the next couple of months, I would see frequent examples of that behavior, as Wyrick alternately tried to befriend and to belittle people who worked for him. He kept staff on their toes, wondering what kind of treatment was coming their way. Following one Advancement division meeting at which Wyrick made jokes at the expense of several staff members present—the amount of hair gel one used, the length of the question another had asked, the discomfort a third one showed in speaking in front of the group—a member of my staff approached me. She said that in the future, when she was in Wyrick's presence, "I'm just going to keep my head down and hope I don't get noticed."

"You did a good job with your remarks," I told Wyrick as I sipped the refreshed coffee during our first meeting after his announcement. We sat across from each other on the east end of the conference room's table.

"Hardin helped me with them." Hardin Young was the executive speechwriter and a member of my RazorWorks leadership team. I was surprised Young hadn't told me he had been given the assignment. We had an understanding within our office called "The Treaty of No Surprises": Please don't let me learn from others something that I should have learned first from you, and I will work equally hard to make sure you don't hear anything from others that you should have heard first from me. It was a practice I had picked up from Terry MacTaggart, my former chancellor at the University of Maine System and a nationally recognized authority on higher education leadership. Young later told me that he had been put in an awkward position the week before the announcement: Gearhart had told him not to tell me that he was working with him or with Wyrick on remarks.

"So how come Dave didn't have you work on the announcement?" Wyrick asked.

"He hadn't told me who he'd picked, and he wanted me to have 'plausible deniability' in case anyone asked who was going to get the job."

"He wanted to keep it a secret," Wyrick noted. "I think it added to the excitement." He changed the subject. "So what's up between you and Dave?"

I thought he was asking about my January 24th trip to Gearhart's woodshed. "He thinks I should be able to keep the media from writing about Advancement," I answered. "Obviously, I can't. It's newsworthy, whether we like it or not. The best we can do is to cooperate with their FOIA requests."

That wasn't what Wyrick had been referring to. "You've got to stay away from Brad," he said, shaking his head as he clarified his intent. "Dave heard you and Pontious were out with him at the country club."

I paused. Judy Schwab had offered me the same caution a week earlier, though more diplomatically. The week of the audit announcement, Bruce Pontious arranged for several couples to join him and his wife Denise at the Fayetteville Country Club for "Pasta Night." His invitation list included me and several other UA employees and their spouses, including Choate (who was the president of the country club's board of directors), Graham Stewart, Tom Smith, the dean of the College of Education and Health Professions, and Jim Rankin, UA's vice provost for Research and Economic Development. During dinner, Gearhart's adult son, Brock, came by our table to say hello—a nice courtesy, as he knew most everyone at the table.

Soon after the event, Brock apparently mentioned to his father that he had seen all of us. Dad wasn't happy to hear that Choate was among our dinner group. The elder Gearhart told Schwab to deliver a message to those of us from Advancement, politely making it known to us that we should consider Choate to be *persona non grata*. Gearhart also mentioned it to UA Provost Sharon Gaber, Tom Smith's boss: Smith later shared with Choate that Gaber told him to keep his distance from his friend. It was a sad turn: once considered a brother figure, Gearhart was labeling Choate a pariah to the UA community, even in social settings. Yet Choate remained on the university's payroll as a vice chancellor, situated and staffed in a corner office on the executive floor of the Admin Building and serving at Gearhart's direction.

Along with his words of advice about Choate, Wyrick also wanted to know about my office's working relationship with the Alumni and Development operations. Moments into the conversation, he offered an observation. "I don't know why Development needs two guys doing what Bruce is supposed to do." The second guy was Mark Power, assistant vice chancellor for Development, who reported to Pontious. "I've never understood that. It's not a two-man job."

Was Wyrick toying with the idea of consolidating the two positions? Everyone understood he would have to adopt all kinds of cost-savings measures to offset his new division's multi-million dollar deficit. However, that particular idea might prove counterproductive. Both Pontious and Power were effective fundraisers and well regarded by donors and deans. I couldn't imagine Wyrick could run a billion-dollar capital campaign without the two of them. Nor did I think Gearhart would let him, despite the chancellor's concerns about Pontious' long-time friendship with Choate. I didn't offer Wyrick an opinion on the subject; I thought combining the two roles was an unlikely scenario. He didn't say anything more about it that day.

With Wyrick's starting date now set for April 1st, Choate prepared to vacate the vice chancellor's suite. Things had not been going as he had expected. After adjusting to the reality of his November reassignment, he committed himself to the two projects Gearhart gave him: creating a brief on each of UA's major donors to help Wyrick and other fundraisers involved in the new capital campaign; and finding another job. He had been having no luck landing a new position; the notoriety of his situation at UA made it impossible for him to land anything remotely appealing. But at least he was making good progress on his fundraising campaign assignment.

Shortly after Choate was removed from his Advancement position, the chancellor's office scheduled a series of meetings between Gearhart and Choate. Choate assumed the meetings related to his new assignment and would include discussions of the capital campaign. But minutes before the first scheduled meeting, Schwab visited Choate in his office. According to Choate, she told him to ignore those calendar items; the chancellor had arranged for them to appear on their calendars just in case the news media FOIA'd Gearhart's or Choate's schedule. These "phantom meetings" would give reporters the impression that Choate was busy earning his salary in his new post.

There would be more such shenanigans. After Choate notified Gearhart's office that he had completed the capital campaign report he had been assigned, UA attorney Scott Varady visited with him. Varady told Choate that, based on advice from UA System Chief Legal Counsel Fred Harrison, Choate should dispose of the report before it could be FOIA'd. Choate did as Varady had instructed, deleting it from his computer. When the time came for Choate to brief Wyrick on the report, he shared it orally from memory. Wyrick took notes.

In late March, Choate was assigned new office space in order to accommodate Wyrick's arrival. Choate was relocated to a windowless conference room across the hall from Gearhart's and Gaber's office suites. He referred to his new quarters as the Cave of Exile—jokingly at first, more ruefully later. He received no further work assignments; only instructions to show up every morning at eight and stay until five. With nothing to do, Vice Chancellor Choate spent the final three months of his UA employment watching various cable TV shows and YouTube videos on the Cave's flat-screen teleconference monitor. He received $87,000 in donor-generated dollars for his time.

Wyrick wanted to hit the ground running. He held his initial all-staff meeting the morning of April 1st, Day One of his new job. He was funny and upbeat, sharing among other things the importance of his upcoming birthday. "Remember my birthday!" he joked several times that day. Wyrick announced that in order to develop a better sense of the division's operation, he had asked UA's Human Resources office to devise an "organizational study." Each of us would be asked to maintain a log of how we spent our time while on the job—everything from meetings, donor visits, and graphic design sketches to phone calls and coffee breaks. The exercise would last two weeks and begin the following week. Several staff members said they were concerned that a two-week snapshot of their activities would not be representative of their overall work. The nature and extent of each of their duties often varied according to the time of month or year. Wyrick assured everyone that the purpose of the exercise was not to judge anyone's performance; it was to help him better understand Advancement's functions. And in a further effort to put his audience at ease, he also promised that no one on the staff would lose his or her job, despite the funding shortfall that he was about to tackle. We all appreciated the pledge.

Meanwhile, the Advancement division's unit directors and managers continued to work on their respective budget proposals for the upcoming fiscal year. Each unit's plan needed to fit within that of the overall division and receive the vice chancellor's approval. After that, it would be submitted to CFO Pederson for incorporation as part of a university-wide budget proposal, which would be discussed by Gearhart and his executive committee before being sent along to the UA System's board of trustees.

Much of my office's budget depended on the priorities of other units within Advancement. We produced news releases, mailings, email blasts, web pages, publications, and videos that were used for fundraising, alumni events, PR, and a wide assortment of event promotions. Sometimes other units within Advancement picked up some or all of the production costs; other times, our University Relations office absorbed those costs as part of our operational support function. For that reason, I needed to know my colleagues' budget priorities in order to set my own.

Each of us was supposed to submit our draft budgets to Denise Reynolds, the person who replaced Joy Sharp as Advancement's budget director. On April 3rd, I sent Reynolds an email, seeking budget information that I understood she had pulled together as part of her post-Sharp budget reconciliation:

> Hi, Denise. To help me provide a comprehensive presentation and case for my FY14 budget requests, it would be helpful for me to have an accurate (well, as accurate as possible! ☺) understanding of the compensation and non-compensation expenditures incurred by each of the Big Three of Advancement [Development, Alumni Affairs, and University Relations] for FY11 and FY12....These will help me keep my requests and expectations reasonable while helping me differentiate the nature of my comp and non-comp expenditures and needs. Please give me a call should you need clarification. Thanks! John

Usually Reynolds would promptly email an acknowledgment that she had received a request. But after not hearing back from her by the end of the following day, I sent her a second email and included my original message:

> Hi, Denise. Just wanted to make sure you received this request. It's possible that the campus email problems delayed its delivery. Please let me know should you have any questions. Many thanks! John

Minutes later, she responded to me and sent a copy to Wyrick:

> John, I did see your request below. However, time constraints simply do not allow me to pull this information together prior to our budget meeting tomorrow. Also, I am not sure what the purpose of pulling this information for Development & Alumni would serve to help you with your budget needs. dr

Dawn Mabry and I were scheduled to meet with Wyrick and Reynolds the next day to discuss the new budget process. I decided to wait until then to explain my need further. Dawn and I arrived early at the vice chancellor's office suite. Reynolds' office door was open, so I tapped on the doorframe and walked in. I reiterated my reasons for needing preliminary budget submissions; Reynolds reiterated her belief that I did not.

"Denise, that's part of the reason Joy got into trouble," I reminded her, referring to Sharp's withholding of budget information. "Do I have to FOIA my own division to see our own budget?"

Reynolds did not appreciate my observation. "We'll take it up in there," she curtly replied, pointing toward Wyrick's office. I returned to the reception area where Dawn was seated.

Soon, Wyrick invited us into his personal office. The four of us took seats at his small conference table. Reynolds appeared agitated; she said there was something we needed to discuss before we started and nodded toward me. I told Wyrick that I had asked for budget information in order to prepare my own office's budget and priorities but that Denise didn't feel I needed it. I told him what I had said to her and why I said it. She said nothing.

I expected him to ask her why she didn't want to provide it and, after hearing her out, to ask her to make the information available. I presumed that he would be sensitive to the need for transparency, given that he and Reynolds, more than anyone else, had inherited a financial and management crisis caused by secrecy and misinformation. But instead, he simply told me to do the best I could with the information I had.

Sharp's practice had been to treat budget information as privileged information, finding excuses not to share details with the division's senior leaders. Now, a year later, it was happening again—only this time with the approval of the vice chancellor. As Yogi Berra would say, it was déjà vu all over again.

Wyrick scheduled a second all-staff meeting for April 16th, two weeks following the first one. By now, I had seen him speak publicly on several occasions, dating back to his introduction as vice chancellor. He always appeared comfortable on stage and also seemed to enjoy it. However, he had a tendency to utter malapropisms, such as saying "awkwardmonious" to describe a situation that was apparently both awkward and acrimonious. On several occasions, when explaining his management style ("Start with the end in mind!"), he labeled it as his "séance" instead of his presumably intended term for focus and repetition, "mantra." In an interview with *Arkansas Business*, he described his plans for leading Advancement this way: "From day one it's going to be about day one."

The primary purpose of the second all-staff meeting was to follow up on his previously announced organizational study. He invited Barbara Abercrombie, the head of UA's Human Resources office, to join us. She reiterated Wyrick's earlier assurance that the work-log assignment he gave us was to help him better understand the division's operation and would not be used to judge any employee's job performance.

Wrapping up the morning's gathering, Wyrick said he and Abercrombie would present their findings at yet another all-staff meeting, to be held in mid-May. Wyrick also reminded us that his birthday was four days away.

Now that we had a vice chancellor on board, we resumed our Monday afternoon leadership team meetings. One of Wyrick's first orders of business was to change the group's name from "University Advancement Cabinet" to "Advancement Executive Staff." It seemed like more than a simple switch in nomenclature; it came across as an attempt to distinguish his role from the rest of us. He didn't need to make that point; we all knew he was the boss, just as we had known it with Choate. It also represented a change in the nature of our meetings: agendas were now longer and focused on reports and updates, not on group deliberations of issues and strategies.

A disturbing exchange took place at our April 22nd weekly meeting. As we worked our way through the agenda, Graham Stewart, the head of Alumni Affairs, reported on the past weekend's "Black Alumni Society" events. BAS was a subset of the Alumni Association; its mission was to "help recognize the history, contributions, and struggles of black persons who have attended the University of Arkansas." One of BAS's events that weekend was a fundraising dinner to support UA scholarships. As Stewart was briefing us about the dinner's program, a voice interrupted.

"Were you the only white guy?" Wyrick asked with a grin.

"Um, no," Stewart slowly answered, taken aback by the question. Continuing with his report, Stewart was again interrupted moments later.

"Brother Honky!" Wyrick exclaimed.

Stewart paused.

"Go ahead," Wyrick said, giving Stewart the green light to finish his report, which he did.

Our meeting continued for the next hour or so. After we completed the agenda, we finished with a "roundtable"—an opportunity to use the time remaining for each of us to share any non-agenda news or announcements. When it was Stewart's turn, Wyrick nodded to him and said, "Brother Honky?"

Is he always this way? I wondered. I wasn't accustomed to hearing jokes about race, nor did I want to. A few weeks earlier, I had been present when Wyrick directed a racially tinged reference to Eric Wood, who was an associate director for Razorback Athletics and is African American. The three of us were traveling together to Little Rock for "Razorback Day at the Capitol." During a conversation with Wood, Wyrick said something like "Your people like that." I turned quickly to Wyrick, who was seated to my right. I gave him a startled look: *Did you just say what I think you said?* Wyrick saw my expression and said, "That's OK. We talk like that all the time." I looked at Wood; he just smiled and shrugged.

After the Advancement meeting, Stewart, Pontious, and I stood outside the Admin Building for a post-mortem. Stewart wondered aloud what his black alumni would say if they heard about the "Brother Honky" quips. Wyrick's tongue could be dangerous, we agreed. He already had a reputation for saying things that should have remained unspoken. For example, during his early fundraising days for the Razorbacks, Athletics Director Jeff Long dressed him down for saying something inappropriate during remarks Wyrick delivered at an event. (Wyrick himself told me about that reprimand, as did others in Athletics.) Now that Wyrick was a highly paid senior officer of the university, would he work harder to keep himself in check? The early indications were not encouraging.

Chapter 9

BULLY PULPIT

News coverage of the Advancement deficit continued like water torture through March, April, and May even though there was little news to justify that coverage. With the Schook memo finally released and the audits finally requested, the *Democrat-Gazette* struggled to find fresh angles. It rehashed stories that had run previously (e.g., "Gearhart Still Rejects Gift Tax on Donations" and "UA Still Firing its Budget Director"). At University Relations, we continued to receive requests for interviews about Advancement's finances past and present. In most instances, we issued our standard response: "We cannot elaborate further in order to protect the integrity of the auditors' investigation."

However, that excuse could not be given in response to FOIA requests. The law did not allow that. Reporters repeatedly asked for budget updates related to the division. I would pass along the request to Pederson and Reynolds and would be given the same response: updated budget information had not yet been assembled. I believed it because that's what I was told. In fact, my fellow associate vice chancellors and I were no longer receiving budget information ourselves;

Reynolds had not given us a monthly budget update since she attempted to do so at the aborted January 14th meeting with Gearhart.

Gearhart remained agitated by the *Democrat-Gazette's* pursuit of something—anything—to report. He viewed the newspaper's efforts as part of a conspiracy to add his name to Arkansas' list of disgraced higher ed leaders. Gearhart made repeated references to the fate of two former colleagues who had once led the University of Central Arkansas, a public institution of about 11,500 students in Conway: UCA President Lu Hardin and Allen C. Meadors, Hardin's successor as UCA's president. In August of 2008, Hardin resigned his position after revelations that he had forged a university document to gain early access to $300,000 in secretly negotiated deferred compensation funds. He later pleaded guilty to wire fraud and money laundering. Three years later, in September of 2001, Meadors resigned after admitting he had entered a *quid pro quo* arrangement with the university's food service provider, Aramark. The company had agreed to "donate" $700,000 to help renovate Meadors' university-owned home if and when UCA renewed Aramark's contract. Meadors had told his governing board about the "gift" but failed to note that it was linked to continuing Aramark's service arrangement with UCA. Intense digging and coverage by the *Democrat-Gazette* played a role in the departures of both leaders.

Gearhart repeatedly spoke in Nixonian ways about the *Democrat-Gazette* trying to "bring me down." On multiple occasions he shared with several of us an exchange that purportedly occurred at the newspaper, something he said he learned from a *Democrat-Gazette* insider. According to Gearhart, certain individuals within the newspaper's organization boasted that "we got two presidents and Gearhart is next." He also claimed that Jennifer Cook, the managing editor in charge of the *Democrat-Gazette's* coverage of the Advancement story, was pushing the story out of spite: in the past, she apparently had applied and been turned down for employment positions within UA. In February, Gearhart told several of us that Cook was again seeking a job at UA. He said her status as a current applicant was a clear conflict of interest. (If indeed she wanted a job at UA, her aggressiveness with the Advancement story was a strange way to promote her candidacy, I thought.)

On March 1, Gearhart sent me an email that contained language for a memo he wanted me to consider sending. His email opened with "Thoughts?" followed by the words "DELETE DELETE DELETE.":

> TO: Jennifer Cook
>
> FROM: John Diamond
>
> RE: conflict of interest
>
> It has just come to my attention that you are a current applicant for a staff position in the law school at the University of Arkansas. I know this is one of many positions you have applied for at the university the last few years.
>
> It is my belief that this fact places you in a position of conflict of interest to be actively assigning reporters to the Advancement story while at the same time seeking a position with the institution. This fact would give the public the appearance of impropriety and an imbalance of judgement and treatment on your part and the *Arkansas Democrat-Gazette*.
>
> I know that when you learned that your former employer, Chris Branum [sic] was an applicant at the university you immediately removed him from any professional dealings with the University of Arkansas. I respectfully ask you to disengage from the Advancement story during the time you are an active applicant at our Law School or any other application for a job you may have with our institution.
>
> Thank you for your consideration.

Gearhart's email also suggested that if I agreed to send his draft message under my own name, I should copy three of Cook's reporting staff and two of her superiors on the email. A day or so later, Gearhart asked what I thought about his request. I was blunt: I said I thought it was a bad idea to send such a threatening message and

I didn't want to send it. He asked me to continue to think about it. (We later discovered that the applicant was a different Jennifer Cook, someone who was seeking a job in the law school's library. Even after being informed of that, Gearhart continued to tell people that the *Democrat-Gazette's* Cook was an applicant and that she had a conflict of interest.)

By late April, all of us in Advancement had completed our daily work logs as part of Wyrick's organizational study. Abercrombie, the head of Human Resources, was expected to digest the information gathered from the division's 150-plus employees and provide her assessment at another all-staff meeting scheduled for mid-May. Given the volume of material, the deadline seemed impossibly ambitious. And it was; soon the presentation was rescheduled to June 20th.

When Wyrick first spoke of conducting an organizational study, he pledged that no one would lose his or her job. But during a May Advancement Executive Staff meeting, he qualified that assurance: he was only promising that full-time employees would be kept on. Some of us in his senior leadership group had part-time employees that we could not afford to lose, and we told him so. He said he would consider keeping them on if they agreed to work full-time—a peculiar decision, given that the additional salary, wages, and increased cost of employee benefits would contribute further to Advancement's funding woes.

Also in May, Wyrick told me that he wanted to add a budget manager to my staff. Following the death of University Relations' in-house budget manager a few years earlier, Joy Sharp took over those responsibilities for us and, now, Denise Reynolds handled them. Restoring the position would ease some of the burden for Reynolds as she managed Advancement as a whole. Initially, I welcomed the idea. But a few weeks later, in a meeting with Wyrick and Abercrombie, they said they wanted to replace my executive assistant, Dawn Mabry, with someone else. The person they had in mind—someone who already was on my staff and reported to Dawn—would handle University Relations' budget and provide administrative support. At first, I laughed in disbelief—not because of the person they suggested, but because Mabry's role was much more extensive than just administrative support. She was my right-hand associate and unofficial chief of staff within our 43-person operation. She was a highly valued member of our five-person marketing team. She worked with others on campus to compile data and produce sensitive reports in response to the many reputational surveys that UA answered each year. Having worked in those roles for eight years, she had a deep institutional memory.

"Why?" I asked.

Abercrombie answered. She said it was based on the other employee's work log; it had impressed her. I was sure that it had, but said that it didn't justify removing the high-performing Mabry, whose responsibilities and experience were much broader. I had not been shown the raw data or the summary Abercrombie said she had compiled; unable to address the specific reasons that motivated the recommendation of change, Wyrick told Abercrombie and me to meet a second time to discuss and resolve my concerns. We did, and I left that meeting believing the suggestion was off the table. We never discussed it again.

Soon afterward, in an Advancement leadership meeting, the issue of part-time employees again came up. Several of us noted that for some half-time employees, their personal circumstances were such that shifting to full-time status would be a hardship for them. In addition, in most instances we didn't think it was necessary or cost-effective to expand their hours. But Wyrick had made up his mind. He held up a large loose-leaf binder, fanning the pages to show us the yellow highlights he had added to what supposedly was Abercrombie's work-log assessment. He was ready to shape the division as he saw fit, which of course was his right as the division head. We just couldn't understand why we, as the leaders of the division's major function and strategy areas, were not consulted as part of his process. We didn't know what conclusions he and Abercrombie had reached nor were we being asked about how any changes might affect our respective offices' ability to perform.

On the morning of June 11th, Wyrick called me. He had just learned that Dawn Mabry was going to be on vacation and would miss the June 20th all-staff meeting. He wanted both of us to meet with him as soon as possible so he could tell Mabry his plans for her. I asked him to tell *me*—her direct supervisor—what those plans were. He said he was reassigning her to the Development office, where she would be a records technician—clearly a demotion. Once again, I had to ask him why. He would not elaborate. I explained that Dawn was at a meeting on campus and would be back around 11 a.m. He said to come see him once she returned. He also instructed me not to tell her why.

When Mabry returned, I asked her to come in to my office and to shut the door. She had a fearful look on her face. "Is this about Richanne?" she asked, referring to a part-time staff member who reported to her. Dawn had been worried that Wyrick would lay off Richanne and other part-time employees as part of his cost-savings plan. I told her that wasn't it; that Wyrick wanted to talk to her and that I was ordered not to be any more specific. She began to cry and tearfully asked if she was being fired. "No," I answered. I also told her I was going to the meeting with her and expected that he would explain what was on his mind.

We headed across the street to Wyrick's office in the Admin Building. We waited briefly in the reception area before he opened his office door and invited us to come in.

"You've been crying," he said to Mabry. "Why?"

Dawn answered that it was because she knew something bad was about to happen. He turned to me. "Did you tell her?"

"Only that you wanted to talk to her about the 're-org'. I didn't say anything more, just like you asked."

He then broke the news to her that he was reassigning her out of University Relations and into Development's Records office. She learned that her new boss would be an assistant director—a position that was lower in the division's hierarchy than the post Dawn currently held. Now it was her turn to ask why. Wyrick simply told her that he thought she would fit better in the Records office.

Once again, Mabry began to cry. She defended her job performance record; her evaluations were always excellent. She talked about her years of service to the division. Then, in a moment of frustration, she noted that others in Advancement were keeping their jobs while she—a person who had played no role in Advancement's mismanagement—was being punished.

"This is tough on *me*, too," Wyrick quickly responded. "You were on the payroll during all of this. I wasn't. I have to clean up the mess!"

"Come on, Chris," I interjected. "That's unfair to her and to everyone else in the division!"

He backed off but did not apologize. He told Mabry that if in six months she was unhappy with her new assignment, she could discuss it with him. She didn't look comforted by those words, still reeling from the shock of his announcement.

"Don't you trust me?" he asked her.

"I don't know you well enough to answer that." Dawn said, still wiping tears from her cheeks.

"I don't want you to tell anyone about this until after the [June 20th] meeting," he told her. "If you do, that's insubordination."

"Can't I even tell my husband?!"

"Yes, but if you tell anyone else, that's grounds for termination." He signaled the end of the meeting by extending his hand to her. She took it and halfheartedly shook it. Wyrick then excused Dawn but asked me to stay. After she left and the door closed, he asked me if I thought the meeting went OK, all things considered. I thought the answer was obvious.

"No, I don't, actually." I told him I thought he was insensitive and unnecessarily harsh. He seemed indifferent to my response. I asked him who would take Mabry's place at University Relations. He said it would be worked out later.

Mabry wasn't the only one having these conversations with Wyrick. Others were being called to his office to discuss their future with the division. Those who made the trip received the same warning that Dawn received: don't tell anyone until after the June 20th meeting.

One of UA's academic bragging points is its law school. Highly regarded and nationally ranked, its graduates include governors, members of Congress, and plenty of women and men who have achieved remarkable success in law and business. Dave Gearhart was a UA law alumnus. So, too, were his brothers Van, the Arkansas district court judge; and Jeff, Wal-Mart's executive vice president of global governance and, for several years, the corporation's legal counsel.

The law school is notable for other reasons. In 1948, it enrolled Silas Hunt, making UA the first all-white public university in the South since Reconstruction to enroll a black student without a court order to do so. Granted, Hunt was physically segregated from other law students when in class, but given the times and locale, it was a relatively progressive step made possible by Law School Dean Robert Leflar. The law school also boasts an impressive list of past and current faculty members. Both Bill Clinton and Hillary Rodham Clinton were full-time members of the UA law faculty early in their careers. In fact, Dave Gearhart was one of Bill Clinton's students.

Physically, the law school facility sits near the center of the Fayetteville campus. It's rectangular with a large open-air courtyard. The complex's most impressive feature is the E.J. Ball Courtroom. Named for a former law professor and Razorback donor, the modern courtroom is used for law classes and moot court trials. It features five elevated, crescent-shaped rows of countertop tables and enough padded seats to accommodate up to 200 persons. The courtroom's focal point sits below in an open well. It's where a law professor would speak or a law student would plead a case. It's also where the state's highest court, the seven-member Arkansas Supreme Court, is seated when it travels to Northwest Arkansas to hear cases.

On June 20, 2013, the well of the Ball Courtroom was occupied by Advancement Vice Chancellor Chris Wyrick. This was the day he would reveal his plans for reorganizing the division. All 150 members of Advancement personnel had been told to attend. Only those members of Advancement who had already scheduled vacations or medical appointments were excused from attending. Wyrick had asked me to have my staff video-record the entire meeting so that it could be shared on DVD with anyone who could not be present. He also asked that we post the video on a restricted-access YouTube site so that he could share it later in the day with Gearhart.

Like many of the attendees, I was anxious to hear what Wyrick would announce. Other than his demotion of Mabry, I did not know what other changes to my areas of responsibility he had in mind. Nor did the two other associate vice chancellors, Graham Stewart and Bruce Pontious. In fact, Pontious wasn't going to be present for the meeting; he was out of town. However, he was present in our minds, having stunned most of us a few weeks earlier by announcing he would retire at the end of September. He was a youthful sixty-three.

I sat in the back, positioned at the end of the last row with another member of Advancement's executive team, Dan Hendrix, the head of the Arkansas World Trade Center. From our corner, we would be able to observe reactions as Wyrick announced his changes. Shortly before the scheduled start of the meeting, Wyrick entered the well of the courtroom and greeted the staff members nearby. He was dressed in a pale blue and white seersucker suit, white shirt, and a red, white, and navy blue bow tie. He was also wearing white-and-tan saddle shoes. As he walked to the podium and rested his hands on its sides, his appearance and the location could have passed for a scene from the TV show *Matlock*, Southern accent and all.

"It has been eighty-one days since we first got together on April the first," he began, following a few housekeeping remarks. "I know to you it feels like one hundred and eighty-one, but it's only been eighty-one since we first got together. And I want to tell you this. I love this job. I love this university. And I love this team.

"Many of you know I wasn't trained for this," he noted, referring to his Advancement position. "It was not my desired outcome for my career. It happened. I took it. I grabbed it by the horns, and I am here.

"Folks, the thing that may be the best news for all of us is, as of July One, we will have a zero-based balanced budget," he announced, with applause following. That was impressive, given that the deficit was in excess of $3 million. "You never want to single out people, but Denise Reynolds," nodding in her direction, "the amount of time and effort behind closed doors, the begging we had to do, the bartering we had to do! The bottom line is this: I am convinced… that we have the money to do our jobs effectively."

This was encouraging news. He was publicly stating that he had balanced the budget. But it was also disconcerting. A "zero-based" budget? If he actually intended to use that term, it meant that Wyrick and Reynolds had put together a $10-$13 million budget from scratch, not one that was based on past years' revenues and expenditures. It also meant something else: they had made decisions about what positions and activities would be funded within each unit of Advancement without any input from those of us who handle the division's day-to-day operations. And, as Wyrick had just said, he had taken those actions after only 81 days on the job.

"So let me say this," he continued. "If you do see Don Pederson, or if you do see any of the deans—and I mean this, OK?—take the time to introduce yourself, walk up, and say, 'I'm with the Advancement division. I know you went to bat for us. You didn't have to. You could have easily tightened that belt and strangulated us, but you didn't. You believed we were going do what we said we were going to do. You took a chance on us, and you're enabling us to do what we need to do.'

"The deans," he added. "Many of you know, they've taken a big chunk of their budget to make this thing work. I'm very appreciative. Every single one of them—to a T, every single one of them—chipped in. OK?"

So the budget was being balanced by reducing funding for UA's academic colleges or by making the deans pick up personnel and operational costs that Advancement had been covering. If accurate, critics could easily cry that UA leadership was remedying the Advancement deficit on the backs of students and taxpayers—something Gearhart had pledged would not occur. Anything that reduced the academic side's revenues or increased its expenses would have that effect.

Wyrick offered no details. Instead, he segued to the HR study. Barbara Abercrombie, UA's head of Human Resources, sat nearby.

"I do want to tell you this about the study. In all candor, it was a lot more detailed than I ever expected. It was amazing what you revealed about yourselves, not only in those logs with those questions that you answered. It was extremely thought-provoking. We spent an inordinate amount of time studying those. And I want to tell you—you know, Barbara is fairly new herself, but we do owe her and her staff a huge round of gratitude for the effort that they put in on our behalf. So with that, Barbara, the microphone is yours."

Abercrombie stepped to the podium and began her presentation.

"Throughout this process—from the beginnings of discussing how we would do this HR review—Chris said, 'I don't want anyone to lose their job.' And he said it over and over and over again. He was steadfast in that leadership. And every time I said, 'But maybe we should think about this,' he said, 'Absolutely not!' That kind of leadership is what you guys have in Chris."

Abercrombie's declaration rang hollow to some in the room, including me. After all, a few in the crowd knew that they would be "losing their job" via reassignment or demotion. But under Wyrick and Abercrombie's definition of the phrase, having a paycheck was the same as keeping your job, even if the nature of the position would provide less stature, professional challenge, or personal enjoyment.

"You guys are a quiet group this morning!" Abercrombie responded to the silence following her reassurances. A few minutes later, as she was wrapping up, she spoke about my area of responsibility.

"Some of you have had some questions about University Relations. We are going to extend the study with them. I've been talking with John and talking with Chris....I really want to do a deeper dive into their positions, how we can help them with that, how we can explain what they do better to the campus, and how we can help them look at what their needs are. So I am looking forward to that, and John and I will be working on that in the future."

That was news to me. No, she and I had not been talking about the organizational study. Wyrick had told me and the other associate vice chancellors not to interfere with her work. I wondered, What were the issues that would preclude her (or Wyrick) from completing the process as they had with the other units within Advancement?

Moments after Abercrombie relinquished the speaker's podium to Wyrick, he quickly undermined her assurances about process and thoroughness.

"You deserve an honest answer," he stated. "Barbara said that the leadership talked about all this," he said, shaking his head side to side. "The leadership team did *not* talk about all of this. We did not come together on our Monday groups and have a group discussion.

"They were upset in some cases with me about this," he admitted, referring to Pontious, Alumni's Graham Stewart, and me. "'You made some decisions about my area without consulting me.' And you know what? They're right. If I were them, I would feel that way.

"But you know something? If you're going to own a process, sometimes you do what you feel you need to do. So if I did not consult, and if it fails, shame on me. But sometimes you just do what you're going to do." So much for the process, I thought.

Wyrick also wanted to address the concerns and criticism he had sensed regarding the work-log exercise. "I don't want you to think this guy isn't hearing what you're saying, OK?" he said, pointing to himself. "I want you to know that I respect some of these comments. Some I don't, to be candid with you. But I want to make you aware of what I have heard. And I want to address them.

"So, a couple of things," he said, nodding to the projection screens overhead and directing attention to the first of a series of presumed staff objections and concerns. "'How could you make a decision on a two-week snapshot of a period of time that may not be my busiest time of the year?' And the answer to that is, That is not what we did! We studied those two weeks. We then took your own evaluations that were done. If there were problems, we did more investigating. I don't know of a single decision that was made in this that I did not interview a neutral party and say, 'This is what A said, this is what B said, can you tell me what C is?' So the idea that this simply was a two-week snapshot is simply unfair. That's not the case."

Not a reassuring statement of thoroughness. Who were these "neutral parties"? And how would they know whether a staff member's assignments over a two-week period were reflective of the nature and totality of her or his responsibilities, especially when supervisors were not consulted? Like others in Advancement, I maintained a work-log during the two-week period, and it was nowhere near representative of my overall duties.

Wyrick moved on to another supposed staff concern. "'This study was mandatory from the chancellor.' The truth is, I was advised to wait a year. Take the time, get to know, and go. But the reality is, when you've gone through what you folks went through, we don't owe it to our constituents and our donors and this university to wait a year. They want action. They want answers. They want to see progress.

"Someone asked me, Did I regret launching this on Day One? Although this is not flawless, some of this probably will prove not to work, but not *One. Single. Regret.* For doing this on Day One."

Wyrick then turned to his next perceived concern. "That Barbara Abercrombie and I had a preconceived notion. 'You put us through this process. There wasn't that much depth to it, sometimes you weren't available to answer questions. You put us through motions.' No. Simply not the case. Other than the budget, I don't know of anything that I've spent more time studying. Including this week, this is all we've done. All we've done is finalize this."

Having responded, Wyrick turned to the specifics of his reorganization plan, working his way through the Advancement division's structure.

First, Alumni Affairs. No changes.

Next, the Arkansas World Trade Center. No changes.

Then to University Relations. "You heard Barbara state very clearly exactly what is going on," Wyrick said. "I can't make you believe it. I don't feel like I need to make you believe it," he added, more agitated than apologetic.

"You know, I will be very honest: I am very aggressive in my management style. Make no mistake about it. You're seeing it today. But the bottom line is, we could have gone in and made some emotional decisions and made some assumptions. It wasn't fair to do. We had inconclusive results. So what we decided to do, we're going back to the drawing board. Barbara Abercrombie is currently working on—and again, I'll let John explain it when the time is right—she is currently working on the best way to get more communications. OK? Plain and simple. That's what it is.

"The one change in there is Dawn Mabry," he announced. "She's going to come with us to University House, and she is going to be working in records and data services for Development. So that is just the one change we did go ahead and make in that area."

That announcement stunned many people, both within and outside of University Relations. Mabry was one of the best-liked and most-respected colleagues in Advancement. Many of her colleagues knew that she had been the one who, following Jeff Long's termination of Bobby Petrino, suggested the "Integrity Goes a LONG Way" T-shirts. After Wyrick's pronouncement, several people in the audience turned my way, offering puzzled looks. *Why Dawn?* I'm sure my expression reflected my displeasure with Wyrick's action.

"Next is Constituent Relations and Special Events," Wyrick continued. He announced he was expanding the responsibilities for a person who was already a unit director. He also announced two promotions: naming Ede Hogue, a part-time employee, to a new full-time position as an associate director. She had called his bluff and taken advantage of the offer to go full-time or go home.

Then, he moved to his second promotion. "Robin Adams! Where's my friend Robin?" he asked, scanning the audience. Adams worked in the Development office as a records technician. Hers would be the position Dawn Mabry would assume. "Robin told me in the hallway that, at the end of all this, she'll be the first one to stand up and say, 'I'm all in.'

"Robin—this is selfish—was hand-picked!" Wyrick said, again pointing a finger back at himself. "I saw that shining smile, I saw that 'I-wanna-do-all-I-can-to-make-it-better' look. Robin is going to be joining this group as a manager."

More puzzled looks among the attendees. Like most public universities, UA required that offices post and publicize any position vacancies or opportunities for promotion. The purpose was to ensure fairness to current employees, to encourage their aspirations, and to make sure that supervisors did not show favoritism or discriminate based on gender, race, religion, or orientation. The policy also required that, in most cases, a time-consuming criminal background check had to be conducted on individuals being considered for promotions. Many in the room realized that those policies and practices had not been followed.

"As I told you before, there is good news in this, things I'm very proud of. And that is promotions," Wyrick continued. "I am ecstatic that—long overdue!—Mark Power is being named associate vice chancellor for University Development. Mark Power! Mark is tremendously talented. He is a great 'ying' to my yang...Mark, I'm very proud of you and certainly looking forward to working side by side."

More awkwardness. Whether a Freudian slip or deliberate jab, calling Power's promotion to lead the Development office "long overdue" was an offense to the absent Bruce Pontious, the current office holder and Power's immediate supervisor. Wyrick announced that Power's promotion and salary increase would take effect in ten days, not after Pontious' retirement at the end of September. In the meantime, Pontious would be given a special assignment related to the fundraising campaign for the remaining three-plus months of his UA employment. Within a few weeks, Pontious would clear out his corner office in University House and relocate to Choate's vacated conference room—the "Cave of Exile"—in the Admin Building.

As with the other announced promotions, Power was the only person considered for, or allowed to seek, his new position. It was not posted or advertised. An associate vice chancellor's position at a research university is highly sought after. Normally, UA would advertise the opportunity nationally and would draw at least 100 applicants with the credentials to do the job. Not that Power wouldn't be the pick, anyway; he was a favorite of Gearhart. But like Wyrick's own hiring, the established process was forsaken to accommodate the boss's personal desires.

Advancement's vice chancellor had additional promotions to announce.

"The next one," Wyrick announced. "Another very selfish decision but hand-picked by the conductor," once again tapping his chest. "Katie Nelson is being named assistant vice chancellor for University Development."

Nelson was a senior fundraiser in UA's Walton College of Business. While qualified, her appointment was yet another one that Wyrick made without allowing, as policy dictates, other development officers and employees within UA to pursue the job. Furthermore, Nelson was taking over Power's position as the top deputy in the fundraising operation. Back in February, Wyrick had questioned whether it was excessive for Development to have both Pontious and Power. ("It's not a two-man job.") Apparently he had changed his mind.

"Denise Reynolds has been promoted to assistant vice chancellor for Advancement," he continued. "Denise has done a great job. She's awesome. She's consistent. I enjoy working with Denise and am proud of this."

More promotions and reassignments followed. All done without any input from Pontious, Stewart, or me, the vice chancellor's three senior leaders. Most, if not all, of Wyrick's actions were done without following university policies and protocol. Usually supervisors get in trouble for that.

"The good news, the good news, the good news," Wyrick proclaimed after presenting his plan. "Every single person in this room—every single person who attended the meeting on April the First—every single one of you—*Have. Your. Job!* We promised that. We fought for it. We told you it would happen."

Perhaps sensing skepticism, he added, "Shame on you of little faith. That is a Biblical verse. I'll quote it to you later. Shame on you, ye of little faith. Every job was saved. We did what we said we were going to do."

Wyrick waited for applause. The audience read the pause, considered it momentarily, and then began a perfunctory handclapping.

Shifting to an exasperated tone, he cautioned all of his staff against overreacting to the changes.

"Nothing is set in stone. What is set in stone is hopefully by August the One, we look like a different organization.

"Don't go pack your office up," he warned, shaking his head. "Don't go pouting that you hear you're moving to the third floor. It hasn't been decided yet. And when it is decided, we will be the first to let you know."

Finished with that remonstration, he took pause to survey the room, corner to corner.

"So," he said with a smile. "The grand finale. The call. I got to get ready for this." Wyrick strolled away from the podium, took a sip from a plastic water bottle, and returned to the microphone.

"The question is, Are you ready?" Several people respond, "Yes!" One person belted out a "Whoop!" Wyrick nodded in approval. "'Cause I'm getting ready to lay one on you! Are you ready?"

Like many in the room, I was ready—ready and hoping for something more uplifting and unifying than the negativity and surprises we had just heard. I expected Wyrick to offer an upbeat, we-can-do-it closing to change the tone and reenergize the staff. We were a diverse group of fundraisers, alumni staff, writers, engineers, clerical workers, records technicians, analysts, graphic designers, videographers, and website developers. There were as many introverts in the group as there were extroverts. Here was an opportunity for our new leader to inspire trust and confidence in his decisions—and to explain the strategic reasoning and cost savings that influenced his thinking. The situation called for a positive, motivational appeal to put the past behind us and to focus on the opportunities ahead.

But that's not what we got. Pausing once again, Wyrick took off his suit jacket, folded it neatly, and placed it on a nearby table. Returning to the podium, he adjusted his bow tie, looked down at his script, and waited. Then, as he cleared his throat, he clasped the lectern frame atop the podium. A PowerPoint slide appeared on the overhead screens, reading, "Call to Action." After 15 seconds of silence that seemed much longer, he began his closing remarks.

"I've listened. I've observed. I've contemplated. I've shared. And most importantly, I've learned." His voice now cracked, presumably from emotion. He leaned forward, tapped the podium, and continued.

"Now is the time to lead. The decisions that have been made have been difficult. They've been thought about. They've been tossed and turned over. But now, they are done. They are not open for debate. They are not going to be discussed further. They are what they are."

Then, attempting to place the Advancement deficit controversy in context, he launched into a twisted metaphor of interplanetary travel, railroads, and highways.

"Eighteen months ago, your train left the station, bound for a billion miles. And unbeknownst to each of you, you had to pull over to the side. You had to have a pit stop about a hundred fifty million miles in. And that was unexpected to all of you.

"It created anxiety. It created a lot of doubt. It ruined momentum. And quite frankly, it hurt. It came as a surprise. And for that all I can say is, I'm sorry, because it was a surprise to me as well."

Dropping the metaphor, Wyrick's voice abruptly turned angry.

"Communication is a great thing. But, my friends! Rumors! Innuendos! Stating things that aren't true! To talk about gossip or to stir the pot will not be tolerated in this organization!

"I want you to enjoy your job. I want you to smile when you see me. I hope we get to the point where we can hug, and you won't turn me in to HR," generating a few nervous chuckles. "But the point is, I don't do drama." Then, dramatically, he continued.

"I addressed your questions earlier," nodding and smirking. "I knew what you had said about this study. Give me a little bit of credit. I had done my homework. But trust me. Going around talking about things that aren't true? We've already beat ourselves down enough.

"This very week, I had coffee with a donor, someone closely associated with this university. And they said, 'You know, It's just really hard to hear that you guys are *down*," dropping his voice to emphasize the donor's tone. "'You work too hard. You're *down*! You're beat. People are questioning. And people are gonna leave!'"

Shaking his head in disapproval, Wyrick offered his closing command.

"Ladies and gentlemen, when you walk out that door today," first pointing to his right, then to his left, then tapping his index finger on the podium. "When you walk out that door today...you are either in, or you are out.

"It's eighty-one days," his voice rising in emotion. "The gavel has been slammed! The questions have been answered!

Marcia and me, July 2013 (photo courtesy of Barbara Owen)

Happier times: Dave and Jane Gearhart with Julie and Brad Choate.

(photo courtesy of Julie Choate)

(photo courtesy of *Northwest Arkansas Democrat-Gazette*/Michael Woods)

Chris Wyrick (left) and Dave Gearhart, February 13, 2013.

(photo courtesy of *Arkansas Democrat-Gazette*/Staton Breidenthal)

Gearhart reacts to my prepared testimony to legislators on September 13, 2013 about document destruction and the culture of secrecy that developed at UA after the Advancement deficit became public.

PLEASE DELETE

(photo courtesy of *Arkansas Democrat-Gazette*/Gavin Lesnick)

Taking the oath at January 7, 2014 legislative hearing. Left to right, Don Pederson, Jean Schook, David Gearhart, Brad Choate, me, Joy Sharp.

"So I end as I began." Suddenly, another, deeper wave of emotion seemed to come over him. He acted as if he was trying to hold back tears and to compose himself. He swallowed hard and sucked in his cheeks. He tapped the top of the podium, apparently unable to put his words to the rhythm. He gazed up at the ceiling, then returned his eyes to the assembly. Finally, he spoke.

"I'm in," he offered softly. "I am in! I'm going for it! One billion miles as the train leaves this station! So, as you walk out of here today, Are you in? Are you on the team? Are you ready to put it behind you? Are you up to bat and ready to go? Because I'm telling you, if you are, we're unstoppable." A brief pause followed.

"Anybody? Are you in?!" Several people respond with words or applause.

"Who's in?! Stand up if you're in!" He scanned the room from left to right, again nodding.

The video operator recording the meeting pulled back his camera, widening the image to pan the audience. He captured the boss's command to staff members and their responses. All stood, displaying mixed levels of enthusiasm. Some clapped. Others simply folded their arms or stuffed their hands into their pockets. A few turned toward the videographer, reacting with unease as they realized his camera had captured their passivity. As the applause ebbed, Wyrick gave his staff a victorious wave.

"Thank you! Thank you very much! I'm headed back over there," pointing in the direction of the Admin Building nearby. "The door is open. Have a blessed day. Go Hogs!"

Annie Dowling was one of the Advancement staff members in the audience at the law school's courtroom that day. Like the others in the chamber, she rose when Wyrick called for employees to "stand up if you're in!" She didn't feel she had a choice.

A research analyst in the Development office, Dowling was disturbed by what she had just witnessed. Seven days later, she said so in an email to J'onnelle Colbert-Diaz, a grievance officer in the university's Office of Equal Opportunity and Compliance:

> At the University Advancement meeting last week, the new vice chancellor [Chris Wyrick] made comments about changes that I just did not feel comfortable with. This also assisted in my decision to leave the university next month. He wants us to be "All in" and is going about it in a very inappropriate, pep-rally, almost-hazing-like way.

Dowling commented further on her reaction in a follow-up email to Colbert-Diaz: "I do not think I am alone in my concerns about the meeting last week. However, I may just be the only one speaking about it."

As for me, I had drawn my own conclusion: the entire handling of the reorganization process and presentation was the most unprofessional example of executive leadership I had ever witnessed.

Chapter 10

UNDER SIEGE

I was ready to get out of town. The events of the past three months had eroded my enthusiasm for my job. The blustery June 20th session was part of it. But other incidents also made me feel that Wyrick's leadership style was not conducive to a healthy, productive workplace. For example, on a couple of occasions in group settings, Wyrick poked fun at me for being Catholic ("Y'all travel in packs" and "Where's the fish fry on Friday?"). Another time, he called an employee to his office and threatened to fire her because, against orders, she had told her boss, Mark Power, that she was being reassigned as part of Wyrick's reorganization. (Power had called her after hearing that she left work distraught after learning of her reassignment from Reynolds; Power insisted that she tell him what had upset her.) Another example involved one of my part-time employees: in separate conversations with me about the worker's performance, Wyrick referred to him as "the old guy who works with Russell." Meanwhile, I remained in the dark about who would take over all of Dawn Mabry's various duties. I still did not know what reasons Wyrick and Abercrombie had for removing Dawn from her position. If the change wasn't based on the work-logs—which both Wyrick and Abercrombie assured us would not be used to judge performance—how in the world could they justify demoting someone whose annual performance reviews were exemplary? In late June I reached out to Abercrombie, directly and through Wyrick, to learn more about her "inconclusive" findings about my part of the division. However, she told me she was not ready to meet with me at the time. We never did.

During the last week of June I drove back to Maine to spend a couple of weeks with family and friends. Marcia's school vacation had already begun, so she had flown to Maine ahead of me. I would drive the 1,800-mile trip to meet her, stopping along the way in Ohio to visit my sister Jean and to catch up with friends in upstate New York. Following our visit to Maine, Marcia and I would drive back to Fayetteville, sightseeing along the way and stopping in Cleveland to catch an Indians game.

We had another part of our excursion that only Gearhart, Wyrick, and a couple of others in Fayetteville knew about. A few weeks earlier I had applied for a vice presidency at the University of Iowa. Soon afterward, I was selected as one of three finalists for the job. This would be a step up professionally: like the University of Arizona, Iowa was among the elite public research universities in the world. A bit of irony was involved in this opening, as the person who had vacated the position, Tysen Kendig, was both a friend and my predecessor as associate vice chancellor at UA. He had recently left Iowa to become a vice president at the University of Connecticut, near where his family lived.

The Iowa search committee scheduled me to be in Iowa City in mid-July for two days of interviews and presentations. I confirmed my plans with Wyrick in emails and separately notified him and his assistant that I would be out of town but available via phone and email should they need me. They acknowledged the messages. Though we had never discussed the topic itself, I suspected Wyrick would not be disappointed if I took another job. But Gearhart might be, I thought at the time.

As with my University of Arizona visits, the interviews went well. However, President Sally Mason offered the job to a higher ed colleague of mine, Joe Brennan of the University at Buffalo, which is, like Arizona, a top research university. As someone expressed to me afterward, there's no shame in being a Silver medalist.

Back in Fayetteville, I returned to work. On July 25th, Tracie Dungan from the *Democrat-Gazette* called me to ask about a document that a colleague of hers had received from UA: an Advancement budget status report dated 6/24/2013. It was one of several items that the newspaper had FOIA'd while I was away. Steve Voorhies, University Relations' media relations manager, had passed it along to the newspaper after Denise Reynolds made it available to him. Dungan had a question that startled me: Why did my office have a deficit while other areas within Advancement were breaking even or have a surplus?

"That can't be right," I told her. I said I'd track down the document, which I had not been given, and would get back to her.

Voorhies forwarded what he had received from Reynolds. It was a budget report similar in appearance and detail to what we used to get on a monthly basis before the January 14th meeting with Gearhart. Sure enough, it showed my office with a $192,603 shortfall for the fiscal year. The amount represented about nine percent of my annual revenues. Except for a negligible shortfall in one office, every other unit in Advancement showed a balanced budget or a surplus. The division as a whole appeared to have nearly $1 million in surplus.

It didn't make any sense. Advancement had received $2 million in centrally held resources in January to make sure we had sufficient funds for the remainder of the fiscal year. All of us assumed that the money would be distributed proportionately across the division based on the relative size of each function area. In addition, I assumed Reynolds would have told me if there were any issues; after all, she, like Joy Sharp before her, managed University Relations' budget along with Advancement as a whole. She, not we, handled our transactions. She had to approve every expenditure of ours. No matter what, Reynolds maintained the controls and responsibility to keep all of Advancement's budget units in the black. So long as the funds stayed within the division, it was permissible to move money back and forth across budget lines, if necessary. Why had she not done so here?

That evening I sent Reynolds and Wyrick an email, with the subject line "URGENT":

> Hi, Denise. Sorry to bother you while you're off, but given that this info is being used right now for a story about the Advancement division, it was necessary to reach out to you. Please look at [the attached budget document], which was FOIA'd last week. I don't understand why there is a deficit in University Relations when every other unit except [Constituent Services, with a $3,000 deficit] has a healthy surplus. As you know, all of us have been dependent on the Vice Chancellor's office all [fiscal year] for budget management, and for us, all of our proposed expenditures were approved by the VC office before we actually made the commitments. I am assuming that the central VC office had simply failed to transfer to University Relations the proportionate share of the [$2 million in one-time funding provided by Pederson and Provost Gaber in January to augment Advancement's operation].
>
> I hope you understand why I am concerned about this. Not only must it be an error but its publication also will make Advancement look like it was not managing its finances properly—even after the leadership changes. Please clarify as soon as possible. I'm cc'ing Chris so that he is aware of this issue. Thanks.

Reynolds responded late morning on the following day:

> As you should know from the monthly statements that I would bring to staff meetings, your negative balance should have been a red flag that would have driven further discussion, since it had

> been there since February....I let the management team know in many staff meetings that I was available to meet and review your budget information at any time. Having made myself available for any detailed discussion, I could have advised you....

Monthly statements at staff meetings? We hadn't received any from her since December! That was a secondary matter at this point, one we would take up later. I responded to Reynolds, noting her role in managing and monitoring University Relations' budget. We depended on her to keep budgets in the black. She had the authority to apply some of the division's centrally held surplus to one of its subunits—in this case, University Relations. Having previously pointed out to her that a reporter was working on a story about this matter, I closed with "I respectfully request confirmation of this today. I see no reason why it cannot and should not be [adjusted]."

She wrote back:

> It is unreasonable to expect me to spend my vacation time working and giving me arbitrary deadlines to meet. Since September, I have done everything I can to support the Division of Advancement and will continue to do so. However, I am now leaving for vacation and will be unavailable for further comment on this subject until I return on August 6th. Feel free to discuss with Chris and/or Don [Pederson].

I tried to. According to UA's email system, Wyrick had read my email on Thursday at 6:48 p.m. but did not call or respond. He had been copied on Reynolds' and my follow-up messages. On Friday, I called and texted Wyrick, initially with no luck. Finally, he called me back late that afternoon and said he'd arranged for Pederson to make the transfer within Advancement's budget to straighten things out. I contacted Dungan and told her that we would provide the corrected numbers at the beginning of the week.

At midday Monday, I had not heard anything from Pederson or anyone from his office. I sent him an email explaining that Wyrick said Pederson would take care of the request. I also pointed out that the newspaper's request was time-sensitive. Apparently, Pederson did not have access to the original document that Reynolds had provided to the reporter weeks earlier. Dungan would have to wait. We were lucky that she didn't press ahead with a story about that original budget breakdown; it would have been embarrassing to many of us, not just to me.

Dungan may have waited patiently because a week earlier she had filed a separate FOIA request—a big one.

> This is a request pursuant to the Arkansas Freedom of Information Act. I would like copies of all correspondence—including but not limited to, emails, letters, memorandums, texts, social media or any other format—regarding the Fayetteville campus Division of Advancement's restructuring and reorganization, and/or its budget deficit, and/or its efforts to revise and/or finalize budget for Fiscal 2013 (the year ending June 30, 2013) and/or its efforts to finalize and/or balance its budget for Fiscal 2014 (the year ending June 30, 2014), dated between Jan. 1, 2013 and the present.

Her request included a long list of UA officials including Gearhart, Wyrick, Pederson, Schook, and Reynolds. It also included the UA System president and board of trustees. After conferring with our lawyers, Scott Varady and Bill Kincaid, I informed her that the request was deemed "overly broad" under the FOIA law; she responded with more specifics and amended her FOIA twice over the next two weeks. Per standard practice, I drafted an email that could be sent to all individuals referred to in Dungan's FOIA by name or by position. My draft explained exactly what the reporter was requesting as well as what Scott, Bill, and I had determined were the types of print and electronic records that recipients of the email should give us for review.

Given the number of people and lengthy period of time covered by the FOIA, on July 29th Varady suggested that we should brief Gearhart and Wyrick before beginning the process of gathering the material. Gearhart's assistant scheduled the meeting for 3:30 that afternoon in the chancellor's conference room.

Prior to that meeting, Wyrick and I had to attend our weekly Advancement Executive Staff session. All members of AES were present except Reynolds and Melissa Banks, the head of Donor Relations and Special Events; both were away on vacation. Wyrick had just returned from his and did not appear to be pleased to be back. Prior to the start of the meeting, my colleagues in the room congratulated me on a recent accolade: Kevin Trainor of Razorback Athletics and I had been named co-recipients of a national public relations award for crisis communications. The award was based on our handling of the Petrino firing in 2012. Conspicuously, Wyrick himself offered no congratulations or acknowledgment.

The first item on the AES agenda was Wyrick's report on Gearhart's weekly executive committee meeting, which had taken place that morning. The pending Advancement audits were among the topics discussed. In June, Wyrick had asked me to prepare a PR strategy in anticipation of the audits' release. At the time, we had no knowledge of what the findings would be or when they would be released; we just knew that auditors would notify UA when their work was done so that Gearhart and Pederson could read it and prepare a formal response, which would be included as part of the materials released to the public. Even without knowledge of the findings, my staff and I put together preliminary recommendations about how to respond when the time came. It included having Gearhart and others hold a news conference to acknowledge the findings and to talk positively about the steps being taken to make sure no such problems occur again. We also recommended that immediately after the release we send an email to alumni, donors, news media, and state policy makers, possibly including a YouTube message from Gearhart. The message would convey the same sentiments that we suggested Gearhart should express in the news conference. It was important for him, as chancellor, to demonstrate that UA was being responsive, accountable, and transparent regarding this unfortunate series of events.

Here, at the AES meeting, Wyrick informed us that Gearhart rejected the response plan. He said the chancellor had decided UA would not respond at all, instead letting the written responses contained in the audit documents speak for themselves. He said the executive committee supported the decision.

I reacted with surprise and offered that I thought that approach would be a big mistake. I said we would be giving up any ability to put the findings, whatever they were, in a context that would demonstrate that Gearhart and Wyrick had regained control and that Advancement's management and oversight issues were things of the past. A news conference and the email communication with stakeholders would provide an unfiltered response that we could control. It would show leadership and accountability, regardless of the audits' findings, I said. I asked if he thought Gearhart would reconsider.

Wyrick raised his voice. No, he declared, then abruptly switched to a separate topic: his frustration with me over my handling of a news release he had wanted issued. In early June, Wyrick asked me to prepare an announcement that Advancement would end the fiscal year on June 30th with a balanced budget. I agreed and worked with my staff to develop a modest rollout plan that included the news release and an email communiqué from him to donors and alumni. However, I explained to him that we couldn't do anything more until we knew exactly what the budget results and breakdown would be. I told him we would look foolish and be embarrassed if we put out a news release declaring we had balanced the budget without being able to show how it was accomplished. Simply saying, "We did it!" without being able to answer "How?" could backfire on us. Per Wyrick's request, I tried to schedule a meeting with him, Gearhart, Pederson, and Reynolds to discuss the content and timing. After Pederson failed to respond, on June 22nd I had sent him and the others a polite reminder that Wyrick wanted us to meet. I figured Pederson hadn't sensed any immediacy; the final budget numbers for Advancement and other divisions of UA would be determined on July 31, a month after the close of the fiscal year, in order to include all end-of-year transactions.

But while I was on vacation, Wyrick told Steve Voorhies, our office's media relations manager, to prepare the release anyway. When I returned to Fayetteville, Steve informed me that the news release was in the final stages of review by Gearhart, Pederson, and Wyrick, being readied for distribution. My advice ignored, I relented. Three days later, we issued the news release. It included a vague explanation of how Advancement managed to balance the budget despite the $3.3 million hole that was reported six months earlier. The news release quoted Wyrick as saying that it was "accomplished primarily by cutting back on expenses… as well as with revenue increases from unrestricted gift funds and university unrestricted revenue and endowment earnings"—which usually means funds from the UA Foundation. The news release begged the question, "Where exactly did you get all that money?"

The media reaction was just as our staff had predicted. Stories in both *Arkansas Times* and the *Democrat-Gazette* pointed out that UA did not provide specifics on Advancement's revenues and expenses. The *Democrat-Gazette's* Tracie Dungan also noted that the total revenues reported was more than $3.3 million above Advancement's budgeted revenue for the previous fiscal year. Something beyond "increased earnings and gift funds" had to have been a factor. Dungan submitted another FOIA to find the documents used to support the news release's claims.

Maybe the news media's skeptical response to Wyrick's budget-balancing boast was affecting his mood at the AES meeting. He continued to go after me for not issuing the news release earlier—as if the media's reaction would have been more favorable had we done so. Then he lashed out at me by saying my emails and calls to him about Reynolds' budget report the previous Friday "ruined" his vacation. "You're lucky I checked my phone!" he barked.

I couldn't continue to take the bullying. I barked back.

"Chris! What was I supposed to do?! You could have told me five, six, seven, eight times to put out a news release, and I'd have to tell you the same thing—[reporters] aren't going to just take your word for it! We got just what I told you would happen!

"And I *had* to call you! That balance sheet was wrong! I was trying to avoid a PR emergency that could have made us all look stupid!"

Angrily, he told me I should have contacted his "second-in-command."

"Who's that?" I responded. None of us had ever been identified as such.

"Mark!" he yelled, referring to Power.

"When did you tell us that, Chris?"

"I'm telling you now!" he answered.

Wyrick continued by defending Reynolds' claim and criticism of me in her email, agreeing with her that I had not been paying attention to the budget reports that she had been providing.

"Chris, we weren't *getting* any budget reports!" I responded. "No one was! How can you say that?"

Graham Stewart, the associate vice chancellor for Alumni Affairs, spoke up.

"Chris, he's right," he offered, much more composed than either Wyrick or I was. "We haven't been given anything since December."

Wyrick acted dismissive. He turned his attention to the agenda, and we moved on. Mentally, I couldn't, though; when he started defending Reynolds, I realized I was being set up as a fall guy.

At the completion of the agenda, Wyrick asked Laura Villines, his executive assistant, to leave the room. (Wyrick apparently didn't trust Villines' ability to maintain confidences; on June 5th he had called her into his office and reprimanded her so loudly that I, waiting in the outer office, could hear him. "He says I talk too much," she told me immediately afterward, embarrassed and upset.) With Villines gone, Wyrick apologized for allowing the meeting to become heated.

He asked us if it was true that none of us had been getting budget updates from Reynolds. Yes, everyone else replied. I didn't say a word. I didn't need to; the others in the room had validated my point. We had gotten no more budget information from him and Reynolds than we had from Joy Sharp.

Wyrick sat quietly for several moments, his lips forming an O shape, shocked—*shocked!*—by this news. Wyrick promised us he would speak to Reynolds when she returned from vacation. On August 19th, we received a monthly budget report—our first since the January meeting at which Gearhart told Reynolds to get rid of December's and to not create any more of them.

Despite the tension that had existed as a result of the AEC meeting, Wyrick and I walked together down the hall and around the corner to the meeting with Gearhart and the lawyers. We went into the conference room, and each took a seat around the large oval table. Don Pederson came in and stood near the head of the table where Gearhart would sit when he arrived. Bill Kincaid and Scott Varady sat on one side; Wyrick and I sat on the other, separated by a couple of chairs.

Gearhart entered the conference room through the pantry that separated it from his personal office space on the other side. *He doesn't look good,* I thought. *Haggard* was the word that eventually came to mind. He opened with criticism of the latest story from the *Democrat-Gazette:* Dungan's July 26th story about Wyrick declaring Advancement's budget balanced. He was angry that the story focused on the fact that we couldn't or wouldn't provide details to back up the claim and that it rehashed most of the details of decisions and events that had occurred since *Arkansas Business* broke the deficit story in December. Much of what he said repeated the reaction he had shared in an email to me a couple of days earlier:

> John: What this says to me is that the *Democrat-Gazette* has no interest in reporting the truth but simply slamming the UA anyway they can. I'm tired of it. I'd like to have from you your thoughts

> on how we can send a message to the *Democrat-Gazette* about our disgust about their biased reporting. I have had numerous calls today, including three trustees that want to know we are countering this. Frankly, this is simply ludicrous and tells me that the *Democrat-Gazette* has a hidden agenda. As out [sic] chief PR person I need a plan to counter this. Dave

In addition, Gearhart was livid about Dungan's most recent FOIA, the one we were there to brief him on. He objected to the FOIA's request for documents and other records from the UA System Board of Trustees. ("You're not going to ask them!" he said protectively, even though that part of Dungan's request was directed to UA System attorney Fred Harrison in Little Rock.) He told us that we were not to seek any more emails or documentation from Choate or Sharp. ("They don't work here any more!" he argued, even though we were still legally responsible for providing FOIA'd emails and records of theirs from the period during which they were employed at UA.) He was fed up with the *Democrat-Gazette*, particularly with Dungan. ("What does she make? *Forty thousand dollars?!*") He talked about Jennifer Cook's "conflict of interest" and repeated the boast that a *Democrat-Gazette* insider purportedly overheard at the newspaper: "We got two presidents, and Gearhart is next." (No one at our meeting mentioned that those two presidents, Hardin and Meadors, had been guilty of the accusations against them.)

He felt under siege. "Who's looking out for the chancellor?" he said, throwing his hands up.

Kincaid and I remained quiet during the meeting as Varady tried to explain the university's obligations. He pointed out that we'd likely be sued again if we didn't respond fully. But Gearhart wanted to take a stand. He argued that complying with a FOIA request that was so inclusive would just fuel more requests. "They're looking for something that's not there." After about 45 minutes, he had had enough. "Go ahead. Do what you want," he said, in a tone that contradicted his words.

Varady, Kincaid, and I left the meeting together. In the hallway around the corner from Gearhart's office, Varady suggested we immediately call the UA System's senior legal counsel, Fred Harrison, in Little Rock. We went to Kincaid's office to place the call. Bill sat at his desk, and Scott and I stood opposite him. With Harrison on speakerphone, Varady related what had just occurred in the chancellor's conference room. Harrison had seen Dungan's FOIA and understood what it was seeking. After exchanging several questions and answers with Varady, Harrison had all he needed to know. "I'll set him straight," he said of Gearhart. "It won't be the first time."

There's a rhetorical strategy that *Mad Men's* Don Draper once summed up nicely: "If you don't like what's being said, change the conversation." At UA, we couldn't dictate what the media reported, but we could give them something different to report about. During the month of July and into August, we conceived of several ways to change the conversation. But despite Gearhart's appeal to us to create "a plan to deal with this," the chancellor himself proved to be our toughest obstacle. At the request of Richard Hudson, UA's vice chancellor for Government Relations, we scheduled a "media event" on campus with the Arkansas Highway and Transportation Department (AHTD). The purpose was to showcase the research collaboration between UA's College of Engineering and the highway department. We planned to invite regional policy makers and business leaders to the event, which we had scheduled for August 8th to accommodate the chancellor's schedule. Faculty and staff from Engineering were working with members of my staff and AHTD on the program and logistics. Both Gearhart's scheduler and chief of staff had signed off on the details.

However, in late July, Gearhart backed out; he didn't want to appear on the platform with AHTD Director Scott Bennett, with whom he apparently had some sort of beef. Instead, Gearhart was willing to attend and be introduced as one of the dignitaries in the audience, leaving it to Provost Sharon Gaber or Engineering Dean John English to represent UA on the dais with Bennett. As these things sometimes go, Bennett's staff notified us that their leader was pulling out of the event shortly after learning that Gearhart wouldn't be on the platform. Our opportunity to showcase intergovernmental cooperation and the results generated from state investment in university-based research had quickly fallen apart. I called Richard Hudson for help.

"Sorry, John," he said. "I've spoken with him. He's not going to change his mind."

There were other ideas we came up with to move the conversation away from Advancement, all of which Gearhart rejected. One was for Gearhart to submit a guest commentary (also know as an "op-ed") to the *Democrat-Gazette* about UA's participation in a new national initiative to promote university-based research as an economic development strategy. ("Don't think it rises to the occasion of an op-ed," he wrote back to me). Another was something that had generated considerable positive press the previous two years: a "back to school" news conference prior to the first week of classes in which we showcase members of our incoming undergraduate class and highlight points of pride about our student body and faculty. ("Frankly, I have not felt we got much bounce out of the press conference. Seems as though a media release is all that is necessary," Gearhart wrote in response.)

However, there was one suggestion he received that he was excited about: something that he thought would expose and embarrass the *Democrat-Gazette.* On July 22nd, Gearhart sent Wyrick an email and copied Varady and me:

> A PR consultant friend of mine advised me today that we start putting on our web site any *Democrat-Gazette* FOIAs we receive or in the alternative send them to all media when we comply with the *Democrat-Gazette* FOIA. His thinking is three fold:

> - It will show how ridiculously over reaching [sic] they are.
> - It will give the same information to all media that we give to the *Democrat-Gazette*.
> - It will show transparency.
>
> Can we implement this practice ASAP? Can we send out an alert to our constituency to this affect [sic] with copies of the last FOIA?

Wyrick quickly responded to all of us: "I like it—John, brainstorm with the staff on this and who in the Communications division would be responsible for this." I forwarded Gearhart's request to our University Relations' leadership team. Charlie Alison, our managing editor of publications, responded with what he labeled as the "Devil's advocate" perspective. In a lengthy email, he noted some of the unintended consequences of singling out the *Democrat-Gazette*. He asked if we would be posting FOIA requests for records that we won't release, and speculated that the public would perceive the university as "spoiled children" throwing a tantrum because it had to comply with state law. He pointed out that a previous UA chancellor during the 1990s tried a similar tack:

> The FOIA list did not, at that time, engender goodwill or sympathy from the public. It made reporters go around the primary sources, get their stories worked out, and then request the documents at the end. It fueled more negative stories than it precluded. Perhaps in this day and age of social media we will whip up a frenzy of people who think the media are being unfair to us, but when one overspends by $3.7 million, that same social media campaign has the potential to be turned into tomorrow's *laugh-at-us* rather than *with-us* meme.

Others on our leadership team agreed with Alison's concerns. He then tried to find similar treatment of FOIA requests among other public institutions and government agencies across the country. He found few examples, and none that concentrated on a single news organization. In light of those findings, we prepared and gave Wyrick and Gearhart a proposal that would include all media FOIAs, not just those from the *Democrat-Gazette*. We also included our rationale for not limiting it to the one newspaper. None of us thought Gearhart's request would improve our media or public relationships, but we thought it would satisfy the chancellor's and vice chancellor's requests, which at that point was a higher priority.

On July 31st, Gearhart responded to me and copied Wyrick and Varady. It began with a phrase that had become more and more common in email exchanges over the past seven months: PLEASE DELETE.

> John: Perhaps I wasn't very clear. The thought was to put up FOIA requests selectively that come from the *Democrat-Gazette* on the Advancement issue. That was the context. See below my email that mentioned *Democrat-Gazette* FOIAs in the context of their ridiculous requests. I never expected we would put up all FOIAs. The suggestion was seen as a way to counter the "exclusivity" element of the *Democrat-Gazette* reporting. It seems to me we must counter the continued harassment and biased reporting about the issue at hand. The latest article was clearly one sided, did not mention anything about our surplus and was slanted reporting. I'm not sure why we don't point that out to editors when that happens. In my email last week, I mentioned to you that three trustees called me about the article in the *Democrat-Gazette* versus what we actually released.

I added this topic to the list of items to share with Wyrick at our next one-on-one meeting. Newspapers and journalists are a competitive lot when it comes to investigative reporting, but they will rally together if a colleague or news organization comes under attack for pursuing the public interest. I hoped I could convince Wyrick that he should ask Gearhart to reconsider his risky idea.

Meanwhile, I continued to refine the email that would be sent out to employees that were covered by Dungan's lengthy July 22nd FOIA request. On August 7th, Varady and Kincaid signed off on it, and I sent it to Gearhart and other senior leaders for their approval. I would not distribute it to its intended recipients without at least Gearhart's and Wyrick's okay. The FOIA request was nearly two weeks old—much longer than what the law permits a public entity to respond within. Because of the delay, Dungan and her newspaper could have taken us to court to force us to turn over the documents. Fortunately for UA, neither pushed the matter, possibly out of laziness rather than disinterest. I didn't know it at the time, but soon I would unwittingly become the catalyst for the newspaper's reenergized focus on Advancement.

Chapter 11

A FAILURE TO COMMUNICATE

Since that day in Gearhart's office back in November—when he told me he was reassigning Choate and Sharp—I had tried harder than ever to serve him and the university in ways that protected his integrity and that of UA. I had given him my best advice, both in terms of public relations and of politics. I tried to provide a different perspective from the insular network of campus administrators and donors he was surrounded with. That's an important part of serving as a CEO's public relations executive. He didn't have to accept my advice, and I knew that. But I would be failing him professionally if I didn't raise certain questions and possibilities or share options that might not otherwise be considered.

The events of July had made me concerned about my relationship with him and Wyrick and my future with UA. Shortly after the meeting with Gearhart and the lawyers regarding Dungan's latest FOIA, I called Judy Schwab, the chancellor's chief of staff, to set up a meeting. Judy—"Jude" as she often signed her own emails—was one of the best-liked people in the administration and someone who had been with Gearhart since his early days as UA's head of

Advancement. She and I worked closely together; in fact, I was her backup on handling Gearhart's public email account, chancell@uark.edu. (He had a different account he used when personally communicating with donors, administrators, faculty, staff, students, and others.) When the volume of email to the "chancell" account was high or when Judy was away, I would respond to them as Gearhart, forwarding a copy to Gearhart's private account as an FYI.

Schwab and I met in her office, located within the chancellor's suite in the Admin Building. I told her I was concerned about "where I stood" with the chancellor and with Wyrick. I filled her in on the disconcerting budget document that Reynolds had produced and of Wyrick's initial defense of it. I shared what had occurred at the July 29th AES meeting, Wyrick's supposed shock in learning that we had not been given budget reports for months, my concerns about the delays with FOIA responses, Dawn Mabry's reassignment, and the other promotions, demotions, and relocations that Wyrick made without the input of the division's management team. (To that point, she told me that the university's Office of Employment and Equal Opportunity also had objected to not being involved in the process—UA System policies required that office's participation—and that it was working with Wyrick's office and Human Resources to retroactively remedy the failure.)

I also told her about my concerns with Wyrick's behavior. The "Brother Honky" references. His remark to Athletics' Eric Wood ("Your people like that."). His comment about me and other Catholics "traveling in packs." His treatment of Mabry and his threats of termination in June to her and to another woman in the division. His demeaning comments at the June 20th all-staff meeting. The repeated use of "the old guy" to identify an employee whose performance he was criticizing.

"I feel like I want to cry," she said in response. Me, too.

Schwab told me that as far as the chancellor's attitude toward me was concerned, she was unaware of anything going on that placed my employment in jeopardy. However, she added that I was fortunate that he did not fire me after what she called the "42-minute" meeting he and I had in his office on January 24th—my trip to the woodshed. I shouldn't have tried to change his mind about the media and FOIA requests, she said. "He doesn't feel he needs to give an order more than once." She was right, but at the time I thought he and I were still in the pre-order discussion stage of the conversation. When I left Judy's office, I felt better than I did when I arrived. Having told the chief of staff (formally titled UA's associate vice chancellor for Administration) what we in Advancement were experiencing, I assumed she would act. I became more optimistic that things within the division would improve, one way or another.

I had to go out of town for three days in August to give a presentation at a national higher ed conference in Charleston, South Carolina. While traveling, I received Gearhart's response to the distribution plan the lawyers and I had prepared regarding Dungan's July 22nd FOIA request. It was addressed to Wyrick and me, with copies to Varady, Kincaid, and Mark Rushing, a director within my office:

> Gentlemen: As you know, I am a firm believer in the Freedom of Information Law and absolutely insist on full compliance in every instance. However, I am not in agreement on handling this latest request in this manner nor in sending the draft email.
>
> Vice Chancellor Wyrick will communicate with all persons listed here and ask for responsive records and then communicate back to John. As you know, similar information has already been requested by Ms. Dungan, but Mr. Wyrick will follow up with all of those mentioned to be absolutely sure we have captured all responsive records. Any responsive records will obviously be sent immediately to Ms. Dungan. He will not contact Mr. Choate or Ms. Sharp. They are no longer employees of the University, and we have absolutely no jurisdiction over them in this matter. You may eventually advise Ms. Dungan to contact them directly if she is so inclined.
>
> Let me know if you have any concerns. Thank you.

Gearhart sent us the email at 8:10 a.m., according to the time stamp. At 10:15 a.m., Wyrick responded:

> Via the chancellors [sic] request, all parties have been contacted by me with the exception of Brad and Joy. The only person with any responsive data is Bruce [Pontious] and he will be getting with Scott ASAP. All others have stated no responsive documents.

Well, that was fast! I thought. Too fast to be believable, actually. How in the world could Wyrick have contacted at least a dozen people in various offices, individually asked them to search through their emails, cabinets, and computer files for content covering the previous seven months on multiple topics, gathered the responses, and offered a Mission Accomplished report, all in just two hours?

It wasn't credible. He hadn't provided anyone with anything in writing that described the types and nature of records that had been FOIA'd. Without that, the results would be similar to the kids' game, Operator: individual interpretations and recollections can quickly change as the message gets circulated. A few days later, while waiting for Wyrick to provide the materials to turn over to Dungan, I suggested that he consider providing an explanation of the request in writing to give to the people he had spoken with. I was giving him the benefit of the doubt that because of his unfamiliarity with FOIA, he wouldn't recognize the need to be clear and inclusive.

"No, I've already told everyone," he retorted. I told him we put ourselves at risk by not documenting that we had performed due diligence in complying with the request. My appeal to him did not affect his decision. Later, I shared my concern with UA attorney Scott Varady, who agreed with me that it would be better for all if we made our records requests in writing. He said he'd speak with Wyrick.

Twelve days passed, and Wyrick still had not provided the documents I was supposed to pass along to Dungan. She called me frequently to check on the status; I kept telling her that "we" were in the process of collecting them. Following a group meeting with Wyrick on August 19th, I asked him for an update.

"I'm done, but I haven't been able to talk with the chancellor about it yet. He's preoccupied with the audit," Wyrick answered.

"We don't have the luxury of that," I reminded him. "The law says we have to multi-task. We're already almost a month late."

"I'll talk with him tomorrow," he replied.

Wyrick and I were scheduled to meet the next day to talk about the Advancement audits. I wanted to go over the draft themes and talking points I had sent him that could be factored into the university's written response. I also hoped he could give me a sense of any issues or concerns we might have to deal with. Given Gearhart's recent behavior, I wondered whether the chancellor was worried about losing his job as a consequence of the audits' findings.

Our meeting didn't take place. At 8:30 a.m. Wyrick sent me an email: "Nothing yet to review on the audit and I could use the hour. OK to circle back up later in week when I know more answers?"

I quickly responded: "Sure. Any word on FOIA?"

No response. That afternoon, I saw Wyrick at a meeting in Gearhart's conference room. We were there to discuss logistics for the September 13th meeting of the capital campaign steering committee. Others in the room were Gearhart, Schwab, and two members of my own leadership team, speechwriter Hardin Young and creative services director Roy Cordell. Early in the meeting, Gearhart brought up the outstanding FOIA—surprising, since neither Young nor Cordell had any involvement in the matter. The chancellor said that if he ran into reporter Dungan, he had a question for her: "Tracie, do you still work for the *Democrat-Gazette*? I thought you worked for the *National Enquirer*." Schwab turned to me and rolled her eyes; Wyrick made a joke about the number of times he'd heard Gearhart say that. We then moved on to the purpose of the meeting, the upcoming capital campaign leadership committee gathering.

After we finished and were all making our way to the door, I pulled Schwab aside. "Any word on whether Chris and Dave have discussed the FOIA?"

"Yes," she said. "Chris brought it up at 'exec' committee. He said that from now on they're supposed to go through Mark."

I was puzzled. "Mark? Mark who?" I asked, thinking she might be referring to Mark Power from the Development office. "Mark Rushing. Chris said that he's now handling them." That was news to me. Rushing was University Relations' director of strategic communications, someone I had hired a little more than a year earlier. He had been a TV sports reporter and anchor before taking a job with a PR firm in Little Rock. He and I had become good friends and was someone I had confided in regarding my concerns about Wyrick and the handling of FOIAs. I also viewed him as the person within University Relations whose personality and talents were best suited to succeeding me whenever I moved on to another job—a possibility that I was now giving even more thought to.

I went down the hallway to the General Counsel's office. Kincaid's office door was closed, but Varady's was partially open. His assistant told me to go ahead in. Scott was at his desk, which was in a perpetual state of disarray because of all the issues that came across it daily. I asked him if he was aware that Wyrick wanted Rushing to take over my responsibilities for handling FOIA. The look on his face indicated to me that this was going to be an awkward conversation. He gave a rambling answer—something about suggestions that more people on campus should manage FOIA requests to decentralize things. He said he thought Wyrick was considering Rushing as someone to be involved in the new process, but that he didn't know much more than that. He wasn't convincing. I told him what Schwab had just shared with me and said that it didn't sound like Wyrick had a plan to "decentralize" in mind. I also told him that Dungan's overdue FOIA request had not been taken care of. He said he would go speak with Wyrick right away and got up from his desk.

As we left his office, he turned back to me and shook my hand—a gesture that we never exchanged except when we unexpectedly ran into each other away from campus. It was unnecessary; we talked with each other daily, often in person. I realized it was a "goodbye" handshake; he knew something was about to happen that would change our relationship.

I went back to my office in Davis Hall. I walked by Rushing's office, where he was seated at his desk.

"Is there something you want to tell me?" I asked. Uncomfortable, he nodded and said yes. I sat down in an empty chair across from him.

He told me that a few weeks earlier, Wyrick arranged to meet with Rushing in the vice chancellor's office in the Admin Building. Once together, Wyrick asked Rushing if anyone knew he was meeting with him. Rushing answered no. Wyrick asked if Rushing had any background in dealing with FOIA, to which Rushing again said no, only what he had picked up from talking with me. Wyrick then told Rushing he wanted him to take over the lead role in handling FOIA. He assured him that he would receive training and support. Rushing told me that he asked Wyrick if I knew Rushing would be taking on this new role. No, Wyrick said. Later, Wyrick set up a second meeting between the two to discuss the topic. Rushing told me that, as before, Wyrick stressed the same expectation of secrecy. "This meeting never happened," Wyrick informed him as he left the office.

"Why didn't you tell me, Mark?" I asked.

"I know what happened next door and didn't want that to happen to me," he said, gesturing to the Development offices in neighboring University House. It was either a reference to Dawn Mabry's demotion to a position with Development or to another incident he, like many in the Advancement division, was aware of: in June, Renea Dillard, a part-time employee who worked for Development, was called to Wyrick's office. Upon her arrival, she met with Reynolds and Villines and was told Wyrick had prepared her termination letter. According to Dillard, Reynolds told her that she would either have to accept a reassignment or would be fired. Like others affected by Wyrick's reorganization plans, Dillard was told not to mention her reassignment to anyone or else she would be canned. Understandably distraught, Dillard called a co-worker after leaving Wyrick's office and asked the colleague to meet her in the parking lot with Dillard's pocketbook and keys; she was too upset to go back to her office to get them herself. On her way home, Mark Power called her to find out what was wrong. "I can't tell you, Mark. They'll fire me!" But Power, her superior, insisted, so she told him. A few days later, Wyrick summoned both Power and Dillard to his office. He first spoke separately with Power behind closed doors. Moments later, Wyrick called in Dillard while he briefly stepped out of his office. "Just listen to him, Renea," Power reportedly said. "Don't say anything." Wyrick returned, whereupon he threatened Dillard with termination for defying a directive not to talk with anyone, including Power. According to Dillard, she felt her job was at risk. To protect herself, she documented what had occurred in case of retaliation.

With those episodes in mind, I reminded Rushing of our office's Treaty of No Surprises and said I would have protected him from retribution. I told him I was mad but not at him; I was mad at the way Wyrick was treating and threatening members of Advancement. I left Rushing's office and went to my own. I checked my iPhone and saw that Wyrick had sent me a text: "FOIA—Scott just walked to my office and I told him there is only 1 document that has caught our eye and I've asked him for a legal opinion."

I immediately wrote back: "Thanks. When were you going to tell me about meeting with Mark Rushing?"

Once again, he chose to not respond. That night, I sent an email to a longtime friend and mentor of mine who was now a university president in another state. I had previously sought his advice about how to cope with Gearhart's combative attitude toward the *Democrat-Gazette* and, more recently, my worries about Wyrick's approach to his FOIA assignment. This time my purpose in reaching out to him was more to vent than it was to seek advice:

> I learned today when I asked the chancellor's chief of staff about an outstanding FOIA that she had been told that my staff person was now in charge (even though he has yet to be trained in it; I've been doing FOIA for 20 years). That's the third member of my staff that's been told not to tell me something. Freakin' unbelievable. I gotta get out of this place.

Shortly after 8 o'clock the next morning, I stopped by Rushing's office and said, "Good morning! Anything I should know?" It was the same way I greeted him every morning, given his role as our strategic communications director. Of course, this particular morning my query reflected a broader scope than simply finding out what might have happened on campus overnight.

"Yeah," Mark answered, leaning forward in his chair. Wyrick called him twice after Rushing and I had spoken the day before, questioning Mark about what I had asked him. I gave a frustrated half-laugh, half-sigh, something I tend to do when I hear something that I'd rather not hear. I didn't ask Rushing for details; no doubt it would have made matters worse for both of us with Wyrick.

Later in the day, Wyrick finally sent over the records that he had gathered in response to Tracie Dungan's July 22nd FOIA request. It contained just one document: a single-paged email from Laura Villines, sent in March, explaining the process Wyrick had in mind for conducting his reorganization plan once he started as vice chancellor the following month. *He can't be serious!* I thought. Dungan had asked for print and electronic records covering more than seven months and multiple individuals and offices on campus. The request had specifically asked for material related to Advancement's budget review and planning process. It also specifically asked for all records related to Wyrick's reorganization plan, which would include the video recording of his June 20th all-staff presentation. (On July 29th, the day of our conference call with UA System attorney Fred

Harrison, lawyer Bill Kincaid told me he had viewed the video and said it was "a problem," presumably because of Wyrick's comments and behavior.) The budget planning book that Reynolds kept in her office was not provided, nor was Wyrick's loose-leaf binder with Abercrombie's organizational study and his yellow-highlighted notes. The FOIA response he was asking me to give Dungan totally lacked believability. But as he had directed, I forwarded the document to Dungan:

> Tracie, attached is the only responsive document to your recent FOIA that the university has identified. As always, the university reserves the right to augment this response should it identify any additional responsive documents. John

Per standard operating procedure, I forwarded the time-stamped email to Varady, Kincaid, and Wyrick. About two hours later, Wyrick sent me a text that read, "You get document?" I wrote back, "Yes and sent it. I shared it with you via email." He wrote back, "I have 39 unread. Thanks."

The next morning, during my 20-minute drive from home west across Fayetteville to campus, I received a phone call. It was Richanne Kegans, who staffs the front desk for University Relations.

"Chris wants you to be at his office at nine o'clock," she said.

"Do you know what he wants?" I asked. It was a little after eight a.m., plenty of time to swing by my office in Davis Hall to pick up any materials I might need for the meeting. No, she responded. Just that Laura Villines called on Wyrick's behalf to make sure I didn't have anything else scheduled for the morning.

"I'm ten minutes out. See you soon." I then called Villines to see if she knew what the meeting was about. She said she didn't.

I turned my attention back to the car radio. I had been listening to *NPR's Morning Edition*. Co-host David Greene had interviewed the writer William T. Vollmann. Taking advantage of the federal FOIA law, Vollmann had discovered that the FBI had kept secret files on him. Many years earlier, the Feds suspected him of being sympathetic to domestic terrorists, he learned. *Harper's* had just published Vollmann's article about what he discovered about himself, or at least the version of William T. Vollmann that the FBI maintained in its files. Those included modest assertions that he had an "enormous ego" as well as more serious and reputation-damaging observations, including one that said his writing style was "consistent with that contained in UNABOMBER's recent letter published in the *New York Times*." (The domestic terrorist known only as The Unabomber, later identified as Theodore Kaczynski, was still at large at the time that an FBI agent recorded the statement.) Furthering the circumstantial connection, the FBI file noted that for a few years both Vollmann and the *New York Times* headquarters co-existed in Manhattan. That, along with other references to Vollmann's career, lifestyle, and writing interests, was enough for the FBI dossier's creator to write, "How many challenges remain for WILLIAM T. VOLLMANN? Serial bombing, perhaps? As a way to change the world?"

If not for his own curiosity and knowledge of public records laws, Vollmann might never have known that someone within a public agency had tried, for whatever reason, to discredit him through secretive, false, and circumstantial claims. Whether intentional or innocent, those efforts steered suspicions toward him while redirecting attention and investigation away from those individuals who were truly responsible for domestic bombings. At the time Vollmann had no idea that false records were being created that could destroy his reputation and livelihood. Decades later, the federal FOIA law provided him a way to find out.

I arrived in the parking lot of Davis Hall with the NPR interview still in my head. I thought more about my nine o'clock meeting with Wyrick. Was it about something new or just a rescheduling of our four o'clock update set for that afternoon? I considered the possibility that it might be related to my meeting with Judy Schwab a few weeks earlier in which I had asked her "where I stood" with Gearhart—and where I reported my concerns and objections regarding Wyrick's offensive behavior. And of course, there was the issue of his meetings with Rushing. We hadn't discussed that yet. There were all kinds of things he could want to discuss.

I went directly to my personal office, skipping my usual check-ins with others along the way. I pulled the file folder containing the printed agenda I had prepared for my afternoon meeting with Chris. (I had added the Rushing matter to it before I left the office the day before.) I then sat down and scribbled notes on a legal pad, listing the things that I had said to Schwab as well as my concerns about the secrecy and behavior that I felt were affecting my areas of responsibility. I felt I needed to be prepared for whatever direction the discussion took.

Just before leaving my office for Wyrick's, I placed a call to Jenifer Tucker, a lawyer with UA's Office of Employment and Equal Opportunity with whom I'd dealt on various issues. I found out that she no longer worked there, so I asked for Danielle Wood, the office's director. She was unavailable, so I left a message for her to call me on my cellphone. I wanted to see whether she had talked with Schwab or anyone else about my complaints about Wyrick. Wood called me back a little before 9 o'clock as I waited in Wyrick's outer office. I told her I could not speak with her at the moment but might call her back later, which I did. I remained seated in the outer office with Villines and Stephanie McGuire, one of Wyrick's clerical assistants, waiting for Wyrick to emerge and beckon me in. When he did, Reynolds was there, seated at the small conference table. Chris shut the door behind me and the two of us joined her.

"You saw the email this morning?" he said, more of a statement than a question.

"No. Why?" I didn't know what he was referring to; I hadn't had time to check email since before I had left home, due to this meeting.

He looked at Denise and then back to me, then made a brief

reference to an email being sent out that shouldn't have been. I later discovered that it was something he had inadvertently sent to all members of the Advancement Executive Staff rather than to just his intended recipient, Villines. It was a directive to remove me from all email distribution and scheduling lists for AES. Wyrick closed the short message with, "This is a MUST."

"I'm reassigning you," he informed me without sharing the nature of the morning email. "Effective immediately, you will be associate vice chancellor for Campaign Communications. You'll have that position only through the end of December. You will be reviewed monthly. You won't be part of the executive staff anymore."

I hadn't been paranoid. He really was going to get rid of me. At least I had given the possibility some thought since my handshake with Varady two days earlier.

"Why?" I responded, surprisingly calm.

Wyrick turned smug. "I don't have to tell you, but you know why."

"I think I do. It's either because of my objections to the way you've mishandled the FOIA or because of my complaints to Judy about your behavior toward me and other employees."

"I don't know what you're talking about," he said, unconvincingly.

I rattled off the issues I had spoken to Schwab about: "Brother Honky," the Catholic jokes, the threats to terminate Dawn Mabry and Renea Dillard, his performance at the June 20th reorganization meeting, the "old guy" references. (I forgot to mention his "your people" remark to Athletics' Eric Wood on our trip to Little Rock in February.) I told him that I felt this reassignment was a continuation of a five-month pattern of imposing serious, disruptive, and secretive changes in personnel appointments with little regard to the stress it placed on affected individuals, their colleagues, and division operations.

His face turned red with anger. "You keep talking, and I'll fire you immediately!"

"You're reassigning me for no legitimate reason," I pointed out.

"It's only fair for me to defend myself." I noted that the unilateral personnel reassignments, including his failure to follow the university's HR and Equal Opportunity and Compliance policies and procedures, had created a hostile and dysfunctional work environment. I also said that holding secret meetings with employees and instructing them not to tell their supervisor was unethical and divisive. "It undermines my managerial authority with my employees," I added.

"They're *my* employees, not yours!" Wyrick snapped. "OK. That's enough!"

"Chris, I saved your ass with that budget report," I pointed out, referring to the document that showed a large deficit in University Relations just days after he told a reporter that "not a day goes by" without him double-checking the division's finances.

"Don't look at me. Look at *her*!" he responded, gesturing to Reynolds.

Huh? Was he trying to place the blame on Reynolds? Or just to have me inform her? I took a second to ponder the directive and then turned toward Denise. "OK. I saved your ass, too."

"The fact is, you've lost the confidence of me and the whole executive leadership," Wyrick claimed. "You've got four months to find another job. I want you to take the rest of the week off. I'll give you your reassignment letter on Monday."

"What am I supposed to say to my staff?"

"Nothing," he answered. "I'm going to talk with them in the morning. Laura's going to schedule the meeting."

"Why can't I tell them myself?"

"*I'm* going to do it."

"Who's going to take over University Relations?" I asked. I assumed it would be Rushing, both because of Wyrick's secret conversations with him and because, among my office's department heads, he carried the most credibility with the office's 42 other employees.

"Roy," he answered, referring to Roy Cordell, another trusted member of my leadership team. Evidently, Wyrick had been having secret meetings with him, too. Feeling betrayed by Roy's failure to say anything to me, I reacted with one of my sometimes untimely half-laugh, half-sighs. Wyrick didn't like my response.

"I am this close to firing you today!" Wyrick yelled, holding his thumb and index finger an inch or so apart. He got up from his chair. Turing toward the door and opening it, he announced, "This meeting is over."

"Leadership," I mumbled, again with my half-laugh, half-sigh. This was not the way good leaders were supposed to act in these situations. As I got up, he turned back toward me and pointed.

"One more word out of you!" he warned.

"Stop threatening me," I responded as I walked through the doorway where he was standing.

"One more word!" He repeated the phrase more loudly and angrily as he gestured again, this time directly in my face.

"I said stop threatening me!" Wyrick is a lot bigger than I am, both in height and weight. As angry as he was, he looked ready to belt me right then and there in front of Reynolds and two others seated in the reception area. But I didn't think about that at the moment. Over the past five months, I had seen and experienced too much of his bullying. It was time for it to stop.

Chapter 12

CHARACTER ASSASSINATION

After leaving Wyrick's office suite, I pulled out my iPhone to check my email. There it was: Wyrick's message from earlier in the morning, instructing Villines to immediately remove me from the AES scheduling and distribution list. Clearly, even before our tense exchange moments earlier, Wyrick had already decided to boot me out of his leadership group meetings despite having given me a new role as one of the division's associate vice chancellors. I presumed that on Monday, when Wyrick was supposed to give me my reassignment letter, he would also tell me he was removing me from Davis Hall and putting me into Choate's vacated Cave of Exile, where Bruce Pontious had taken up residency after relinquishing his leadership office in University House. The conference table in the Cave would likely be my new desk, something Bruce and I would have to share.

I took the stairs and headed two flights down to UA's Human Resources office. Halfway down I stopped and jotted down, on the legal pad I had brought with me, notes about my meeting with Wyrick. When I entered the HR office, Debbie McCloud happened to be standing near the reception desk. She was the person I was hoping to see. McCloud had been the interim head of Human Resources until Don Pederson hired Barbara Abercrombie in September of 2012. McCloud had since become Abercrombie's director of Employee Relations and Services. I liked McCloud and trusted her; she and I had dealt with a couple of difficult HR issues over the previous three years, and I found her to be professional and ethical. Coincidentally, she and I had just been appointed by Gearhart to lead UA's annual United Way charitable campaign on campus.

"Got a minute?" I said to her after entering the reception area. "Sure," she replied. Then, recognizing from my expression that it might involve a sensitive subject, she invited me follow her to her office. Once there, I told her I had been reassigned and given four months to find another position. She seemed stunned, which indicated to me that she, a prominent personnel administrator within the HR office, hadn't been involved in any discussions about my reassignment. I told her about my meeting with Wyrick, his morning email, my previous meeting with Schwab, and my concerns about Wyrick's treatment of employees. I also informed her about the mishandling of FOIAs and asked what my options were; I felt my reassignment was related to that particular issue. She advised me to again call Danielle Wood at UA's Equal Opportunity and Compliance office, which I did from outside the main entrance of the Admin Building as soon as I left McCloud's office. I summarized for Wood the exchange in Wyrick's office and the issues I had been dealing with. I told her I felt he was retaliating against me for speaking to Schwab. She said she would have a compliance officer call me as soon as possible. I hung up and headed back to my office in Davis Hall.

When I returned to the office, the first person I saw was staffer Richanne Kegans, who was seated at the reception desk.

"How'd it go?" she asked.

I didn't say anything. I just shook my head and made a throat-slashing motion with my finger as I walked past her toward the stairway. Steve Voorhies, our media relations manager, had his office at the head of the stairs on the second floor. I went in and told him that I was being reassigned and had four months to find another job. He flipped the pencil he was holding in the air in an obvious expression of frustration. I told him that I was instructed to leave and not come back until Monday. Voorhies would have to handle any media calls that came my way.

I then left Steve's office for my own, passing by the now-vacated office and desk where Dawn Mabry used to work. I checked my to-do list and began packing up things I could work on at home. I put my laptop and a notebook in my briefcase and took them to my car. In the parking lot, I ran into a colleague from the Development office, who casually asked how things were going. "Well, Chris just told me I had four months to find another job." Sincerely taken aback by the news, she made some remark about the craziness that was swirling around within the division. "Hang in there," she offered in support, putting her hand on my arm.

I went back in to get a box of papers and files to take home. Before I left, I stopped by the first floor office of University Relations' managing editor Charlie Alison; he and I were supposed to meet that morning about a project he was working on. I told him what had occurred and that we'd have to have our discussion the following week, if that was possible. While talking with Charlie, Richanne came down the hall and said something that I interpreted as "Your 'BFF' is on hold for you." I, of course, thought the "best friend forever" she was referring to was Marcia, whom I hadn't called yet; I wanted to tell her the news in person. I told Richanne I'd take the call in a minute. Moments later, I walked back toward the reception desk to pick up the phone. Richanne asked if I wanted to take "his" call somewhere else.

"It's not Marcia?" I asked.

"No, it's Chris."

Startled, I asked her to tell him I couldn't talk right now, and with the box in hand, I headed to my car. Dawn Mabry came out to the parking lot as I was getting ready to leave. She had already heard the news in University House—not surprising, given the email that Wyrick had inadvertently circulated in the morning. "I knew this was going to happen," she said, not because she had any inside information; she had just sensed it was the inevitable after she had been removed as my executive assistant. I told her I'd let her know what I learned about my future, my assignments, my office space, etc., after I talked with Wyrick the next week.

As I held onto the box and headed across the parking lot to my car, a wave of nausea came over me, clearly stress-induced. My mind was swirling: *What should I do? Who do I call after I talk with Marcia?* I loaded the box into my car and slumped down in the front seat.

I picked up my phone, which I had left in the car along with my briefcase several minutes earlier. I had a missed call from someone from Wyrick's office. There was no message, so I didn't call back. I then called Marcia at her school and told her what had occurred. I was feeling too miserable to stop by St. Joseph's to tell her in person but couldn't hold off sharing the news until she got home after work. She was justifiably upset by the news. After I gave her a short overview, she said she would leave work and meet me at home.

Even with four months to find a new job, I was concerned about how that short amount of time—and potential employers' reaction to my reassignment—would affect us professionally, financially, and emotionally. Once we both got home, I forwarded an unrelated media query to Steve Voorhies. Then Marcia and I shut off our computers and phones and spent the rest of the afternoon trying to make sense of what had happened. We also began laying out how and when we would share the information with our family and friends.

When I checked my phone that evening, I saw that I had missed a call from *Democrat-Gazette* reporter Tracie Dungan. She had also sent me an email at 3:46 p.m.:

John: I've been trying to reach you today. Is everything okay? Tracie

I also had received a text message from Wyrick, sent at 3:07 p.m.:

> I tried to call you after a conversation I had with Tracy (sic) of the *Democrat-Gazette* who called asking me if you were fired. I have no idea where this is coming from? I believe it would be mutually beneficial to talk before the days end? Please call me.

It was well after hours by the time I saw those messages, and I didn't have the energy or proper state of mind to respond. Marcia and I were emotionally drained and still had not called our kids to tell them the news. (The Treaty of No Surprises covered our home life as well.)

I didn't know it at the time, but Wyrick had contacted Richanne Kegans at home. Earlier in the day, after I had left, my creative services director, Roy Cordell, had asked Kegans what was going on with me. She shared with him what she knew, based on what she had seen and heard. Cordell evidently contacted Wyrick and passed along what he had gleaned from Richanne, prompting Wyrick to call her after work. When he reached her, he questioned Richanne and then directed her to put what she saw in writing and to send it to him.

The following day was Friday, August 23rd. Though Wyrick had told me not to return to work until Monday, I had a nine o'clock doctor's appointment to have some stitches removed at the campus health center. The health center was on a corner, diagonally across from the Admin Building in one direction and, in a different direction, across the street from Davis Hall, the home of University Relations. The health center's waiting area featured a long wall of floor-to-ceiling windows. While listening for my named to be called, I saw both Wyrick and Gearhart cross the street together, heading toward Davis Hall. Wyrick had told me he would be meeting with the University Relations staff on Friday morning to tell them about my reassignment. *Was Gearhart going to join him for the announcement or were they just both walking in the same direction?* I wondered. The receptionist called my name before I could see when or whether they returned to the Admin Building together. I turned off the ringer on my phone and went in to see the doctor.

After my appointment, I went back to my car and turned on my phone. I had a couple of voicemail messages; they were from members of the University Relations staff, expressing sorrow about the news that Wyrick *and* Gearhart had shared earlier in the morning. A little while later I received a phone call from Darinda Sharp, the communications officer for UA's Fulbright College of Arts and Sciences (and no relation to Joy Sharp). She, too, said how sorry she was to see me leave and, wishing me well, offered appreciation for the support I had given her over the past two years.

"Thanks, but I'll still be around for a few months so we'll being seeing each other before I leave," I reassured her.

"You will?" she responded, sounding puzzled.

"Yeah, I'm being reassigned for the remainder of the year." I answered. "What did you think?"

Wyrick and Gearhart made it pretty clear you were gone immediately, she said. That was the impression everyone got, she added.

"No, Chris told me I had until the end of December. I'm getting my reassignment letter on Monday." I thanked her for the call and said we'd talk soon.

Still in the car, I drove to McDonald's on College Avenue to have lunch and to read the newspaper. While there, I received a text message from Wyrick, sent at 11:28 a.m.:

> John, I just sent you two emails containing letters that you need to review immediately. If you prefer to resign, rather than be terminated with 30 days notice, please contact me by 12:30 p.m. At 12:30 p.m., it is my plan to do a press release announcing your departure from the university. Next week, I will send you an email about your work from home assignment. I will be available until 12:30 p.m. should you have any questions. CCW

After I read the text message, I checked my iPhone for the emailed letters. I could not read them very well on my phone's screen, so I forwarded them to Marcia at her office, called her and asked her to read them aloud to me. One letter was a standard termination notice that Human Resources generates. It informed me that my employment would end in 30 days. It also outlined the various support resources on campus and procedures I would follow. However, the second letter was unlike anything I had ever known an employer to provide a dismissed employee: a lengthy citation of accusations and criticisms of me from Wyrick. Normally when employers want to fire someone, they avoid getting into any specifics that could later be dissected and challenged in court or through some other appeals process. *UA's lawyers and HR office would never sign off on such a letter!* I thought.

"You're not going to resign!" Marcia urged. "They won't let him get away with this!" The "they" she was referring to was System President Bobbitt and the trustees. She was convinced they would investigate and determine that Wyrick—and possibly Gearhart—had violated the law. I thought they would, too. I hung up with Marcia and sent a text to Wyrick in response:

> I just read your text and letters. You have fabricated details of our meeting. Giving me less than an hour to process your change from yesterday is unethical and unprofessional. I will respond as quickly as possible.

He texted back minutes later:

> I disagree with your response. My summary of our meeting is accurate. I will await your response.

I didn't know what to say. I didn't want to get into another argument, but I also didn't want to make a hasty decision to resign. This was clearly retaliation for what I had said to him at the meeting the day before; I needed to get some professional legal advice before doing anything more. With that in mind, I responded to him with a short, nonthreatening text: "Agree to disagree."

Sure enough, UA issued its news release as Wyrick had said:

> Chris Wyrick, vice chancellor for University Advancement, announced today that John Diamond, associate vice chancellor for University Relations in the Division of University Advancement, will be leaving the University of Arkansas at the end of September

> 2013…."I wish Mr. Diamond the best in future endeavors and thank him for his service to the UA.""

I needed to find a good lawyer who would follow up with the university on my behalf—not an easy thing to find in a "company town" like Northwest Arkansas. Reporters started contacting me shortly after the announcement appeared on UA's website and in its news feed, asking why I was leaving. The news release didn't address that point. I didn't want to get into any details, but I knew that in the absence of something, there would be speculation about all sorts of things. That could be more damaging to my reputation than being fired. In response, I sent the reporters who contacted me a short statement:

> I learned of this action in a text message from Chris Wyrick at 11:28 this morning. I believe it's the result of strong philosophical and material differences over what it means to be a transparent and publicly accountable university. My wife and I love Northwest Arkansas and UA. We need some time to process this news before saying anything more. I hope you and others understand.

Afterward, I resumed my search for a lawyer. Late afternoon, around 4:30 p.m., Mark Rushing called me to say that the news media had FOIA'd my letters of termination. He said he thought the letters had to be released and wanted me to know. I knew that the law, in its silence on the matter, permitted me to submit a formal response to the termination letters, and I wanted to do so. I needed time to prepare it and thought I could have it done by morning. Rushing said he wasn't sure whether waiting was permissible, so I asked him to have Scott Varady or Bill Kincaid call me. Varady called a little before five o'clock. He said the only way that UA would withhold release of the termination letters was if I exercised an option in the law that allows an employee to seek a state attorney general's opinion on whether the documents' release would constitute an "unwarranted invasion of privacy."

I told Varady that I didn't object to releasing the letters, but I wanted UA to release my response as well. Varady said that wouldn't be possible; if I didn't want the termination letters released that evening, I would have to tell him I was contacting the attorney general. I told him that if that was the only option I had in order to make sure my response to Wyrick's letters was released simultaneously, I would do so.

"However, I want to make it clear that I don't object to the release on Monday," I emphasized. "I'm only doing this to give me an opportunity to give my response to the university." By making this point, I was trying to make sure neither Wyrick nor UA said or did anything that would suggest I had something to hide.

But they did it anyway. At 6:48 p.m., UA issued a statement from Wyrick:

> Mr. John Diamond was terminated from employment with the University of Arkansas today, with 30 days notice. The reasons for his termination are contained in correspondence Mr. Diamond received from me today.
>
> The university informed Mr. Diamond that it believes the correspondence is subject to release under the Arkansas Freedom of Information Act. In response Mr. Diamond declined to allow release of the documents and wishes to seek an opinion from the Arkansas Attorney General.
>
> Accordingly, the University of Arkansas cannot release the document until an Attorney General's opinion is rendered or until Mr. Diamond gives his permission to release the documents.

The next day, when reporters called me, I explained what I had told Varady and that on Monday I would provide UA with both my response and permission. I also told them that Varady had known that—and that I had asked him on Friday to say so to reporters seeking the letters. Though relaying that detail was the honest and honorable thing to do, Varady and UA had chosen not to do it.

To no surprise, my dismissal was featured prominently in Saturday morning's news media:

> "University of Arkansas Sacks John Diamond, Top University Relations Official" (*Arkansas Times*)
>
> "UA Spokesman Fired; Boss Cites Irreparable Rift" (*Democrat-Gazette*)

Arkansas Business provided a headline that presented a slightly different emphasis:

> John Diamond, Man Behind Jeff Long Speech, Leaving UA.

Over the weekend, I heard from lots of people through email and calls. Most of them I knew; some were strangers. Three UA deans contacted me to express their regrets—one by phone, two by email. The first one read:

> I am very sorry to hear that you will be leaving. You have been a tremendous asset to the university, and your departure is a great loss. I have greatly admired your creativity and integrity, and have seen firsthand your skill in leading communications.

The second one stated:

> I was sorry to hear today about your departure from the university. You did a great job and were unfortunately in a no-win situation. Please let me know if I can be a reference for you or assist in any way with your transition.

One prominent UA alumna from Little Rock—a former officer of the university's alumni association board of directors—took to social media to share her reaction to the news with her large Facebook following:

> I am shocked and stunned. John Diamond has been a rock and a force as head of University Relations, etc. for the University of Arkansas in one of the darkest, if not challenging, PR years I can remember....I cannot say enough praise for his leadership...and especially how he reached out to alumni and volunteers as a voice of reason and encouragement. He was also always willing to give us the words to use so that we could remain vocal supporters of

> our alma mater...even on the dark days. He is simply first class. It is unfortunate that he has not been treated with the same dignity and class he has treated all of us and the U of A. Best of luck to a great man and a great leader. Thank you for everything you did for the U of A.

Meanwhile, Gearhart had been busy composing an email, which he sent to UA System President Bobbitt and the Board of Trustees Saturday morning. He also shared it with an unknown number of recipients:

> Over the past several days I have been in close contact with several members of my senior staff as well as Dr. Bobbitt over the personnel issue surrounding Mr. John Diamond. Any time we deal with issues of termination the accounts of the actions taken are paramount. I wanted to send you this email to insure (sic) that you too are in the loop on what already has become a public issue. The purpose of this email is to give you some important background information in advance of any further media articles.
>
> For many months Chris has attempted to build a relationship with Mr. Diamond as his new supervisor. Diamond was hired by Choate three years ago and has found it difficult to accept our new advancement leadership team. It has been a particular concern to me for many months. Mr. Diamond has been argumentative, inflexible, insubordinate and aloof with his direct report. He consistently refused to take direction from Chris or many of the senior leaders of my team on a variety of issues.
>
> As you may know, since Brad Choate's dismissal, Mr. Diamond has been interviewed for at least three positions at other institutions in the last several months and has been unable to land a job to date. Diamond has been very defensive of his former boss, Brad Choate, who hired him, and continued to maintain a very close and inappropriate relationship with Choate during a time he was serving as our chief spokesperson, a clear conflict of interest.

Over the last several months the relationship with Diamond and Chris, and my senior leadership, has deteriorated to the point of irreparable damage. Thursday, Chris met with Diamond and told him he felt a change was necessary and that his relationship with him was beyond repair. Chris told Diamond that the senior leadership had lost faith in him for a variety of reasons, including his inflexible attitude and his inattentiveness to his daily duties, including his refusal to answer emails and phone messages from myself, Vice Chancellors and Vice Provosts.

Chris told Diamond that he wanted to give him more time to find a job, but he should expect to conclude his position by the end of the calendar year. He made it very clear to Diamond that he did not want to harm his reputation or embarrass him.

Diamond became very agitated, hostile and exhibited aggressive behavior bordering on rage. In what appeared to be a premeditated, emotional rant, Diamond accused Chris of racism, harboring ill will toward Diamond's religion and told him his management style was "laughable".

This was all witnessed by one of Dr. Pederson's staff members, Ms. Denise Reynolds, who sat in on the meeting. Ms. Reynolds personally felt threatened by Diamond. Diamond stormed out of Chris's office and within minutes an ADG reporter called Chris with knowledge of the meeting.

Chris attempted to call, text and email Diamond throughout the day in hopes he had cooled down, but Diamond refused to take the calls or respond in any way. On Friday, Chris gave Diamond an opportunity to resign but only received a combative text in return. After discussions with me and senior officers, Chris terminated Diamond with 30 days notice. He also asked him to leave his office and finish his 30 days from home so as not to continue his creation of a hostile and threatening work environment. Diamond contacted several members of the media and has yet to respond to his supervisor. Diamond is claiming to the media that he was fired because he had a different philosophy of transparency with the public. In reality, Diamond has always insisted that all communication with the media come through him and that my senior team should not answer any media inquiries directly.

Any lack of transparency with the media or the public can only be attributed to Diamond's own failings as that was his primary responsibility. Diamond also refused to allow the university to release the termination letter which describes the reasons for his termination.

My apologies for the length of this message but you needed to have these facts. Please call me or Chris should you have questions.

Thank you.

Wow! I thought after reading Gearhart's screed, a copy of which was sent to me by a sympathetic official who had received it. *If I had been guilty of all that, I would have fired me, too!* But I wasn't. Among many falsehoods and distortions in Gearhart's email, the one most easy to document and discredit was his statement about UA's accountability: "Any lack of transparency with the media or the public can only be attributed to Diamond's own failings." *You've got to be joking—or delusional,* I thought, when I read that line. I quickly discovered that Gearhart's disparaging email to the board and others was the first salvo of a public campaign of character assassination, with me as its target.

Sometime that weekend, Development's Bruce Pontious called Wyrick and told him he was quitting, effective at the end of the coming week. Officially he was "accelerating" his retirement date, which he had previously announced as September 30th. On Monday, he gave Wyrick a letter he had drafted to send to Advancement employees, saying thanks and farewell. Pontious wanted to have Laura Villines, who managed intra-division communications, send it out on his behalf. For whatever reason, Wyrick rejected the letter. Pontious produced a revised version and shared it with Wyrick; he refused to approve that one as well. Consequently, Pontious did his best to personally inform as many members of the 150-person division as he could in the few days that he planned to remain on campus.

Meanwhile, Wyrick instructed Mark Power, the person he had appointed to replace Pontious two months earlier, to issue a notice to division employees informing them of Pontious' imminent departure. Wyrick himself apparently couldn't or wouldn't do it, despite the fact that over the previous five years Pontious had played a leading role in raising over $400 million for UA. With that kind of performance, one would have expected Gearhart, Wyrick, and other members of UA's top brass to issue an announcement to publicly thank Pontious for his years of service. Or to honor him with a plaque in University House acknowledging his work, like UA had done for one of his predecessors. Or at least have a reception at which deans, directors, and others whose programs had benefited from Pontious' fundraising efforts could stop by and say thanks. Even if Pontious himself didn't want the fuss, he was deserving of such praise.

Instead, word was distributed through the grapevine after Power sent his email to Advancement division employees. When contacted by *Arkansas Times*, Wyrick denied that Pontious' sudden departure had anything to do with my firing. He said that Bruce just decided to leave a week earlier than originally planned. Not true: Bruce had told everyone, including Wyrick, that his final day would be September 30th. In fact, Pontious was supposed to take part in the September 13th campaign steering committee meeting, where that group was expected to pay tribute to him upon his upcoming retirement. Wyrick also claimed that Pontious had to rush back to his native Ohio sooner than expected to start a part-time consultancy job. By the time the news story about his abrupt departure appeared, Pontious was already gone. He had spent his final week contacting key donors to say goodbye before he quietly and unceremoniously left town, much to the disappointment of his many friends and UA colleagues.

On Monday, August 26th, I emailed my response to my termination letters to Wyrick, Varady, and others at UA. The response was in the form of a four-page letter and included the details I had expressed to Wyrick—and, previously, to Judy Schwab—about his offensive and threatening behavior and his failure to abide by Arkansas' FOIA law. My email cover message reiterated what I had told Varady three days earlier: that my authorization to release the termination letters was contingent on UA simultaneously releasing my response letter. They did so around mid-afternoon, shortly prior to holding a hastily called 3:45 p.m. press briefing.

It was highly unusual for a university to hold a news conference related to the firing of any official other than the school's CEO, athletics director, or a coach. A terminated academic dean doesn't get anything more than a news release, if that, even if the dean contests the action. My firing apparently had struck a nerve with someone, and UA overreacted. The rawness of it was evident when Gearhart proactively distributed to reporters the email he had sent to trustees about me on Saturday. (A week later, he handed out the email at a meeting of the Chancellor's Administrative Policy Committee, a group of approximately 40 senior leaders, faculty, staff, and students who met with him once a month for campus updates.) It was an incredible display of hubris: he was publicly circulating information about an employee—much of it false and some of it libelous—in violation of university policies and procedures. It was hard not to see the hypocrisy when juxtaposing that act with Gearhart's months-long refusal to release the Schook memo, claiming that he and UA couldn't do so without violating Choate's and Sharp's privacy rights as employees.

At the news conference, Gearhart was joined by Wyrick, Pederson, Reynolds, Provost Sharon Gaber, and HR's Barbara Abercrombie. To the likely disappointment of those officials, the news coverage that appeared that evening and the next day focused as much, if not more, on the contents of my response to Wyrick as it did on the content of the termination letters or the explanations provided at the news conference. The *Arkansas Times* coverage was representative of what other print and online publications provided:

> Diamond responded in a four-page letter, which begins by noting the omission of context and "relevant details." He focused on two things: "...a purposeful effort to interfere with the university's obligations to respond to Freedom of Information Act requests from the news media ..." [and] "....impulsive, threatening and offensive statements and actions you have engaged in affecting me and other members of the university community." Diamond specifically notes his disapproval of response [sic] to *Arkansas Democrat-Gazette* requests for information in its ongoing review of the budget deficits and fallout in the university Advancement division. He said some responses were not legally justifiable or [were] incomplete.
>
> Gearhart said the university was careful about compliance and thought it had always followed the law. "We don't know of anything you have requested — or anyone else has requested — that we have not released."

In her story, the *Democrat-Gazette's* Tracie Dungan quoted extensively from Gearhart's Saturday email, correctly pointing out that "[t]he memorandum to trustees and Bobbitt appears to have been written before Fayetteville campus administrators secured Diamond's permission to legally release correspondence about his termination from his personnel file." Her story also emphasized the section of my termination response that dealt with Wyrick's handling of her July 22nd FOIA request:

> Diamond said his protocol included consulting with legal counsel for the best way to put instructions in writing to comply with Freedom of Information requests, but that Wyrick had asked individuals orally to comply.
>
> "I believe the negative consequences of orally and individually asking for responsive records are obvious: It becomes very easy for individuals to misinterpret exactly what is being asked for as opposed to giving them specific written instructions that are shared

> uniformly with all possibly affected parties," Diamond wrote. "That might explain why only one item was submitted to you in response to that request."
>
> During the news conference, Gearhart disputed this, saying the university had only one responsive document to the newspaper's freedom of information request and that the request had been so broad as to be "ridiculous."

Dungan also delved into the inconsistencies between my version of Thursday's meeting in Wyrick's office and his.

> Both Diamond and Wyrick wrote that each had felt threatened by the other during their Thursday meeting. When questioned by reporters Thursday, Wyrick said: "I'm a pretty big guy; I'm not easily threatened." When pressed about what it was that he found threatening about Diamond's response, Wyrick said: "He took an aggressive step towards me is how I'm going to answer that question."

A few days later, revisiting this issue in his Saturday morning commentary, *Arkansas Times'* Max Brantley offered this take:

> I do find laughable the notion that John Diamond was an intimidating and threatening figure who — according to Gearhart in today's *Democrat-Gazette* story — dominated meetings. Chris Wyrick, a former jock who dwarfs Diamond and is the Advancement division leader who fired Diamond, is particularly inapt to make such a charge. He is comfortable enough with locker room talk to make racial and religiously charged 'jokes' to subordinates in the presence of many other subordinates. That is intimidating. Diamond, as one university insider remarked, is more of a 'Mr. Peepers' character in demeanor.

At the news conference, Wyrick tried to explain or reject the offensive comments I had complained about. *Arkansas Times* reported Wyrick's responses topically:

> CATHOLIC: Wyrick disputed saying Catholics travel together. He said a co-worker Wyrick had worked with previously at the athletic department was a Catholic and they'd long had jocular exchanges.

> In April, Diamond was present when Wyrick said he remarked, "What time is the fish fry on Friday?" Said Wyrick, "If that was offensive, it took him until August to complain and that was after he was reassigned."
>
> HONKY: Similarly, on the Brother Honky remark, Wyrick said that was a nickname given him and used frequently by black former athletes with whom he'd worked on fund-raising. He said he'd been told, but didn't remember, that he might have used the nickname referring to the work of another staff member, again at a meeting in April. He said he didn't remember it, but, if so, "it's kind of ironic that he didn't mention it until August."
>
> OLD MAN: He categorically denied having referred to the part-time employee as an old-man. He said he had been exasperated while working in the hot rafters of an arena preparing for graduation to see the employee sitting in a chair "and do virtually nothing."

If Gearhart and Wyrick had wanted to limit the attention my firing received, calling a news conference to elaborate and pose new accusations was not the smartest way to do it. It was an invitation to the news media to restate quotes and context in ways that kept the story on the front pages. It also prompted another FOIA request from the *Democrat-Gazette's* Tracie Dungan:

> This is a request pursuant to the Arkansas Freedom of Information Act, as amended. I am resubmitting my July 22, 2013, FOIA request that produced one responsive document roughly one month after I submitted it. Feel free to use the most recently amended, and narrowest version, of that request. I ask that you try another method this time, such as giving uniform, written instructions to employees on the kind of information being sought, or other method other than the one used on this request the first time.

Unlike its original response to the FOIA, this time the university provided scores of print and electronic records related to Advancement's budget and reorganization, including HR documents and the video of Wyrick's June 20th staff meeting. As expected (or feared, depending on your perspective), this second response generated several new stories, much of which would have been less newsworthy had the FOIA'd records been gathered and turned over when originally sought. Once again, by trying to avoid negative media coverage, UA had acted in ways that actually fueled it.

Over the next week *Arkansas Times* and the *Democrat-Gazette* submitted FOIA requests for my entire personnel file. Rushing and Varady notified me of the requests; I told them I would grant my permission to release them only after I was given the opportunity to review the file. I was actually pleased my file would be released because it included my positive annual performance evaluations.

However, when I received a copy of the file, it included a document that I had never seen: a purported summary of the July 29th AES meeting at which we disputed Reynolds' and Wyrick's assertions that she had been circulating monthly budget updates among division leaders. However, a handwritten message on a Post-It note attached to the document stated it was created at Wyrick's request by Mark Power and Laura Villines on August 23rd, the day Wyrick fired me. I notified Varady that I found it suspicious and disingenuous for UA to both create a document about an event a month after the fact and add it to my file only after I had been fired.

Days later, I learned yet another document had been added to my personnel file after I had already given permission for it to be released. It was a memo Wyrick had written, dated Tuesday, August 27th, but not placed in my file until August 30th. It stated that I had failed to properly notify Wyrick or gotten his approval for some of my time away from the office in July. (The memo also indicated he had instructed the office's new HR manager, an assistant to Reynolds, to dock my August pay.) It wasn't accurate, and I called him on it in yet another written response on September 3rd. "This was the second document in five days that was added to my personnel file without my knowledge [prior to] releasing my file per Arkansas' FOIA law," I wrote. I attached copies of email exchanges between Wyrick and me from June and July. Those emails documented the notification I had provided and Wyrick's acknowledgment that he received them. I pointed out that he had told me in July to count my days at the University of Iowa interviewing for the vice president's job there as paid "professional development" days, not as vacation days. I provided to Wyrick a copy of the email I had sent him in response, in which I said I did not feel that would be proper, as I was in Iowa for personal interests unrelated to my employment with UA. My September 3rd message also questioned why no one in Wyrick's office bothered to tell me he had docked my upcoming paycheck.

The manipulation of my personnel file was "a very disturbing action on the part of a senior officer of our university," I wrote. It was hard for me to believe that Varady, Rushing, and attorney Bill Kincaid, three confidants I respected and had trusted, were aware of how Wyrick was mishandling my file.

The last week of August, Wyrick embarked on a sort of apology tour across the Advancement division. The purpose was to "accept full responsibility" for the remarks and behavior I had objected to. Wyrick granted an interview to the *Democrat-Gazette* to talk about his workplace visits. The story and Wyrick's photo appeared on the newspaper's front page under a bold double headline:

"Rues Remarks, Learned Lesson, Wyrick Says;
UA Official, Fired Aide Expound on Religious,
Racial References Called Offensive"

The drawn-out report—what journalists sometimes call a "Second Coming" story when its length or headline goes well beyond the newsworthiness of its contents—focused on Wyrick's efforts to explain himself and to seek the sympathy and forgiveness of those upon whom he brought disgrace. "I've learned the lesson. I've accepted the responsibilities of those consequences, and it will not happen again," Wyrick pledged. The story quoted me explaining why jokes directed at Catholics about fish frys and traveling in packs would be deemed offensive; it was the same reaction that members of other religious groups would have in response to comments that stereotyped and mocked their appearance or traditions.

Other than the embarrassment of public disclosure, I wasn't sure what other "consequences" Wyrick was accepting. He did not contact me via letter, phone call, or text to apologize. However, he did have someone call my church on his behalf to see if our priest would allow Wyrick to address parishioners, many of who were large donors to UA and to Razorback athletics. Our priest declined the request, understanding that Wyrick's presence would be inappropriate under the circumstances. Furthermore, given that the church and Marcia's school were part of the same building complex—and Marcia's fear of Wyrick's unpredictability—our priest told Marcia she could call the police if Wyrick showed up unannounced.

During this period, a couple of media commentators expressed skepticism that jokes about a person's Catholic faith could be interpreted as offensive or disrespectful. Catholics were mainstream in America now, though it was hardly the case in Arkansas, where Catholics made up less than seven percent of the population. That kind of media skepticism wasn't expressed in Maine, where news media coverage of my termination in Arkansas included more about the Catholic references than about my complaints about FOIA violations. That distinction was understandable: a large percentage of Maine's population consists of first-, second- or third-generation French-Canadian and Irish immigrants who are Catholic in heritage if not in actual faith practice. In fact, many schools in Maine teach about the historical discrimination against Catholics in Maine that occurred in the 19th and 20th centuries, including demonstrations against Catholics and immigrants in Maine by white-robed Ku Klux Klansmen in the 1920s.

I wasn't the only one in Northwest Arkansas who didn't see the humor in jokes about Catholics. A conspicuous example of this point appeared a few months after my firing when Danny Pugh, UA's vice provost for Student Affairs, added a Facebook post for his hundreds of followers to read:

> Been a long time since I've heard the expression "Good Catholic" used in a discriminatory and bigoted fashion. Thank goodness for idiots. It was said to me yesterday! Don't worry. I'll pray to Mary for your soul and eat some fish in your honor to complete the stereotype!

By the time Marcia saw the post and took a screenshot of it, seven people had "liked" Pugh's remark, including John Erck, who was one of the Catholics in attendance when Wyrick made his first Catholic joke in my presence. In response to Pugh's post, a mother of a UA student posted a two-part comment regarding her own experience: "Being Catholic in the Bible Belt with 4 kids has drawn that comment more than once....If that happened in the workplace it could be harassment."

"Or not—at UA," added another Catholic, a member of the university's faculty. Minutes after the reference to UA appeared, Pugh removed his post and the comments. But I sympathized with their sentiments.

Chapter 13

OPACITY

The week after I was fired, I received a text message from Lisa Hammersly, the *Democrat-Gazette* reporter who, earlier in the year, had been reporting on the emerging Advancement scandal. I hadn't heard from her in months, which had not bothered me in the least; back in January and February, she had been relentless in her pursuit of documents, interviews, and answers and, unlike Dungan, had a good understanding of finance and management principles. Mark Rushing, Steve Voorhies, and I had met with Hammersly for a get-acquainted visit shortly after she was assigned to the Advancement story in January. She was all business, as were we.

It was Hammersly who, on January 22nd, had first questioned the reasons why Advancement had a multi-million dollar "accounts receivable" on its books at the end of June. Pederson had given me an answer to pass along to her, but when she asked for a more specific response, she had received the same answer in return. Looking back, she might have touched a particularly sensitive point with Pederson: the next day, he sent me the memorable email in which he instructed me to tell her, with Gearhart's blessing, that her FOIAs "border[ed] on the absurd and frankly, harassment." My unforgettable visit to Gearhart's woodshed had occurred the following day; it was the session during which he told me to stop responding to reporters' questions about Advancement.

Hammersly's text in late August was short. Identifying herself, she wrote, "Want to talk?" Marcia and I discussed the possibility; we had scheduled a meeting with a UA compliance officer and hoped (unrealistically, as it turned out) that UA System President Bobbitt and the trustees would investigate my charges. Had they done so, I was confident that they would realize I had been looking out for UA's interests in the face of unresponsive leaders. However, given the recent manipulation of my personnel file and public trashing I had received by Gearhart and Wyrick, I was quickly losing hope that Bobbitt or the trustees would do the right thing. Hammersly, an investigative reporter who had dogged UA (and me) months earlier, might be someone who could hear my story and treat me fairly, I thought.

I agreed to see her and arranged to meet with her at Marcia's school at 4 p.m. on August 29th. Marcia and I spent a couple of hours with her. She was attentive as I rattled off details about my concerns about UA's weak compliance with FOIA and its relevance to my short-lived reassignment. I also explained why I thought my complaints about Wyrick's treatment and comments triggered my actual termination. She listened politely, accommodating my need to purge those memories, then asked a series of questions related to document preservation within the division. I told her about the January 14th meeting with Gearhart, Reynolds' subsequent suspension of providing us with monthly budget reports, the sudden appearance in July of a budget document that alleged a deficit in my University Relations accounts, the July 29th meeting about FOIA compliance that Gearhart, Wyrick, Pederson, the lawyers, and I had, and the events of the recent weeks that led to my dismissal. I also offered to provide her with copies of documents that should have been included in Wyrick's one-page response to Dungan's July 22nd

FOIA. She asked me how I happened to have them.

"I was often copied or blind-copied on emails and received them myself."

"How come you didn't turn them over?"

"Wyrick never asked me if I had anything" related to the FOIA, I answered. Besides, if Wyrick had performed due diligence, he should have received everything I had from one or more of the people specifically covered by Dungan's FOIA request. I agreed to talk with her again after the audits were issued.

Two days later, reporters learned that the Arkansas General Assembly's Joint Legislative Auditing Committee would meet on Friday, September 13th to take up the Advancement audits. They expected the reports—conducted in tandem by state auditors and the UA System's internal audit team—to be released publicly a few days before their hearing. Gearhart, Pederson, and other UA officials would attend the session to answer legislators' questions. Though legislators said they had not yet been informed of any findings, UA had; following their protocol, auditors had given their findings to the university so that it could prepare its written and public responses. Gearhart and Pederson had conducted at least one exit conference with auditors; it was learned later that the state audit was completed and signed on August 22nd, the day before I was fired.

At noon on September 10th, the Division of Legislative Audit publicly released the audits it conducted in concert with the UA System's Internal Audit office. The 48-page report was organized in two parts based on a previously agreed upon division of labor: the first section, completed by state auditors, represented their "review of selected financial records as well as internal controls, policies, and procedures at Advancement," while UA System auditors "would focus on budgetary controls over Advancement's operation." Both sections included UA's written categorical responses to the respective findings.

The front page of Legislative Audit's section of the report

included a sidebar titled "Highlights of Report," which was enclosed appropriately, if not intentionally, in a box outlined in red ink. The short summary of findings appeared on Page 4:

> [Legislative Audit's] review of Advancement financial records revealed deficit cash balances and incorrect journal entries for accounts receivable at June 30, 2011 and 2012. Other matters discovered were non-compliance with generally accepted accounting principles and university polices and procedures; deficiencies in internal controls; and lack of oversight by the VCAD [Vice Chancellor for the Advancement division]. In addition, information contained in an internal report prepared by the Treasurer relating to Advancement was not disclosed to [state] auditors during the exit conference for the [university's] financial audit.

At first glance, the casual reader might have looked at that paragraph and assumed all of it was referring to failures or misbehavior by Choate, Sharp, or both. After all, until now, they had been the ones in the spotlight regarding mismanagement and overspending, and the new report didn't dispel earlier reports of their complicity; if anything, it added to it. Auditors blamed Advancement's deficit on five causes, four of which were related to failed controls within Advancement itself: Choate's failure to personally provide fiscal oversight to Advancement's operation; Sharp's "inaccurate and inadequate accounting and reporting" of Advancement's financial condition; the Division's "failure to appropriately budget and account for" direct payments to vendors that Advancement had instructed the UA Foundation to make on its behalf; and increases in staffing without having the funds necessary to support the growth. Schook's October memo and Gearhart's subsequent public statements had offered those reasons months earlier; the audit seemed to confirm them.

However, state auditors pointed out a fifth contributing factor to Advancement's deficit: "Inaccuracies in Advancement financial statements prepared by the Treasurer's office relating to accounts receivable."

> "In noncompliance with generally accepted accounting principles, the Treasurer's Office posted the following Advancement accounts receivables [$2.1 million on June 30, 2011 and $2.5 million on June 30, 2012], which partially obscured the deficits in [Advancement's] financial statements....Both of these receivables were reversed in July, without verification that funds had been received. The Treasurer indicated to [Legislative Audit] staff that this is the university's typical practice to eliminate deficits on the financial statements as of June 30 [of each year]."

In other words, two years in a row the UA's Treasurer's Office, led by Schook, enabled Sharp to balance Advancement's revenues and expenses at the end of the fiscal year by recording for her, on Advancement's books, that a scheduled payment from the UA Foundation had not yet been received. The problem was there was no such payment due. Additionally, Schook's office had exercised that budget-balancing maneuver two years in a row and had attempted to do it a third time two months earlier—with a June posting of a non-existent $3.2 million obligation from the UA Foundation—in a way that would aid the new Advancement regime of Wyrick and Reynolds. Auditors flagged it, and UA removed it before the audit findings were issued, according to the audit reports.

According to the auditors, Schook claimed that these end-of-year bookings were indeed legitimate "receivables." However, auditors disagreed and listed their reasons:

> The Foundation's own books showed no such payments due nor did Advancement or the Treasurer's office ever ask for them to be paid. Furthermore, by the end of each of those years, Advancement had already spent all of the money it was scheduled to receive from the Foundation.

Another problem was that the financial report that accompanied Schook's October 19, 2012 review of Advancement's finances showed no outstanding $2.5 million payment due from the Foundation on

June 30, 2012, the date the Treasurer's Office booked one as a "receivable." If UA was indeed owed that money, why did the record of it not appear in Schook's financial report?

If that wasn't criticism enough, the audit report also faulted the Treasurer's Office for failing to include, in UA's annual financial statements, two outstanding loans that Advancement had received from the UA Foundation. The Foundation's own financial disclosure records had acknowledged the existence of those loans.

The report also listed a third finding that should have been particularly disturbing to Gearhart, Bobbitt, and System trustees: Pederson and Schook's failure, in October, to tell state auditors about the accusations and findings contained in the Schook memo when the two UA officials met with them.

> On October 25, 2012, during the exit conference for the University's financial audit report for the fiscal year that ended June 30, 2012, neither the Treasurer nor the Vice Chancellor for Finance and Administration disclosed to [Legislative Audit] staff information about the Treasurer's report on Advancement issued six days earlier.

The report pointed out that at the exit conference, Pederson had signed the management representation letter attesting that he had "no knowledge of any allegation of fraud or suspected fraud affecting [UA] received in communications from employees, former employees, analysts, regulators or others."

To underscore the point, the audit report cited, at length, Schook's October 19th memo in which she wrote of "an overwhelming amount of evidence that points to a lack of management oversight, non-compliance...and deliberate efforts to disguise poor financial management." It also included Schook's acknowledgment in that memo that she had not yet examined Advancement's books to determine whether or not any university resources had been misappropriated.

Along with state auditors, the UA System's own auditors identified concerns and shortcomings related to the university's financial management. Their findings, contained in the second part of the joint audit of Advancement, identified several weaknesses and failings related to the university's system of checks and balances:

- The campus' budget management system did not align employee salaries with the budgets they were paid from, which made it difficult for someone reviewing Advancement's budget to spot that there were more people on the division's payroll than there was money to fund them.
- System auditors also faulted the university for not having written instructions to guide UA's college and division budget managers on how to maintain proper, uniform budget monitoring procedures.
- The auditors also questioned UA's annual practice of leaving millions of dollars unbudgeted and instead allocating chunks of money over the course of the year in a separate distribution process that the report said only Pederson and Gearhart controlled.
- The auditors also determined that, remarkably, Pederson's division, Finance & Administration, each year waited until May—the next-to-last month of the university's fiscal year—to survey each of UA's colleges and divisions to determine whether or not they were in danger of ending the year with a deficit.

In the course of identifying how Advancement's deficit occurred and went undetected for so long, UA System auditors also found a couple of instances outside of the fundraising division that called into question the adequacy of the university's overall financial management practices. Auditors found an $8 million deficit in a university account that funded improvements to the university's IT network and data systems. The deficit on that project, which began in 2001, was repeatedly carried forward from year to year, growing to a shortfall of more than $15 million in 2010 before being whittled down to the $8 million deficit that existed as of 2013.

System auditors also found a second deficit that had been carried forward from year to year: it involved Garvan Woodland Gardens, a 210-acre botanical garden that UA owned in Hot Springs, Arkansas. Auditors said the facility was operating with a deficit that had grown in five years to $5.9 million. They also pointed out that little effort was being taken by UA's senior leaders to reduce the deficit; Pederson's office had transferred just $300,000 during the previous two fiscal years to reduce the red ink despite the fact that UA held more than $30 million in university reserves, including $19 million that had not been budgeted for anything. In their conclusions, auditors wrote:

> [UA's] established system of internal control over the budgeting and financial reporting processes needs to be strengthened [according to the auditors' recommendations] in order to enhance the adequacy of safeguarding assets, ensuring that the university's financial records and reports are accurate and reliable, and ensuring compliance with applicable university policies and practices.

One didn't have to be a CPA to realize, when reading the report, that auditors were placing part of the blame for Advancement's deficit on Pederson and Schook.

Shortly after Legislative Audit issued the joint findings, UA posted a news release to respond. Under the heading "Joint Legislative, UA System Audit Confirms University Findings," the university spun the auditors' findings into a victory statement:

> An audit report released Tuesday by the Division of Legislative Audit confirms an earlier review by the University of Arkansas, finding that the deficit in the university's Division of Advancement's budget was the result of mismanagement that led to overspending. ...Like last year's university review, the audit report indicates no fraud, theft, or misappropriation of public or private funds.
>
> The auditors found that the deficit was caused by overspending by managers who failed to maintain proper budgetary oversight. While there is some disagreement on technical accounting

principles mentioned in the audit report, the university recognizes the recommendations and continues to make adjustments based on those recommendations and the findings of its own internal review.
"Our own review and now the legislative and UA System audits found that the division was, in effect, borrowing on anticipated revenues to pay current bills – that's unacceptable and it cost two employees their jobs," said Chancellor G. David Gearhart. "But no taxpayer dollars or private funds were lost, not one penny.
Based on its own earlier review and in anticipation of the audit report, the university has already taken steps to enhance its accounting procedures and system of checks and balances to prevent an issue like this from happening in the future. The university is also creating a new position in the administration focused solely on budgets and financial planning to strengthen the finance and administration division.
"Since becoming aware of the problem last fall, Dr. Gearhart and his team have worked steadily to identify the causes of the overspending and have taken steps to ensure this does not happen again," said Donald R. Bobbitt, president of the University of Arkansas System. "I want to reiterate and confirm my full support for Chancellor Gearhart in this effort. In calling for these audits, Dr. Gearhart invited a transparent review of the Advancement division finances with the goal of determining steps needed to correct the problem."
"No question, mistakes were made before I assumed leadership of the division and we have identified those errors," said Chris Wyrick, vice chancellor for Advancement."....Under Wyrick's leadership since April, the Advancement division balanced its budget for fiscal year 2013 with a combination of cost containment, sharing of revenue between academic units for the benefit of the university, and increases in revenue needed to support the unit...."
"I want to thank our legislative and UA System auditors for their efforts in helping us resolve this issue and bring it to a close," said

> Donald O. Pederson, vice chancellor for Finance & Administration. "We are in essential agreement with the auditors in regards to the cause of the deficit and the corrective steps needed moving forward."

As is usually the case, news releases are written both to inform and to frame the way the topic will be presented in the media. UA's emphasis on some of the causes of the deficit—Choate, Sharp, over-hiring, overspending, and mismanagement—attempted to guide attention in that direction. Similarly, UA's response silently steered attention away from auditors' criticism of Pederson and Schook's accounting and oversight practices. The closest anyone from the university came to acknowledging those factors was a passing reference to "differences on technical accounting principles mentioned in the audit." In truth, they were more than "mentioned" in the audit findings and were more than technical differences.

Late that afternoon, UA called a news conference to answer reporters' questions regarding the report. (A month earlier our University Relations team had recommended this activity as part of UA's response plan, but Gearhart and Wyrick had rejected it.) Afterward, the resulting media coverage of the audits highlighted the increased size of the deficit—$4.16 million, about $750,000 more than what reporters had previously cited—as well as Choate's and Sharp's breaches of policies and practices.

One section of the findings received less attention initially, but it did catch the attention of a few employees in Advancement's Development office:

> [Legislative Audit] staff experienced difficulty obtaining Advancement financial records, which potentially limited the scope of this review. For example, a total of only 20 payment authorization forms were maintained by the university for fiscal years 2010 and 2011. Approximately 765 payment authorization forms located for the fiscal year ended June 30, 2012, were not maintained in any order and appeared to have been haphazardly placed into boxes. It was the

university's practice to not retain payment authorization forms.

Sometime that afternoon, I received a phone call from Renea Dillard from the Development office. She and a co-worker had been talking about the auditors' findings. When the topic of missing payment authorization records came up in their conversation, Dillard's colleague reminded her "that those were the documents that [Dillard] had shredded based on the information given to me by Denise [Reynolds]." Dillard said she was contacting me because "it appeared that the blame was being put on Joy Sharp for destroying those documents" when she, Dillard, knew otherwise. Dillard also told me she was worried that she and her colleagues might be in legal trouble for having shredded those payment authorizations.

She walked me through the events that led up to the document destruction. Dillard said that in December, she and a few others in Development had been told to start cleaning out the various storage units that Advancement maintained on campus and in privately owned storage facilities around Fayetteville. However, the assignment was put on hold for some reason shortly thereafter. According to Dillard, during the week of February 4th, Reynolds asked Dillard and the others to clean out a storage unit at University House containing documents that were no longer needed. Dillard said she was instructed to shred the documents, which she realized were payment authorizations. On February 11th, Dillard emailed Reynolds to have the budget director clarify which of the university's records retention policies applied to payment authorizations; she wanted to make sure she preserved the proper years of those records. After not hearing back from Reynolds, Dillard called her to get an answer, which she wrote down on her desk copy of UA's records retention policy. According to Dillard's notations, Reynolds told her to save "current year plus one," meaning those payment authorizations covering the current fiscal year and the one immediately preceding it. The rest should be destroyed. Reynolds also told her to treat documents marked "travel claims" the same way.

After Dillard had dumped "five or six" bank boxes full of records into the shredding bin, a senior officer in the Development office, Brenda Brugger, saw her and realized what had taken place. Citing the recently announced audit investigations, Brugger told her not to shred any more documents.

As Dillard was recounting her conversation with Brugger, I remembered that in separate Advancement Cabinet meetings back in October and December, Reynolds had brought up the possibility of eliminating off-campus storage units as a way to reduce the division's operating costs. At the first meeting in October, Choate was still the division's vice chancellor; I remembered that he said we shouldn't do it because of "the optics"— i.e., the appearance that Advancement might be trying to get rid of some kind of paper trail related to Sharp's recent demotion. We all chuckled with nervous relief at Choate's observation, realizing the unintended PR consequences such a housekeeping effort could have produced if we had proceeded with the idea.

In December, after Choate had been removed from the division, Reynolds again brought up the issue of off-campus storage units at a UAC meeting. Pontious mentioned he had talked about it with someone in his office (who proved to be Dillard) but that the work had not yet begun. Laura Villines then pointed out that in light of the recent news stories about the deficit, there was a real possibility that auditors or other investigators would want whatever records we had. "That would look real bad if we had the shred truck pull up to our doors!" she joked. She was correct, of course. Pontious agreed and said we shouldn't do anything more.

Now I was learning that Reynolds proceeded with the purge even after the leadership group twice rejected the idea, that the record destruction occurred even after Gearhart invited auditors to investigate Advancement's finances, and that it included some of the very documents that auditors had been told were not available, presumably because Sharp had taken them with her or had destroyed them.

Shortly after our conversation Dillard contacted me again, this time seeking my advice on to whom she should speak in order to protect herself. I gave her the name of a System-level compliance officer in Little Rock I had dealt with. When the person didn't promptly respond to Dillard, I called the compliance officer myself and asked for advice. She suggested that I contact Roger Norman, the director of the Division of Legislative Audit, which conducted the UA audit. I sent him an email:

> Hi, Mr. Norman. Today I was contacted by a University of Arkansas employee who was looking for a safe place to report information. The employee shared first-hand information about the destruction of documents that were reported as missing in the Advancement audit. She is fearful of losing her job and was hoping I could steer her to an appropriate person to whom she could report this information. She has witnesses and documentation to support her accusation, which she said occurred immediately after Chancellor Gearhart announced he was going to seek the two audits. Please call me at your earliest convenience and I will share more. Her information may be helpful to Friday's hearing. Thank you.

I quickly heard back from Norman, and after explaining in greater detail what I had been told, I provided the contact information to allow Dillard to share her knowledge directly.

The following day, Marcia and I headed southwest to Dallas, where we were planning to celebrate our 27th wedding anniversary. Along the way, I received a phone call from Norman. He told me that the chairs of the Legislative Auditing Committee wanted me to attend Friday's hearing at the State Capitol complex in Little Rock, at which the committee would discuss the UA audit. He wanted to know if I would be willing to testify; Gearhart, Pederson, Schook, and System President Bobbitt were also lined up to do so.

"Sure," I said. "Just let me know when and where." Later, he called me back with an additional detail. "The committee chairs want to swear in all of the witnesses, just in case there's conflicting testimony. Are you still willing?"

"Absolutely," I replied.

I didn't know if anyone from UA was aware I had been invited to speak. The university had many alumni and allies in the Arkansas General Assembly who likely would take it upon themselves to inform Bobbitt, Gearhart, or Richard Hudson, UA's lobbyist. I learned much later that someone had indeed tipped off Hudson. In a mid-afternoon email to Gearhart—"Subject: Please Delete"—Hudson sent the following message in boldface type: "I learned that John Diamond apparently will be attending and speaking at some point during tomorrow's meeting."

Things hadn't been getting any easier for UA in the days leading up to and following the audits' release. People on campus were talking about a story in the *Democrat-Gazette* that cited former UA records analyst Annie Dowling's July emails complaining about Wyrick's "almost hazing-like" behavior at the June 20th Advancement meeting. Members of UA's faculty and staff were reacting to a *Democrat-Gazette* report that more than $500,000 of Advancement's annual personnel costs had been shifted to the academic colleges and to a few other campus units. The newspaper pursued information about the shift after reporters finally received the FOIA'd video of Wyrick urging Advancement staff to thank Pederson and the deans for helping the division balance its budget. On September 12th, the *Democrat-Gazette* reported that the Division of Legislative Audit had referred three items to the Washington County prosecutor for consideration: the double-reimbursement of $2,050 to Choate; Sharp's misdirection of $1.35 million in restricted funds donated by the Tyson family to an unrestricted account that had a large deficit; and Schook's posting of the two budget-balancing "accounts receivables" that auditors said never existed. Then, on the day of the Legislative Auditing Committee hearing, newspaper headlines prominently reminded UA officials, state legislators, and taxpayers of details that went beyond Advancement itself:

"State Audit Report Critical of Top UA Finance Officials"

"Actions of Pederson, Schook Questioned"
"Lack of Records Hinders UA Probe, Reports Say"

I picked up a copy of the September 13th newspaper in the hotel lobby that morning and read the stories. The articles focused on several questions that the audits themselves had only alluded to: Pederson's and Schook's lack of forthrightness with state auditors at the October 25, 2012 exit conference; Gearhart's decisions not to immediately seek an audit and to keep Choate and Sharp on the payroll; UA's weak financial controls and record keeping; and the university's use of unconventional accounting practices to balance its books. With news reports highlighting those aspects on this morning, the hearing could easily turn contentious for Gearhart, Bobbitt, and the others—even with the help and protection of committee members friendly to UA.

We left our hotel on Little Rock's West Markham Street and drove the mile and a half to the State Capitol Complex. Once there, we followed a one-way loop road past commemorative statues of the "Little Rock Nine," the black students whose attempts to integrate Little Rock's Central High School in 1957 met with white outrage stoked by Arkansas' notorious governor, Orval Faubus. Forty-five years later, those events remained an indelible stain on the reputations of Little Rock and Arkansas.

We found a place to park the car just beyond the statues. Entering the Multi-Agency Complex (better known as the Big MAC building), we took the elevator to the public hearing room. As we stepped off the elevator and looked toward the lobby area outside of the meeting room, we saw the UA entourage of Gearhart, Richard Hudson, and others. UA System officials also stood by, although Bobbitt and spokesperson Ben Beaumont were the only ones I could identify by sight. We went inside the hearing room to find Kimberly Williams, one of the state auditors I was told to connect with. The hearing room was large and fairly modern. A low wall with a swinging panel that could be opened to allow entry to the other side separated seating for committee members and the public gallery. On the committee side, there were more than three dozen desks in multiple rows. A long table was positioned in the foreground of the committee section to accommodate individuals called to testify and respond to questions. For today's hearing, four chairs had been placed at the table and set to face the committee.

As a joint committee of the General Assembly, "Auditing" consisted of 39 members from the House and Senate. The committee was led by two co-chairs: State Senator Bryan King and State Representative Kim Hammer. On this day, Hammer was scheduled to preside over the hearing. Both men were positioned in the center of the elevated row in the rear, with Roger Norman seated nearby. Kim Williams spotted me first and came over to introduce herself. Marcia remained in the public seating area as Williams took me through the swinging door and up to where Norman and the committee chairs were chatting. After introductions, Hammer asked if I planned to make an opening statement (I did, I said) and confirmed that I was still willing to testify under oath. With the hearing about to begin, I joined Marcia in the gallery. Gearhart and the rest of the university contingent were already seated on the opposite side of the room.

Hammer rapped the chairman's gavel three times. "OK, members of the committee. Please come to order as we begin the audit meeting at this time." As an American flag appeared on the hearing room's video screens, Hammer led attendees in the recitation of the Pledge of Allegiance. Immediately afterward, he asked State Senator Gary Stubblefield to provide an opening prayer. Then Hammer got down to business.

"Ladies and gentlemen, if there's no objection we're going to do things a little out of order," he said. "We've got members here from the University of Arkansas who have come in early this morning to speak to the audit report. They have a meeting to get back to in Fayetteville....I want to ask at this time that the representatives from the University of Arkansas would come forward to the table."

Bobbitt, Gearhart, Schook, and Pederson stepped through the swinging door and took seats at the table.

"Is there anyone else who is going to speak to the report?" Hammer asked. "I know that Mr. Diamond is here. Mr. Diamond, where are you, please?"

I stood and raised my hand. "Mr. Diamond, would you come to the table please at this time?" Then, noticing Gearhart and the others repositioning their seats, Hammer added, "Y'all don't have to make room. He's going to stand there for just a second." I stepped to the witness table and stood at the end of the table alongside the seated Bobbitt.

"Somewhere during the course of the morning, Mr. Diamond is going to be given an opportunity to speak," Hammer announced, addressing all in the room. "I want to tell you upfront that there may be conflicts of statements that are going to be made." Turning to the five of us, "So, at this time, as chair, I want to ask each of you to stand, and I'm going to swear you in under the oath. Would you please stand?

"First of all, Mr. Diamond, if you would please, state your name, the agency you represent, and your position please, and then I'll swear you in."

"My name is John Diamond of Fayetteville. I'm with the University of Arkansas, and I'm currently associate vice chancellor for University Relations." I waited until later in the hearing to point out that I'd be losing that title in nine days, something most, if not all, already knew.

Hammer continued. "Would you please raise your right hand and repeat after me: Do you solemnly swear and affirm that the testimony you are about to give will be the truth, the whole truth, and nothing but the truth?"

"I do."

"Thank you," Hammer said, before asking the same questions of Bobbitt. Then it was Gearhart's turn.

"Mr. Gearhart, do you solemnly swear and affirm that the testimony you are about to give will be the truth, the whole truth, and nothing but the truth?"

"I do," the chancellor replied.

"Thank you, sir."

After Schook and Pederson affirmed their oaths, a member of the committee posed a belated question to Hammer.

"Mr. Chairman, I don't recall us ever swearing anyone in before. I'm not being disrespectful, but I would have thought we would've waited until we had some discrepancy before we did that instead of at the start. Tell me what you're thinking."

"Sure," Hammer responded. "Because Mr. Diamond is here, and because of things that have been reported in the press and things that have been stated in other sources—whether they're credible or not, they have been stated—it is the opinion of the chair that there's potential for conflicting statements. I felt that instead of getting halfway through the meeting and [then] having to stop and swear them in, it would be better to go ahead and just do it on the front end.... One of the things that I will want to see achieved...is that the truth will be maintained and that accountability and transparency would always be brought into each meeting."

With that clarified, attention was directed to Kim Williams, who presented the main findings of the two audit reports. Highlights of the findings appeared on the video monitors in the room as she walked the committee through the reports section by section. Fourteen minutes later, she wrapped up her presentation. Hammer then invited Gearhart to make an opening statement.

"Thank you, Mr. Chairman. I appreciate the opportunity to make some brief opening remarks. I thank you for that. I want to begin by thanking the auditors for the performance of their duties. When I asked for the audits, it was my hope that their independent investigation would help us to be certain that our university review was accurate and correct. We also hoped it would confirm our determination of exactly what happened and make recommendations for future action to ensure that it will not happen again. They have done that. And I am grateful for their efforts.

"Now, I have thought long and hard about what I could say to this committee and to all members of the General Assembly that would give you some level of comfort about this issue as we move forward. I have thought about what I would want to know if I were sitting in your chair, representing the people of Arkansas. I have thought long and hard about what the people of Arkansas would want to know and should know. And here is what I would want to know if I were on your side of the aisle.

"Number one. Do I, as chancellor, take full responsibility for what has happened? My answer is, absolutely. It is on my watch, and it happened under my leadership. And I accept full responsibility for any and everything that happens at my campus. While I am confident I understand the basic causes as to why it happened, it is indeed my responsibility to alleviate the cause and to fix the problem. I accept that responsibility as part of the job of managing a campus with an $800 million budget, 5,000 faculty and staff, and 25,400 students. As you say, the proverbial buck stops here, and I do not shy away from that responsibility.

"Number two. If I were in your shoes, I would want to know if the University of Arkansas were putting in place controls and appropriate changes to ensure that this will not happen again. My answer is an unqualified, absolute yes. The audit has suggested a number of controls that we are already implementing. And we are strengthening the oversight and responsibility of the university as well as the training of staff and system operations. We have replaced personnel. We have changed reporting lines of budget officers to ensure more stringent accountability.

"Number three. If I were you, I would want to know if the state lost any money. If there was any fraud. Or any private benefit. Or private inurement to anyone. Or if the university lost any public or private funds. Was a single penny misspent? Misappropriated? Or, for that matter, wasted? I'd want to know, Did anybody steal anything? I believe I can answer with confidence—and I think that the audits confirm—that expenditures were for legitimate campaign needs in preparation for a major fundraising campaign. We don't see any evidence of misspending or misappropriation of funds or theft or loss of state or private funds. It is our opinion that the previous vice chancellor inappropriately added much needed staff for a fundraising campaign prior to the budget being in place. These people were needed but should have been added over a period of years, over a period of time.

"Number four. If I were you, I would want clarification about reports in the media that the size of the Advancement deficit was larger than we reported previously. My answer is that the size of the deficit is the same as the auditors found. And it is not larger than we previously reported....

"Number five. If I were a member of the General Assembly, I would want to know about the financial viability of your flagship and if this unfortunate event has damaged the fiscal stability....Your university is in the best shape financially that it's been in years—perhaps in its history. This has always been about a deficit in a unit of the university. There has never been a deficit at the university level as a whole.

"Number six. If I were in your chair, I would want to know about reports about transparency. And accountability. And adherence to Freedom of Information laws. My answer to this is that we will, and always have, adhered to the laws of the State of Arkansas. We take the Freedom of Information law in particular very seriously. On the Advancement subject alone, we have received over 100 FOIA requests and released thousands—*thousands!*—of documents in our efforts to comply with the law. We have staff dedicated almost exclusively to answering FOIA requests, not to mention three full-time attorneys in Fayetteville and two in Little Rock that spend hours and hours being certain the law is followed to the letter.

"And number seven. Finally, and certainly not to the exclusion of any questions you may have of us, if I were a member of the General Assembly, I would want to know if this whole ordeal has damaged the reputation of the University of Arkansas and hurt our standing among alumni, students, faculty, and staff. Obviously, I cannot speak for these groups. But I can say that the evidence, the facts, show that our alumni and friends are supporting the university with their gifts at a higher level than ever before. Last fiscal year, when media carried numerous stories on the subject, our private gift totals were at record highs with over $108 million. Our enrollment pipeline for students in Arkansas and beyond is at an all-time high. And the morale of students, faculty, and staff as related by their representative leadership is very high and they feel valued and appreciated.

"Thank you, Mr. Chairman, for letting me make these brief remarks and I will answer any questions."

After an opening question about Gearhart's annual $225,000 deferred compensation payment, Hammer asked the first of several questions about the Schook memo and UA's commitment to transparency. "Why did the *Democrat-Gazette* have to sue the university in order to get the information that they were seeking in the lawsuit?"

"We were advised by our attorneys that that information was protected under the law," Gearhart responded, "and we would have to get the people that were affected by that document to get their sign-off....We did that, and that's the reason we did release it. We had no problem with the contents—the contents we felt bore out everything we had said. But it was critical of some employees. We felt it was in the personnel file and that it was protected under the Freedom of Information law. That is what our attorneys advised us."

"Why was it placed in the personnel file, where it couldn't be accessed without such great length to go to get the information?" Hammer asked.

"Because it was the document that led us to decide that we were going to not allow the people that were affected to stay in employment," Gearhart replied.

"Is that referred to as the Schook report?"

"Yes sir, it is."

"I have to ask: Was that just an effort to hide information from being FOIA'd?" questioned Hammer's Senate co-chair, Bryan King.

"No, absolutely not," Gearhart answered. "As a matter of fact, I was fine with releasing the Schook memo, and I told our attorneys at the time—and I know they will verify this—that my opinion was, 'Release it! Send it out!'"

In saying this, the chancellor apparently forgot about his November 29th email to me and UA's attorneys in response to the initial *Arkansas Business'* FOIA request: he encouraged us to broadly apply FOIA's exemptions provisions when reviewing documents. ("Anything that can be interpreted as protected due to personnel in nature should be given consideration," Gearhart had written.)

"There's not anything in there that shows that we tried to hide anything," Gearhart continued in response to King. "Our attorneys advised us that it could open the university up to a cause of action from the employees that were mentioned. So when we were sued, we went to the employees and asked them if they would allow us to release it. We asked for signed waivers, and they both gave us signed waivers. And we released it. But I think the record will show that we had no problems releasing it all along."

"Why was Mr. Choate allowed to stay on as long as he did?" a committee member asked Gearhart.

"Well, for several reasons," the chancellor replied. "Our initial investigation did not show he committed any fraud. It did not show that he had stolen anything. It did not show that one penny was misused. He simply overspent his budget. Not a good thing. Not acceptable. But he had been a prolific fundraiser. He was engaged with our very highest benefactors to the university. We were raising well over a hundred million dollars a year in private gift support. And our feeling was, we could not find where he did anything illegal or inappropriate in terms of graft, in terms of anything corrupt, in terms of stealing money. And I made a conscious decision that because of that, we would allow him to stay as a fundraiser, helping us with our major capital campaign, but remove him from the day-to-day operations of the budget. The best way I would say it to you is that Mr. Choate is—*was*—a proven fundraiser, not only at our institution but at a lot of places around the country. If we felt he had done anything illegal or improper in terms of fraud, he would have been dismissed immediately." Gearhart was trying, more diplomatically than he had in other situations, to reiterate his claim that Choate may have been "a lousy manager" for allowing Sharp to mangle Advancement's finances with arguably little oversight, but he could still make it rain as a fundraiser and therefore was too valuable to let go—at least for a while.

For the next hour, questions focused primarily on the accounts receivable issue. Legislator after legislator probed the university's use of booking a supposedly unpaid obligation of the UA Foundation at the end of two fiscal years to balance Advancement's budget, even though the audits and the Foundation said no such obligation existed. The audits also pointed out that UA's treasurer's office attempted the same maneuver a third time, just a couple of months prior to the release of the audits, posting a non-existent $3.2 million unpaid obligation that it claimed the UA Foundation owed Advancement.

Schook took the primary lead in defending the practice, continuing to declare that she and Pederson had based their actions on a different interpretation of "the available literature" on accounting from that of state and UA System auditors. No legislator offered support for Schook and Pederson's position; plenty criticized it. Finally someone asked Legislative Audit Director Roger Norman to offer the definitive interpretation, as he had done in the audit report itself.

"The purpose of an accounts receivable is to record, at a particular date, the amount of revenue that's due from another organization," he explained. "The expenses [UA] incurred had nothing to do with the amount of revenue that was due from the Foundation....[T]here was no agreement between the university and the Foundation as far as [a] contract; it was not a grant, where they would spend and be reimbursed. It appears to us that under this scenario that the more you expended, the more revenue you could recognize [as a payment due]."

It reminded me of the old joke about bank accounts: "How can I be out of money if I still have checks left?"

Still, a strident Schook continued to defend the practice before finally agreeing to follow the auditors' "interpretation" in the future.

Committee members also wanted to press the university on the audits' finding that Pederson and Schook withheld their knowledge of Advancement's financial and management problems during their October 25th exit conference with state auditors.

"What concerns me, sitting here listening to the testimony today, is that some of the questions don't appear to be being answered directly," Representative Nate Bell offered. "I go to page 12 and 13 of the report. I draw your attention to that. I believe the most significant issue in my mind rests right there: 'Issues not disclosed at the exit conference.' As recently as just about a year ago, [Pederson] signed an exit conference representation letter for our auditors that said, Look, we don't believe there's any suspected fraud here. Then, your own internal documents directly conflict with that....[H]ow can this body have any level of trust that you all are going to be open and transparent with us when you clearly didn't in this case following this scandal? You talk about 'transparency'! There's a high degree of opacity in how you misrepresented this to our auditors. I would like to hear from somebody about what assurances this committee and the public and this state have, going forward, that y'all are going to be transparent with us and that you're going to—when you're directly challenged about an issue—that you're going to come clean. It's bothersome to me."

Pederson responded with a failed attempt to mollify Bell. "The document you're quoting from that appears to show a conflict states that there were risks of fraud—not fraud or suspected fraud—and I signed the document that I had no knowledge of any allegation of fraud or suspected fraud because I believed that to be the case. We did not believe there was fraud or suspected fraud, that there was any fraud at that time. We had already determined that the risk of fraud did not lead to fraud or suspected fraud."

Bell was unmoved. "Do you understand how difficult that is [to accept]? We depend on having an honest and fair and open representation, not parsing words. Any fair-minded person would look at what you just told me and say, 'That's walking a very narrow line and parsing words.' While I understand that in the strictest technical definition you're correct, it's very opaque. That's not indicative of transparency.... You know the old proverbial question, It depends on what your definition of 'is' is. Sometimes I'm feeling I'm playing that game here. Why do we have to narrow you down to the most infinite detail to get a truthful answer?"

Gearhart spoke up to rescue Pederson. "Let me say that the fact is, there is no fraud, and the legislative auditors showed us that there is no fraud. Dr. Pederson made a statement that he did not believe there was fraud. Now, I understand what you're saying, sir. But I would just counter that by saying that the reason that I asked for a complete investigation of this by Legislative Audit and by the System auditors was so that we would be totally and completely transparent. I don't want it to be lost on this committee, members of the General Assembly, or the people of Arkansas that we asked for that audit."

Gearhart failed to qualify that statement: he asked for the audit a full seven months after he first learned of Advancement's financial mismanagement, and finally did so only after weeks of public pressure and just four days after meeting with Bobbitt and the board of trustees.

"We did not see any private inurement," Gearhart repeated. "We did not see any fraud. We did not see any misspent money. And I believe we can stand by that statement today."

Bell agreed with the chancellor on some, but not all, of those assertions. "As we sit here as a committee, I believe that it is fair to say that there was a fraudulent misrepresentation of the facts—on more than one occasion. We can define fraud in various terms, and in the strictest legal interpretation, you're correct. That is my point here: There was 'no fraud' in a very narrow determination. But the fact of the matter is, the facts were misrepresented."

"Sir, I appreciate your comments," Gearhart replied. "As you would expect, I don't agree with them. I think we are very transparent. There was no allegation of fraud. To suggest that we have been fraudulent, I just have to disagree with you. I don't think you can point to any place in the audit that suggests that. That is a pretty serious charge to make of somebody who's been at the university for 43 years [referring to Pederson], somebody who was a member of this committee—a staff member for 25 years [Schook]. So all I would say to you is, if you can point us to where that is said, then I'd be happy to have you do something."

Committee Co-chair Hammer spoke up. "I'd like to ask you a point on that, Mr. Gearhart. I'm looking at a copy of the Schook report, as it's referred to. It's page 3. In a letter that you received on October 19, 2012, the third bullet down on page 3....It says, 'In what appeared to be an intentional effort to disguise a prior year account receivable balance that had been cleared, the director deposited restricted funds—a gift for capital purposes—totaling 1.3 million dollars'." He stopped in midsentence to get clarification. "Is that referring to the Tyson donation?"

"Yes," Schook answered.

Hammer resumed reading aloud from Schook's memo. "—in May 2012 into the same unrestricted general operating account with the same delinquent account receivable balance.' Now, maybe there are different ideas about fraud, but it seems to me that that one falls close enough to it that there should have been some follow-up action that would have addressed this. Ms. Schook, you wrote this into the letter upon your own investigation as you were directed to do so. By who? Who directed you to compile this report, Ms. Schook?"

"Dr. Pederson," she replied.

"Dr. Pederson, when you received the information that was in this report, who did you give it to?" Hammer asked.

"I shared this with the chancellor," Pederson answered.

"At that point, what happened to this report?"

Pederson deferred to his boss.

"'What happened to it?'" Gearhart said, repeating Hammer's question. "Well, it went into the individuals' personnel file, and then it was released after we had the authority from the individuals to release it."

Hammer wasn't satisfied with the answer. "Ms. Schook wrote into this report—and it's mentioned on several occasions—that there's at least the appearance of fraud, if not a direct accusation. But I think the bullet I just read was pretty straightforward that there may have been some fraud. Why was this handled in the way that you handled it, knowing the strong language that was used in this letter in reference to fraud?"

"Well, I can only say to you that I did not believe there was fraud," Gearhart responded.

Meanwhile, throughout the hearing, legislators' questions of transparency continued to pop up. One committee member, Representative John Walker, tried repeatedly to understand UA's assertions of openness in the face of contradictory evidence. "How can the university say it's been transparent when the audit indicates it can't find records for expenditures, according to the legislative audit, and when it fired a chief spokesman who objected to the reluctance to release those records?" he stated rhetorically.

It was a theme that Representative Andy Mayberry had raised minutes earlier. Mayberry pressed Gearhart about the university's obligations to be accountable to the committee and to the public. "How do you address that perception that the university is not being as forthcoming with information as it should be with the people of the state?" he asked.

He received a conditional assurance in response. "I do believe we are transparent," Gearhart responded. "I do believe that we work very hard to comply with the law....We have open books. We believe that we are as transparent as is required by the law."

Chapter 14

NOTHING BUT THE TRUTH

Two hours into the audit hearing, questions and answers were becoming repetitive. In such situations, legislators sometimes wander off to make calls, engage in side conversations, or just leave altogether, believing they had heard enough. Possibly with that in mind, Hammer decided it was time to bring me to the witness table. There were only four chairs at the table, so Hammer asked if someone would clear a seat for me. Bobbitt did so, giving up his chair located immediately to Gearhart's left. I sat, took my written testimony out of its folder, and placed it in front of me.

"Mr. Diamond, let's start off by asking, Is there a statement you'd like to make or anything you'd like to say, please?"

"Yes," I answered. "Thank you very much." With that, I began to deliver my 850-word opening remarks. "Chairman Hammer, Chairman King, and members of the committee. Thank you for the request to join you today. My name is John Diamond, and I reside in Fayetteville...."

For the next several minutes, I explained what my role and duties had been at UA and highlighted my direct involvement in ensuring

UA's compliance with FOIA law. I told the committee about my fears that the audits would have whitewashed the facts, and my relief that they didn't. But I also pointed out weaknesses in the audits that resulted from missing documents and the blame assigned for their absence. "I believe I can help address some of those gaps, based both on my role as an officer within the division and on my familiarity with the way the university has handled documents of value or interest to auditors and to the media.

"The points I will make can be corroborated by witnesses and/or documentation. I will address these topics briefly and will elaborate on them further during the question and answer session, should the committee so desire."

I proceeded to outline three areas of concern. First, auditors' heavy reliance on the Schook memo, which I said was "of questionable value in that none of the associate vice chancellors or unit managers within the [Advancement] division was ever interviewed as part of that review." Understandably, auditors would have assumed that Schook had done so.

Second, the representation or presumption that Joy Sharp was solely responsible for the missing payment authorizations. "Many of those documents did indeed exist after Ms. Sharp left the division and were in the division's possession until immediately after the request for these audits was issued in February," I reported.

Third, the university's failures, at various times, to properly respond to FOIA requests, a result of the "culture of secrecy that developed and grew" in response to discovery of the Advancement deficit, I offered.

"Members of the Advancement division's leadership team and staff received directives from key individuals that resulted in the destruction of documents relevant to the audits and to FOIA requests," I explained. "This occurred both before and after the February request for the audits. Those two reasons are in part why auditors could not find documents they sought, and that's why so few responsive documents were given to the media during the past several months." I closed my prepared statement by repeating that I had documentation and witnesses that I would provide to the committee to support my assertions.

As far as I knew, only King, Hammer, Norman, and possibly Kim Williams knew I would mention the destruction of documents in my opening remarks. Without a doubt, Norman informed the chairs about Dillard's call to me and, later, to him; most likely that was one reason for asking me to testify. And once I had done so, the attention level among committee members increased noticeably.

"Mr. Diamond, thank you very much," Hammer said. "Would you mind sharing copies of what you just read with the committee?"

"Sure."

"I want to ask you a couple of questions," he began. "You still work for the university right now?"

"Until next Friday," I answered.

"And why are you leaving the university?"

"I was terminated for what I believe were a combination of things," I responded, "...practices related to transparency and public accountability—differences with my superiors."

"Is that going to go on your personnel record?" Hammer asked.

"Yes."

"OK," Hammer continued. "I'm going to ask you some questions about things you just said—and for the record, you are here at the requests of the chairs, is that correct?"

"Yes."

"You referred to witnesses. Are you saying that there's others that feel the same way that you do?"

"Yes," I responded.

"Why are they not here today?"

"Several of them are still employed," I replied. "Several of them are fearful about their jobs. There has been, in recent months, a series of promotions, demotions, and reassignments that have people concerned. And disciplinary actions that have people concerned about their employment status."

"And what documents were you referring to in what you just said?" Hammer continued. "None of us have a copy of that. So, in the document you just read, what are you referring to as far as documents being destroyed?"

"There are several. I'll start with the payment authorization forms that were noted in the audit. The audit refers to those as not being available beyond a certain period of time and limited availability during the two years [for which] the committee received them. The week that the chancellor asked or announced he was going to request the two audits, a directive was given to certain members of the Advancement staff to destroy boxes of records as part of a housekeeping matter. Employees asked what specifically should be included, what should be retained or destroyed, and specifically asked about payment authorizations. They were told to retain the current year—FY13 at the time—and FY 12, and to destroy the others. So they went to the shredder."

Marcia observed that the room became abuzz with muttering and side comments on both sides of the short wall separating the public gallery from lawmakers and witnesses. I sensed an agitated Gearhart stirring in his seat next to me.

"I noticed in the audit report," Hammer said, "that during 2010 and 2011 there was a relatively small amount of payment authorization forms, but then in 2012, it seems like it went up to around 765. And I'm going to ask you this and give any of the other three folks at the table an opportunity to respond. What's the explanation for why for two years they only had that few, and then in 2012 all of a sudden it spiked up to 765?"

"I don't know," I responded. "The maintenance of those records is handled by others within the Advancement division. But this information, like some of the points I'm making here, came to me after my termination a couple of weeks ago. People were concerned [before the audits were made public]—and even since the report came out, people were concerned that there were things that were missing from the report."

"Did you ever personally destroy any records yourself?" Hammer asked.

"One," I answered. "One that I know of. Actually, two." They were emails between Gearhart and me speculating about the source of leaks to Chris Bahn regarding the gift tax proposal. "At that time there was discussion brought up by two members of the [Advancement Cabinet], including the person who is now the assistant vice chancellor for Budget within Advancement, related to documents that were trying to make sense of the financial situation facing the division. Again, this is in January of 2013. This is very awkward for me, sitting next to the chancellor, but he got angry at the fact that there were documents that had been maintained about the so-called gift tax and various options that had been proposed about that. And a financial report distributed by at that time the new budget director, Ms. Denise Reynolds, about where she saw the financial situation of the division at that time. The chancellor got very upset, got angry, and made several statements which concluded with an instruction to all of us to get rid of those documents and not to produce anymore. Because—"

"OK, let me stop you right there," Hammer interrupted. "I've only got one other question. I want to ask Dr. Gearhart; I want to give you an opportunity to respond, please, sir."

"I categorically deny that we have ever said to anyone to destroy documents," Gearhart declared. "That is not true. And I would be delighted to see the evidence that he has for that. Mr. Diamond is a disgruntled employee that was dismissed from the university for a number of reasons. He is an at-will employee. We tried to give him time to find a job. We told him we didn't want to embarrass him. That we did not want to hurt him in any way. That we would give him plenty of time to find a position. Mr. Diamond, ever since Mr.

Choate [and] this whole issue came about, was a very disgruntled employee. He tried to find a job. We know of three different times; it was reported in the media that he tried to find a job, he was not able to find a job. We went to him and said, 'We do not believe you want to be here and frankly the senior management of the university doesn't think that you should be here.' His accusations today are astounding to me. They are not accurate, and I hope he has proof of them, because it's a pretty serious allegation for him to make.

"I deny that we have ever told anybody to destroy any documents," he continued. "Now, I will tell you that there are times we have working papers that we do not keep. But if we have been FOIA'd for a document, we always comply with that document. But every day of my life, there are things that I tear up. There may be plans. They may be thoughts about certain issues that we have. There may be personnel items. We have to be able to do our business at the university. But we have never, ever refused to send some to whoever asked for it if we have it in our possession if it is releasable. And I stand by that.

"And I am shocked and I find it pathetic that we have a person here who has been dismissed from the university making allegations. There is no proof of that. He cannot prove it. He is a disgruntled employee. He cannot find a job. I really don't have much else to say. That's sort of the issue. And he can sit here all day long and express his opinions. He is entitled to his opinions, but he's not entitled to his facts."

Gearhart's attack on me as a person was not surprising; it was a defense he often employed when on the ropes, as he had shown previously in his dealings with Greenberg and other critics. But given that Richard Hudson had told him the previous day that I would be testifying, one would think he would have offered substantive arguments that he himself could back up. Other than his references to me applying for other positions (higher level posts at more academically prestigious universities, he failed to note), he would not have been able to substantiate his claims.

I was hoping that Hammer would allow me to respond because I was prepared to present the very proof that Gearhart challenged me to offer: the specifics of the documents he told us to "get rid of" on January 14th; Reynolds' subsequent and abrupt halt to the distribution of monthly budget reports to Advancement's department and unit leaders; and details about Wyrick knowingly withholding the June 20th video and many other FOIA'd documents related to his reorganization plan and budget reconciliation efforts.

Before that could occur, Schook asked permission to respond. She insisted that auditors could have gotten the information recorded on the missing payment authorization records from the private UA Foundation, and that she had told them as much. That may have been true, I thought, but the fact was that payment authorizations were indeed destroyed at someone's instruction after the call for audits and that UA officials led auditors to believe that it was Joy Sharp who had committed the act months earlier.

Gearhart asked permission to make another point.

"Mr. Diamond claimed that there was no interviewing," he stated, even more heatedly than before. "That is absolutely false. I interviewed Mr. Diamond. I interviewed every member of the senior Advancement team, and I asked them questions such as this: 'Were you given a budget by your supervisor? Were you given a budget to follow?' Mr. Diamond answered that question, No, he was not. I asked the associate vice chancellor for Development, Did you have a budget? And that person looked at me and said, No, and it was a source of concern for me for a number of days, a number of months. His name, by the way, is Bruce Pontious. I'm sure he will confirm that. I asked the assistant vice chancellor whether or not they had a budget, and he told me –his name is Mark Power—and he can confirm that. There was no budget given by the senior management. And that was part of the problem. And Mr. Diamond told me the same thing. And for him to claim today that nobody interviewed him is ridiculous. It is absurd."

"Sir, if I could clarify," I said to Hammer. "The chancellor and I did have that conversation—*after* the Schook memo came out, not before. My point was, if there's an investigation of what happened and whether there was any fraud or any malfeasance, and a report came out that was deemed so severe that it resulted in two people having disciplinary action taken against them at the time, you would think that the people who worked directly with those people would have been interviewed *as part of* what Ms. Schook put together, not after the fact. And that was my point."

Hammer's co-chair, Bryan King, spoke up. Reiterating that the audit reports determined that payment authorization records were indeed missing, he asked if Gearhart would allow his committee staff to interview the people who allegedly took part in the document destruction.

"I don't have a problem with you talking to anybody, sir," Gearhart replied. "But let me say this: the records they are talking about that were missing are the records that were with Ms. Joy Sharp, who has been dismissed by the university. Those are the records they were not able to find. What she did with them, if there were any, I don't know."

"That's what we'll find out," King responded.

Uncertain about how far to go with questions in light of the conflicting testimony, Norman, King, and Hammer huddled off-microphone for two minutes to discuss their next steps. Reaching an agreement, Hammer addressed the committee.

"In light of what's come out today, we'd like to seek a motion to ask that this report be given as 'not presented.' Basically what that's going to do is allow for the committee to continue [to investigate]." It also would mean that the committee was not ready to accept the conclusions in the audit. Before a vote could be taken, Representative John Walker asked committee leaders to clarify a point.

"If this motion passes, we won't have a chance to ask Mr. Diamond any questions?" he asked. Hammer told him that the committee could, if it wanted, have me return to testify at a future hearing on the audit reports. Walker pressed to make sure that everyone's intent was on the record, evidently concerned that something might keep me from being allowed to speak further. He asked permission to pose one question before the committee voted.

"It goes to Mr. Diamond, and it goes to Chancellor Gearhart," Walker stated. "Mr. Diamond, did you receive work evaluations of your work the year before last?"

"Yes," I answered.

"Were they satisfactory or above?" he followed.

"Yes."

"Have you ever received an unsatisfactory work performance evaluation?"

"Not until a couple of weeks ago," I replied.

"I see," Walker acknowledged.

"—and I released my entire personnel file, even things that would normally be privileged," I added.

"Thank you," Walker said. "Is that right, Chancellor Gearhart? He never had, until after this matter became public, an adverse evaluation of his work performance?"

"I had a number of sessions with Mr. Diamond where I made him aware that I was not pleased with his performance that go back some time ago," Gearhart claimed. "I did not do the evaluations of Mr. Diamond. I can tell you that there was an evaluation done by our Department of Human Resources that indicated that there were management issues and morale issues in the department. That was done by an independent evaluation of Mr. Diamond's area. It was done by Barbara Abercrombie, and I'm sure she would be happy to testify to that effect."

Fortunately, I was able to suppress my habit of expressing disagreement with a half laugh, half sigh. Gearhart was referring to the employee time records—the work logs that Wyrick and Abercrombie had all employees across Advancement complete in advance of Wyrick's reorganization plan. That exercise wasn't an assessment of me personally; it was designed to capture time use and working conditions within the Advancement division itself. Wyrick refused to let any of the supervisors review those work sheets—and he never acknowledged their existence when reporters first FOIA'd them in July. Months later, when I used FOIA to access those work logs, the complaints staff members listed dealt with disappointment and frustration regarding the division's hiring freeze and budget cuts, not toward me.

Walker didn't let Gearhart get away with evading the question. "I'd just like Chancellor Gearhart to answer directly whether or not a written evaluation was ever given to Mr. Diamond before this time last year noting his work performance deficiencies, irrespective of what people may have thought about him."

"Would you answer that?" Hammer instructed the witness.

"I don't have knowledge of those performance evaluations," Gearhart replied.

Hammer was ready to move on. He restated the motion, explaining that a "yes" vote would allow the committee to hold further discussions and hearings in the future, if it chose to do so. The motion passed unanimously.

After the hearing, Hammer addressed reporters. "Are we dealing with a 'disgruntled employee' who has legitimate claims or a 'disgruntled employee' who doesn't have legitimate claims?" he remarked to *Democrat-Gazette* reporters Hammersly and Chad Day, invoking Gearhart's description of me. "The magnitude of what Mr. Diamond was saying...warrants at least keeping the door open to where [Hammer's committee] can get to the bottom of it."

Outside the committee room, reporters asked me to elaborate about the destruction of documents. I explained that a university employee involved in the process told me that days after Gearhart agreed to the audits, she had been instructed by Denise Reynolds to go through a particular storage unit and shred certain records as part of what I described as a "housecleaning." I didn't reveal Dillard's name to reporters but told them I had provided the employee's identity to the Auditing Committee's staff.

A few hours later, Reynolds issued a statement to the media through UA's Mark Rushing, denying the assertion in my testimony. The allegations "are false," she said. "I did not order a 'housecleaning' of documents and no one told me to do so." She stated that she was trying to reduce costs by cleaning out storage areas but that "none of these records [in the storage unit being emptied] was requested by persons conducting the university's internal review or auditors. Additionally, we maintain electronic copies of all payment records, including Foundation payment authorization forms."

Her statement about payment authorizations was in direct contradiction to what auditors reported. It also directly conflicted with Renea Dillard's statements to me and to Legislative Audit Director Norman about what she and her co-workers had been told. As had been the pattern over the course of this day, evidence was accumulating about failures to tell the truth, the whole truth and nothing but the truth.

Following the Auditing Committee's session, the UA System Board of Trustees cancelled that day's scheduled meeting of its own audit committee, which was to discuss the auditors' reports. Jane Rogers, the board's chairperson, was quoted as saying the meeting was called off because the legislature wasn't done with the audits. I assumed there was at least one other possibility: Bobbitt and the board's leadership might have been concerned about what individual trustees, unscripted, might say in the presence of reporters and the public about the morning's unexpected turn of events.

The front page of Saturday morning's *Democrat-Gazette* confirmed the power of a picture. Under the headline, "Ex-UA Aide: Budget Files Shredded," Arkansas' newspaper of record published a color photo of Gearhart and me. I appear in the foreground, my image a little out of focus as I read my statement to the Legislative Auditing

Committee. Gearhart was in sharp focus, scowling at me from his seat to my immediate right. He is leaning on his left fist, with his middle finger extended and pressed against his left temple. A sidebar story adjacent to the photo appears under the headline, "Lawmakers Raise Issue of UA 'Trust'."

Even the regional *Northwest Arkansas Times*, a descendent of the newspaper that Gearhart's late father once served as publisher, pointed out "a lack of accountability" on the part of UA. In its Saturday editorial, it opined that the audits showed that UA "has operated in a loosey-goosey fashion, perhaps by design, regarding the Advancement division's finances for years."

> UA can sit comfortably trying to fend off criticism only because donors have been so generous to the state's flagship university. But can those donors be comforted that UA leaders see blame only for two fired employees? Can they rest easy knowing that auditors faced missing documents and record-keeping tantamount to throwing bills in a shoebox? The expectation for UA accountability must be stronger.

Meanwhile, the *Democrat-Gazette's* editorial writer and Gearhart antagonist, Paul Greenberg, excoriated UA's chancellor for his attempt to spin the audits' findings. Greenberg cited several of the auditors' critical conclusions and noted that Gearhart failed to acknowledge them in his post-audit news release.

"As for minor desiderata like transparency, accountability, responsibility and so tediously on, well, anyone can see what's happened to them at [UA]—even if its chancellor can't," Greenberg wrote. Deeper into his editorial, he addressed the chancellor, Pederson, and others who were mentioned in the audits.

> None of these worthies felt any need to offer their resignations, or even a public apology to the taxpayers, donors, faculty and students whose faith in the university has been so sorely betrayed. That would have been unspeakably accountable. The chancellor did note in the course of this long and all-too-defensive press

conference that all this "happened on my watch." Some watchman.

Greenberg's editorial was accompanied by a pointed cartoon. It featured a partially open door with a sign on it, saying "UA Fayetteville Advancement Division Bookkeeping: Authorized Personnel Only." The image revealed what was on the other side of the door: a toilet, plunger, and towel.

On Monday, Washington County Prosecutor John Threet told *Democrat-Gazette* reporter Bill Bowden that he would be investigating the claims of document destruction as well as the audits' previously reported findings regarding Sharp's misdirection of the Tyson donation, Choate's receipt of a duplicate reimbursement payment, and Schook's listing of non-existent accounts receivables to balance Advancement's end-of-year books. According to Bowden, Threet's decision was related to Legislative Audit Director Norman's email to legislators that same day in which he said he was required by law to inform the prosecutor on all matters that "appear to involve a criminal offense."

"We're going to stay after this thing and make sure the prosecutor does due diligence," Senate Co-chair King told Bowden. "If there is something wrong, we're going to make sure they're held accountable."

I was feeling optimistic about the direction in which things were moving. If the prosecutor interviewed everyone who attended the January 14th meeting where Gearhart issued his "get rid of" directive, it would validate not just what I said in my testimony but might also motivate the UA System trustees to look into my claims more seriously. After all, they had legal responsibility for protecting the public interest in its state universities, and that included making sure they operated according to the letter and spirit of the law.

However, one factor gave me pause. A news report noted that chief prosecutor John Threet's involvement might be a conflict of interest, or at least give the appearance of one. He was married to the stepdaughter of Frank Broyles, the legendary Razorback coach and athletics director who was now, in his semi-retirement, on the payroll of the Razorback Foundation as a speaker and goodwill ambassador. In that role, Broyles worked with Chris Wyrick in the latter's recent jobs as the Razorback Foundation's executive director and as an athletics fundraiser. Furthermore, I soon discovered that Threet also was on UA's payroll as an adjunct member of the law school's faculty, earning $8,000 per academic year for that part-time role, according to UA records. Despite these connections and appearances, Threet said he would not recuse himself from the investigation; instead, he would delegate responsibility to one of his deputy prosecutors, David Bercaw.

Soon, Bercaw heard from Christopher Plumlee, a partner in the Northwest Arkansas law firm Mitchell-Williams, who followed up that initial communiqué with a letter to Bercaw dated September 18th. In it, Plumlee stated that Mitchell-Williams was representing Gearhart and that the firm believed I had made "false and baseless allegations" about its client at the Legislative Auditing Committee hearing. Plumlee also provided a list of attendees present at the January 14th meeting "to facilitate a prompt review of the events by your office."

For whatever reason, Plumlee's list of names left off two attendees: Judy Schwab and Laura Villines. Around the time that Plumlee sent the letter, word was circulating among employees on the Admin Building's executive floor that Gearhart and Schwab had had a falling out. Was the absence of Schwab's name on the list deliberate? Was she unwilling, at the time, to back her boss's contention that he never uttered the "get rid of it" remark? As for the failure to include Villines on the list, was Gearhart worried about what she might say? As a longtime Advancement division employee who had worked closely with Sharp, Villines had intimate knowledge of the division's workings, history, and its relationship with the Chancellor's office. For example, Villines was aware that until the deficit was discovered,

Joy Sharp continued to manage Gearhart's own use of, and access to, UA Foundation funds provided to the chancellor. Was Gearhart worried about Villines' candor with prosecutors?

Meanwhile, I, too, was in contact with Bercaw's office. With my time on the UA payroll ending in a couple of days, I needed to return my university-issued laptop, cellphone, and iPad. However, I feared that UA would tamper with it, either deleting or adding things in an attempt to undermine or embarrass me. (I wasn't being paranoid, as UA's manipulation of my personnel file had already shown.) For that reason, I wanted to turn over all of that equipment to the prosecutor's office for safekeeping. Bercaw agreed to help and made arrangements for the Fayetteville Police Department to "image" (i.e., copy) my computer's contents and retain the equipment while the investigation was underway. Before I turned over my equipment, a friend of mine who works in the IT field duplicated my email and computer files so that I would have them to load onto my new personal laptop and review for whatever lay ahead.

I met Bercaw in person for the first time on September 19th. His office was located in the Washington County Courthouse, about a mile east of the UA campus. I checked in with the receptionist and waited in the small reception area for about 15 minutes before Bercaw arrived. He introduced himself to me, apologized for the wait, and led me to an interview room on a lower floor. Bercaw was a tall, lean man and, like me, in his late-fifties. He had a deep, husky voice, possibly related to the pack of cigarettes I noticed in the breast pocket of his white dress shirt. We were joined by another deputy prosecutor, Mieka Hatcher. I later learned that Hatcher, like her boss John Threet, also moonlighted as a UA faculty member.

Bercaw positioned himself across the table from me; Hatcher sat diagonally to my right. Bercaw led the meeting and invited me to say whatever I wanted to share, which I did at great length. Bercaw took extensive notes as I spoke; Hatcher took fewer. Though I understood their routine—just listen and learn—I was disappointed that neither one asked many questions during the hour or so that I spent with them. I was hoping to gain a sense of what they thought was important.

Before we finished, Bercaw asked me to go through the list of January 14th attendees (including Schwab and Villines) and indicate which of them I thought would be truthful with him about what was said at that meeting. I responded and also urged him to add another person to the list of interview subjects: Scott Varady. Earlier in our session, I had told Bercaw and Hatcher about the July 29th phone conversation Varady, Kincaid, and I had with UA System attorney Fred Harrison regarding Gearhart's objections to the *Democrat-Gazette's* FOIA. In fact, I indicated that over the past nine months I had told Varady just about everything I knew related to the Advancement situation—including Gearhart's January outburst and directive regarding budget documents. Varady also had first-hand knowledge of the discussions related to Wyrick's one-page response to the newspaper's FOIA. Kincaid was another worth considering for an interview; as I had told Bercaw and Hatcher, Kincaid had seen the video of Wyrick's June 20th all-staff meeting and told me that Wyrick's comments on the FOIA'd video were "a problem." Varady and Kincaid both knew that in mid-August Wyrick deliberately withheld the overdue FOIA response because Gearhart supposedly was "preoccupied" with the anticipated release of the audits. Varady, UA's formally designated "custodian" of the university's records, possessed knowledge and records that would help Bercaw complete his investigation, I told the prosecutor.

After finishing the interview, I returned to my car and called Marcia. "I think it went well," I told her. "They didn't ask many questions but said they'll probably have more to ask me after they interview others."

"Did they seem to take it seriously?" she asked.

"I think so," I said, adding, "but it was hard to tell."

I went home and took a long walk on the trails surrounding nearby Lake Fayetteville to clear my head. I had hated reliving, once again, the details of what I had experienced over the past several months. But I was cautiously hopeful that this particular recitation would result in a proper investigation. If Bercaw did a thorough job, he and Hatcher would discover for themselves the incongruence between what Gearhart had said to the Advancement leadership staff in January and what he said under oath to the legislative committee in September. Presuming Bercaw and Hatcher pursued the question of missing documents, they would also learn about the existence of dozens of documents and electronic records that Wyrick knowingly failed to gather and provide in response to the *Democrat-Gazette's* July and August FOIA requests. Additionally, the prosecutors' investigation should position them to determine whether Pederson, Schook, Choate, or Sharp was guilty of any criminality related to the audits' findings. With all of that in mind, I began to feel somewhat optimistic that as a result of this inquiry, UA System trustees and Bobbitt would respond and demonstrate, through both words and actions, the commitment to public accountability that had been missing as this scandal roiled.

A few days later, I learned from UA employees who worked or had business to conduct on the executive floor of the Admin Building that there was unusual activity occurring around the chancellor's office suite. One by one, members of the Advancement division's leadership team were being paraded in and out of the chancellor's office every half-hour or so. The reason, some quickly learned, was to be questioned about what Gearhart had said at the University Advancement Cabinet meeting on January 14th. However, the division heads were not there to meet with the county prosecutor; instead, the chief inquisitor was Varady. He was accompanied by a lawyer from Mitchell-Williams, the law firm representing Gearhart.

According to two of the individuals interviewed, Varady told them that System President Bobbitt had instructed him to investigate my allegations about the January 14th meeting. Those individuals told me that Varady asked them a series of questions, with Gearhart's personal legal counsel occasionally asking them to clarify certain responses. "There was an air of mystery" about the purpose of the interviews, one participant later told me. "Supposedly, it was for Bobbitt's benefit but [Gearhart's own lawyer] was there."

I had no trouble confirming the report. On Saturday, I sent Bercaw an email to share that information. It seemed to me that the interview location—the chancellor's own conference room, which adjoined Gearhart's personal office—and the presence of one of Gearhart's personal attorneys would have a chilling effect on participants' candor. After all, why would an employee in that situation put himself or herself at risk by validating the claims of a colleague who had been fired four weeks previous?

Shortly thereafter, Bercaw and Hatcher began meeting with some of those who were present for the January 14th meeting. Each person was accompanied by Varady or another UA lawyer. Gearhart, of course, also had his own lawyer present when he met with the two prosecutors. For some of those meetings, a third person was present for the questioning: Robert Cessario, an agent with the FBI. His supposed role was to help Bercaw and Hatcher understand some of the technical financial processes and terminology that might come up in the course of the interviews.

It would take Bercaw and Hatcher about two and half months to conduct and complete the four-part investigation that legislators had charged them with. However, about halfway through their effort, I began to get concerned. I heard through several friends on campus that the prosecutors still had not contacted some of the January 14th witnesses. By that point, I had already been interviewed by Bercaw and Hatcher a second time and had delivered over 100 pages of email and documents that substantiated the inadequacy of Wyrick's FOIA response and the atmosphere in which he had pursued the assignment. I had also told the prosecutors that Wyrick's limited response was a residual effect of Gearhart's orders in January and beyond related to

FOIAs and the news media. Furthermore, Renea Dillard had told prosecutors about the shredding episodes (without Varady present; apparently he didn't know she was on the prosecutors' interview list), which would have added further validation to my assertions. I didn't know how to interpret the failure to interview all of the January 14th witnesses. Did that signal that the prosecutors had heard enough to confirm my account of the meeting? Or, more disturbing, did it indicate that they didn't want to hear anything more?

Chapter 15

DON'T ASK, DON'T TELL

The fall of 2013 was not kind to UA. While the reverberations of the audit report and the legislative hearing no doubt troubled university administrators and trustees, of greater concern to most Arkansans was the performance of UA's football team under new head coach Bret Bielema. After starting the season with three wins, the Razorbacks would lose their next (and last) nine games as autumn arrived in Fayetteville. Bielema's performance and leadership, not Gearhart's, were of greater interest to the UA faithful.

Still, the sports pages were not the only place where disconcerting headlines appeared. Throughout the fall, the *Democrat-Gazette* and, to a lesser extent, *Arkansas Times* featured stories and commentary that raised questions about UA's leadership and management. In an editorial titled, "Steady as She Sinks," Paul Greenberg wrote:

> [T]here's no longer any denying the mare's nest that's called administration at [UA]. The secrecy, the backbiting, the scapegoating, the conflicts and confusions, the screwed-up accounting....It's all coming out, and it sounds like there's a lot more where that came from.

In his opinion blog, the *Times'* Max Brantley began referring to Wyrick as "Brother Honky," the nickname Wyrick himself twice ascribed to UA Alumni Association head Graham Stewart but which Wyrick later claimed was his own appellation; apparently Brantley wanted Wyrick to experience what it really felt like to publicly wear the label.

A few stories were particularly troublesome for anyone who cared about UA's credibility and accountability. Just two months after Chris Wyrick issued a declaratory news release announcing he had balanced Advancement's budget "primarily" through austerity measures and budget cuts, *Democrat-Gazette* reporter Bill Bowden discovered that, in reality, it took a previously undisclosed $4 million transfer from UA's centrally held reserves to accomplish the feat.

> A July 25 news release about the balanced budget didn't mention the $4 million transfer. When asked about the omission in the news release, Vice Chancellor for Advancement Wyrick responded by email: "I did not write the release therefore do not feel I am the correct person to offer a response."

It was a disingenuous reply: according to UA's online news archives, Wyrick was both quoted extensively in the July news release and was listed in it as the lead contact for reporters seeking elaboration. Emails showed he reviewed and approved the release and insisted on issuing it despite staff concerns that reporters and donors would expect specificity about revenues and expenses—details he was unwilling to provide. Bowden's article about the $4 million transfer (which represented nearly 30 percent of Advancement's total revenues) also explained the auditors' findings that in June, UA had once again attempted to book a non-existent accounts receivable—this one for $3.2 million—in order to eradicate the division's ongoing deficit.

The *Democrat-Gazette* followed that story with the first of several news reports over the next few months that explored the validity and possible effect of Gearhart's January instructions to Denise

Reynolds to "get rid of it" and "don't create any more" documents. Shortly after the legislative hearing, reporter Lisa Hammersly asked me what evidence I had to substantiate Gearhart's directive beyond the university's failure to provide budget updates in response to FOIA requests. I rummaged through my computer files and found Reynolds' email to Pontious and me, the one prefaced with an instruction to delete it after reading, in which she compared her request for secrecy to the behavior of fictional secret agent James Bond. I copied the message, which Pontious and I received three weeks after the January 14th session with Gearhart, and sent it to Hammersly. I also agreed to be interviewed about it, saying that it exemplified the change in behavior that resulted from Gearhart's outburst.

Hammersly's article appeared under the front-page headline, "'Delete After Reading,' UA Budget Officer Emailed."

> An email sent Feb. 6 to two administrators of the deficit-plagued fundraising unit of the University of Arkansas at Fayetteville told the recipients to "Please delete after reading," records show. The sender, the Advancement division's budget officer, Denise Reynolds, said Friday that the electronic message had nothing to do with a disputed January meeting at which Chancellor G. David Gearhart is accused of directing officials to destroy and stop creating budget documents… Asked why the electronic message opened "Please delete after reading," Reynolds responded by email: "I don't specifically recall, but I was attempting to gather information for a monthly spreadsheet that was routinely updated." Asked about the reference to James Bond, she wrote: "This was simply an attempt to be humorous." Asked if she had deleted her own Feb. 6 email or saved it, Reynolds responded: "I deleted it."

Another Hammersly story ("Records Show Gearhart Halted Group Meetings") told of Laura Villines' January 25th email on Gearhart's behalf in which he cancelled all future meetings of the University Advancement Cabinet. The story also quoted UA spokesman Mark Rushing as initially telling Hammersly he would not respond to questions about the email "no matter how sensational the allegations may be." However, he changed his mind later in the day, writing that Gearhart cancelled the meetings "in the interests of using his time most appropriately" through separate meetings with each of the eight members of the Advancement leadership team.

In August, Gearhart cancelled another meeting, this one involving himself and legislative auditors, according to a story that reporter Bill Bowden broke in mid-October. As Bowden explained, prior to the completion and release of the Advancement audits, the chancellor wanted Roger Norman, the head of Legislative Audit, to interview him. The session would be in addition to those Gearhart had already had with UA System auditors, who had been assigned responsibility for examining Advancement's budget management processes as part of the larger joint auditing assignment. Norman agreed to meet with Gearhart a few days later in Fayetteville. However, Norman soon learned that Gearhart planned to have Pederson and Schook accompany him. In response, Norman emailed the chancellor:

> Our purpose is to interview you, not to discuss the [pending] report with other individuals at this time. Once the report is completed, Legislative Audit will be available to meet with Don Pederson, Jean Schook, or other university officials at the exit conference or subsequently to discuss the report. Therefore, I need clarification on the meeting Thursday. The [Legislative Audit] Division would like to meet with you alone....If that is not possible, I do not see a need to meet.

Gearhart responded by saying thanks, but no thanks.

> My thinking for the meeting was to answer any questions your team might have of me. [UA Government Relations Vice Chancellor] Richard Hudson said the two of you talked and agreed that you really don't have any questions of me. Therefore, I agree that a meeting is not necessary.

After reviewing copies of the FOIA'd email exchange in October, Bowden wrote that he attempted to reach Gearhart to ask about the cancellation. "As I have said previously, it is not appropriate to comment while the audit is still open and the prosecutor is doing his work," Gearhart replied in an email. His refusal to explain, two months after the joint audits were completed, why he didn't want to be interviewed without Pederson and Schook present was puzzling. It suggested that his decision might be related to matters of concern to prosecutors or legislators.

Or to trustees, as a little-known backstory to Gearhart's request for a meeting reveals. On a late Saturday afternoon in early August, Gearhart sent an email to Jacob Flournoy, the UA System's director of Internal Audit. At the time, Flournoy was leading the review of Advancement's financial management and practices as part of the joint audit with Norman's office. The message read:

> Jacob: One thing I meant to bring up at our meeting [on August 1] is the fact that no one ever asked to interview me? Neither the System or legislative auditors. Seems rather bizarre that they would not want my perspective as CEO. Any explanation?

Flournoy disagreed with Gearhart's claim that he had not been interviewed. He responded the following afternoon with a courteous, detailed, 400-word recitation of the dates, times, and purposes of his phone calls and meetings with Gearhart: February 25th. April 16th. June 27th. July 16th. August 1st. He also indicated that as part of those interviews, Gearhart had provided him with "advice on who to interview and areas that needed to be addressed. You have also provided your perspective on the draft findings [of the audit] and other recommendations."

Gearhart disputed Flournoy's response, despite the documentation the veteran UA System official provided to substantiate it. Within an hour, the chancellor provided his own account of what had, and had not, transpired:

> Mr. Flournoy: My recollection is different than yours. I do not ever remember being asked for a list of people to interview. I certainly never received a formal request and have no evidence of a response.

> I was never asked a single question from you, your auditors or legislative auditors on my perspective of what happened. I was never interviewed directly by your staff conducting the audit, specifically on the cause of the deficit, or by Mr. Norman's staff. That just seems very odd to me.
>
> Probably more than anyone else, I have the most knowledgeable perspective on the causes of the Advancement deficit, yet neither team [of auditors] ever reached out to me for those perspectives during the entire audit.
>
> You will recall that I asked you some weeks ago why I had not been contacted. You did not know. I'm not understanding how your audits can be complete having never directly interviewed the chancellor about causes and effects.
>
> I would be pleased to meet with both teams at a time convenient if you believe it relevant to your findings. Thank you.

In response, Flournoy expressed "regret we are in disagreement" but did not back away from his assertions about the meetings and conversations that had taken place. Flournoy said he would set up another meeting for Gearhart, this one with Norman and his auditors present as well as Flournoy and his audit team. He did so, scheduling it for August 8th to accommodate Gearhart. But as the *Democrat-Gazette's* Bill Bowden reported three months later, Gearhart, the person who professed to have the "most knowledgeable perspective about the causes of Advancement's deficit" and the man who asserted he had "never been asked a single question" by auditors, would not agree to be interviewed without Pederson and Schook present.

In reviewing the email exchanges myself a year later (I obtained them through a public records request), I spotted something that I had not previously seen reported. At 8:37 a.m. on August 7th, Norman informed Gearhart that the auditors "hope to be able to conduct the exit conference [with UA] next week...The report will be presented to the Legislative Joint Auditing Committee on Friday, September 13 at 9 a.m." Norman's information arrived around the same time that day as when Gearhart would have seen my email to him and Wyrick—the one laying out the procedures for gathering emails and documents related to Tracie Dungan's lengthy July 22nd FOIA regarding Advancement. A couple of hours later, the lawyers and I received Gearhart's carefully worded profession of respect for the FOIA law, his rejection of the record-gathering plan, and his designation of Wyrick as the person to take over the assignment. Looking back, I wondered whether his decisions that day were influenced by a spike in angst over what he knew could be revealed in the report, the release of which he now knew was imminent. It might explain why, two weeks later, Wyrick claimed he still had not talked to Gearhart about finally responding to Dungan's FOIA request because "he's preoccupied with the audit." A year later, as I read the erratic, accusatory, and provocative language in his email exchanges with Flournoy and Norman, it reminded me of the more public behavior he had exhibited toward me at his late-August news conference and at the September 13th legislative hearing. I took a bit of comfort in knowing I was not the only person whose veracity or character Gearhart attacked or recast when they said something the chancellor didn't want to believe or acknowledge.

In November, the Legislative Auditing Committee once again changed the date of its next public hearing on the Advancement audits. The committee wanted Choate and Sharp to testify and December 13th worked for both of them as well as for the committee and staff. Meanwhile, Prosecutor Bercaw was still interviewing individuals related to the four issues he had been asked to investigate.

For me, the events of the past year had been disconcerting, to say the least. In the summer of 2012, about the time the Advancement deficit was uncovered, Marcia and I seriously thought we would stay in Northwest Arkansas for the rest of our careers. We would likely retire around 2020 at the end of the UA's nascent capital campaign, spending summers and holidays back in Maine and the rest of the year in Fayetteville. We had made wonderful friends in the region, many of whom we considered extended family. And Marcia was loving her job as principal of St. Joseph Catholic School.

However, by the time Choate was reassigned, we had changed our minds about that plan. Like most everyone else on campus, I expected Gearhart to conduct a national search for a new vice chancellor for Advancement. Pontious would have been the most qualified internal candidate, and even though UA and Gearhart had a history of promoting from within, I didn't think Gearhart would want someone so closely associated with Choate professionally and personally. I didn't consider myself a possibility; I lacked the big-time fundraising experience necessary to raise a billion dollars. Rather than risk staying on with a new vice chancellor who might not be as supportive and strategically simpatico as Choate had been, Marcia and I agreed that we'd consider a professionally superior possibility if and when one came along. Three did, between late November of 2012 and June of 2013: I had applied for senior vice presidencies at Arizona, Iowa and Marquette and was a finalist at all three. But now, as a result of being fired, my options suddenly were quite limited. I looked into other higher ed positions that would be more lateral moves than what I had already pursued. However, the taint of UA's scandal and my high-profile association with it made it difficult to attract interest. "You've got a great track record," an executive search consultant told me, "but unless the Arkansas thing blows over soon and you're vindicated, people are going to Google you and the scandal's going to come up."

Now, with Thanksgiving approaching, my day-to-day routine had changed dramatically from what it had been three months earlier. Weekdays consisted of driving Marcia to work (just for the fun of it) at seven a.m., spending the morning reading and hyper-caffeinating in a coffee shop somewhere away from campus, getting dinner ready, and reviewing my UA emails and documents. In addition to my own computer files, I had copies of all the documents I had received and processed in response to FOIAs. I was hopeful I might find something that would be of further help to the only remaining parties that could help clear my name: the prosecutors, the Legislative Auditing Committee, and the Arkansas news media.

On December 12th, the day before legislators were going to meet to continue their review of the Advancement audits, Deputy Prosecutor Bercaw issued his report in the form of a 14-page letter to his boss, John Threet. He prefaced his findings by recapping the scope of the assignment and listing the names of 17 individuals he and fellow deputy prosecutor Hatcher had interviewed. That list confirmed my earlier suspicions: they did not interview everyone who attended the January 14th meeting. Aside from Gearhart and me, the only attendees the prosecutors spoke with were Pontious, Reynolds, Graham Stewart, and Kris Macechko. Bercaw and Hatcher did not include four others who were present when Gearhart issued his directives: Mark Power, Melissa Banks, Judy Schwab, and Laura Villines. Granted, Schwab and Villines were not on the list of attendees that Gearhart's lawyer provided to Bercaw in September; however, they were on the list that I provided to the two prosecutors.

Also missing from the list of interview subjects was UA attorney Scott Varady. I had emphasized that Varady, if asked directly, could verify several aspects of my account related to the mishandling of FOIAs over the course of 2013. Varady's name did appear in the report but only as someone with whom Bercaw and Hatcher had "frequent contact" as they conducted their work. Reading that they chose not to interview him as a witness, I saw an early signal that I would be disappointed with the findings presented in the upcoming pages.

To no surprise, the prosecutors concluded that the duplicate $2,050 reimbursement to Choate was an administrative error on Joy Sharp's part, as one disbursement had gone to Choate directly and the other to the vendor who provided the service. Prosecutors also agreed that at the time of the error, Choate was due over $7,700 in reimbursements for other university expenditures he had personally covered.

Bercaw's findings regarding Sharp's mishandling of the $1.3 million Tyson donation were less clear-cut. The prosecutors explained how Sharp prepared a payment authorization, obtained Pederson's authorization to submit it to the UA Foundation, and received a check a few days later. The paperwork and check all listed the proper fifteen-digit account indicating that the money was for a restricted purpose (construction funds to help pay for the Jean Tyson Child Development Study Center on campus). However, when Sharp deposited the check with the university's cashier's office, she provided a substantially different account number, one whose funds could be used for unrestricted purposes. A year earlier, in her October 19th assessment, Jean Schook had labeled this move an apparent "intentional effort" and "misdirection of funds" on Sharp's part. Sharp's response was that it was simply a mistake.

In their report, prosecutors accepted Sharp's admission, saying they were "not persuaded that this transaction was an intentional effort to cover the deficit in Advancement. There still would have been a deficit in Advancement, just a smaller one." Plus, they said, "there was no personal benefit to Ms. Sharp from the transaction." I found those conclusions to be peculiar, given the situation at the time the redirection of funds occurred. In May of 2012, no one other than perhaps Sharp herself knew that Advancement was, as auditors later discovered, $1.6 million in the red as the end of the fiscal year approached. By depositing the Tyson funds into an unrestricted account, that shortfall was reduced to a much more manageable $300,000, with time remaining to eradicate that—as Sharp attempted to do at the end of June, when she submitted multiple requests to the UA Foundation for funds in $100,000 increments that, to her shock, the Foundation rejected. It was only after the Foundation's "freeze" that

UA discovered that Sharp had mishandled the Tyson money. True, she didn't pocket any money, which seemed to be the only measure of fraud that prosecutors and UA applied. But it's hard to argue she didn't benefit from her action; she was able to maintain her budget director's job and paycheck only until, with no other options available, she confessed her mismanagement of funds to Choate.

The report also found no criminality related to the university's use of accounts receivables to temporarily balance Advancement's books. However, it did fault Pederson and Schook's attempts to justify the practice. Prosecutors pointed out that the "available literature" Schook had cited at the legislative audit hearing did not support the accounting tactic she employed to even out Advancement's annual revenues and expenses. They also noted an obvious flaw in Schook's approach: intentionally or not, her method of washing out shortfalls by booking a comparable amount in accounts receivable concealed the reality that a deficit existed. Furthermore, in light of the way deficits were accumulating—rising to $3.2 million as of June 30, 2013—"sooner, rather than later, the amount of the accounts receivable entries (and the deficit) would have been larger than the amount expected to be received from the University Foundation for a full year." In short, it was unacceptable to use the accounts receivable maneuver to balance Advancement's books, as it camouflaged Advancement's true finances for anyone who looked at the end-of-year books.

Prosecutors also determined that Joy Sharp violated university policies, though not state law, in authorizing her sister Betty to approve transactions on Joy's behalf. Pederson's office had okayed the designation, which resulted in "a serious violation of internal control," something that was not confined solely to oversight of the Sharp sisters.

Prosecutors labeled the fourth and final matter of their investigation "FOIA Issue." After explaining the root of the request—testimony at the September 13th hearing—Bercaw wrote that "if anyone did perjure themselves at the hearing, jurisdiction would properly lie in Pulaski County as the hearing took place in Little Rock." With that, the report avoided any reference whatsoever to the question disputed by Gearhart and me: did the chancellor tell Advancement's budget director, in front of eight others on January 14, 2013, to get rid of a budget document and instruct her not to create any more?

Instead, the report focused only on my assertion that UA withheld FOIA'd documents and destroyed payment authorization documents that auditors described as missing. The only exploration of the January 14th meeting dealt with whether Reynolds' budget document was subject to an outstanding FOIA request at the time. In their report, prosecutors said it wasn't.

> The document was clearly a monthly update of the Advancement division's budget and should be characterized as a budget activity report. The documents requested were for the period between January 1, 2012, and June 30, 2012. The report handed out at the meeting was for December 2012, outside the time frame of the request.

As for the missing payment authorization forms, Bercaw wrote:

> [T]here were conflicting statements given by witnesses as to the disposition of [UA] Foundation payment authorization forms held within the Advancement division....We did not find evidence that the Foundation payment authorization forms were disposed of with the intent to frustrate the audit or to frustrate any FOIA requests.

This second part didn't surprise me, as it narrowly looked at the question of whether the payment authorizations had been destroyed specifically for the purpose of concealing them from auditors and FOIA requests. But that had never been my point. When I brought up the shredding at the September legislative hearing, I was responding to the claim that Joy Sharp was responsible for destroying the payment authorizations that auditors said were missing. That is what the auditors indicated they had been led to believe, and Gearhart reiterated the point during his legislative testimony. But as Renea Dillard reported to Norman and me (and, apparently, to

Bercaw and Hatcher), it was Reynolds who was responsible for the documents' disappearance; she specifically instructed Dillard and others on what to keep and what to destroy just days after Gearhart called for the audits. My remarks to legislators about shredding were in the context of UA's misrepresentation of facts about payment authorizations that auditors incorporated into their reports.

However, I was astonished by prosecutors' conclusions regarding FOIA'd documents. Setting aside the question of Gearhart's perjury, Bercaw and Hatcher had applied the wrong part of the January 10th FOIA request mentioned in their report to determine whether the budget document Gearhart said to "get rid of" was part of an outstanding public records request. The prosecutors cited a paragraph in the FOIA that asked for budget documents related to a six-month period in 2012, and correctly determined that the document Reynolds gave to Gearhart and the rest of us was produced outside of that time period. But it was the preceding paragraph in the FOIA request that actually applied to the budget document:

> We ask for detailed, complete, line-by-line budgets of Advancement and its units--that go beyond the framework of total salaries, total wages, total fringes, total M&O and grand totals—for Fiscal Years 2011, 2012, and 2013 (as the latter stands now).

The document Reynolds tried to share on January 14th—a budget report, dated December 31, 2012, that presented the most recent compilation of budgets for Advancement and its subunits—met the description of Advancement's Fiscal Year 2013 "as the latter stands now."

In addition, Bercaw and Hatcher failed to consider a similar FOIA request, this one filed by Lisa Hammersly on January 11th. She asked for "copies of documents indicating where the Advancement division's budget stands, including for each of its arms, including Development." On that same day, she wrote to Gearhart and Pederson to tell them that she was working on a story about Advancement's budget and that she had contacted me for information. She wanted to interview each of them but they both declined, in writing. (Pederson directed her back to me for answers.)

Those two public records requests were among the outstanding FOIAs that Bill Kincaid and I discussed with Gearhart and Pederson on Tuesday, January 15th in the Chancellor's office. As was our routine, Bill and I had gathered potentially relevant documents from various campus sources. The documents we had been given did not include Reynolds' budget breakdown from our Advancement Cabinet meeting with Gearhart the day before. However, at the time of our meeting on the 15th, Kincaid and I were focused on the documents we had been given, rather than on what might be missing. When it comes to handling FOIA requests, UA operates on an unreliable self-policing honor system, one that can be abused by someone with something to hide.

On Thursday, January 17th, Hammersly sent me a long list of questions about Advancement. After receiving them, I forwarded the request to Pederson and asked that he and I discuss them the following morning. As we had been doing on a regular basis, the next day he provided his answers and, with his permission and encouragement, I tweaked them as necessary to put them in layperson's language. In that situation, as in all involving Advancement's finances, Pederson signed off on the responses before they were given to the reporter.

Though several of Hammersly's questions were complex, one was simple and straightforward: "Is the Denise Reynolds Dec. 15 budget document the most recent FY2013 working budget for Advancement?" (That document broke down the division's and subunits' revenues and expenses as of November 30, 2012.) Having conferred with Pederson earlier in the day, I answered, "Yes." It was a failure to acknowledge the existence, at least on January 14th, of an updated version that Reynolds attempted to distribute in Gearhart's office. I was uncomfortable with that statement but, having not received the updated budget summary in response to recent FOIAs, I believed the hard copies and electronic version of that report had indeed been deleted in keeping with Gearhart's instruction to "get rid of it."

I had documented the inadequacy of these responses for Bercaw in November. I gave him a 155-page packet of emails and attachments that related to FOIA requests about Advancement's budget, the deficit, and organizational changes. I provided a five-page summary index explaining the relevance of each section to UA's handling of FOIAs since the disclosure of the Advancement deficit. In light of that documentation, I was stunned that Bercaw limited his investigation of FOIA compliance to one question and did so by erroneously aligning a single aspect of one public records request with Reynolds' January 14th revoked budget handout.

The Legislative Auditing Committee was scheduled to discuss Bercaw's report the day after it was issued. On the morning of the hearing, I sent an email to Audit Division Director Norman and Deputy Auditor Kim Williams, pointing out Bercaw's citation and application of the wrong section of the January 10th FOIA:

> I am hopeful that you will bring this to the attention of the committee chairs and the committee itself during today's hearing. Furthermore, it should keep open the question of whether or not the chancellor's directive to "get rid of" that document was a violation of Arkansas' FOIA law. The prosecutor's error in applying the wrong paragraph (cited in his report) when reaching his conclusion should result in the committee setting aside that particular finding until it can be revised.

In my closing, I added another request, which I hoped they would share with the legislative committee:

> I also respectfully request that you ask the Pulaski County prosecutor to investigate the conflicting statements made to the Legislative Audit Committee on September 13 regarding what Chancellor Gearhart said to the Advancement division's leadership team on Jan. 14. This matter is important to the credibility of the investigation, the management and governance of the university, the

> taxpayers and tuition payers, and to the reputations of Chancellor Gearhart and me.

The afternoon before the hearing, Marcia and I drove south to Little Rock, a three-hour drive. We planned to meet Brad and Julie Choate for dinner that evening at a Chinese restaurant. We hadn't seen them in months. Once together, we exchanged updates on children, grandchildren, and our mutual friends back in Fayetteville. We of course talked about the prosecutor's report and the next day's hearing. Brad summarized the key points he was planning to make, and the four of us speculated about what Joy Sharp and Gearhart would say. I had not prepared testimony but expected to be asked questions, based on the committee's request that I return. We also wondered how aggressive the committee members would be as a result of Gearhart's belligerent responses at the last hearing, Pederson and Schook's strident defense of their unorthodox accounting practices, and the media scrutiny and revelations that had occurred since the committee's September 13th meeting. Who else would testify? Would Wyrick be asked why he withheld the documents and video that had been part of the *Democrat Gazette's* July 22nd public records FOIA? Would Joy actually show up?

Marcia and I stayed at the same hotel at which the Choates were staying. In the morning, we met in the lobby to share the seven-mile ride to the State Capitol campus. Outside the Multi-Agency Complex, where the hearing would be held, we spotted Joy and Betty Sharp. The four of us greeted them, sharing hugs. We all walked together into the "Big MAC" and took the elevator up to Room A. Across the lobby outside the hearing room, we saw the UA cortege of Gearhart, Richard Hudson, System spokesperson Ben Beaumont, trustee John Goodson, and others. Joy and Betty took seats a far distance away from that group while Marcia and I went directly inside the hearing room. The Choates were already in there, with Brad restlessly motoring around the room. I checked in with auditor Kim Williams to make sure she and Norman had passed along my email about the mistakes in the prosecutor's report. They had, she said, adding that it was likely I would be asked to elaborate on it.

Shortly, Senate Co-chair Bryan King called the committee to order, and the four of us, plus the Sharps, took seats in the public gallery. King led the committee through quick action on several reports and other routine items of business. Seven minutes into the hearing, he turned control of it over to Representative Kim Hammer, who had presided at the September 13th discussion of the audit reports.

Hammer reminded committee members why they were once again taking up the audits. "First of all, you have the report from last time. It was left 'open.' We did not file it," he explained. "The content of that was referred to the prosecuting attorney up in the county that the U of A resides in. And that report came out yesterday.

"As we left the meeting last time, there were requests from members of the committee to extend an invitation to Ms. Sharp and also to Mr. Choate to come before the committee....Are Ms. Sharp and Mr. Choate in the audience today? Would you raise your hand? OK. We're going to have you come up here in just a minute."

But first, Hammer had an introduction to make.

"Committee members, we've been asked to give Mr. John Goodson, a U of A trustee, an opportunity to come and address the committee....After that, I'm going to invite Ms. Sharp and Mr. Choate to come up. We will give them a chance to make a statement....And then, committee members, we're going to open it up for questions, either of them or of anyone else from the previous meeting.

"Mr. Goodson, thank you for being here today," Hammer said. "State your name, and introduce yourself for the record."

"My name is John Goodson. I live in Texarkana, Arkansas, and I serve on the University of Arkansas Board of Trustees."

No introduction was necessary. Every politician, lawyer, and court watcher in Arkansas knew John Goodson. He was a heavyset man in his mid-50's with white hair, and his slow Southern drawl bespoke his ties to the small city that literally straddles the Texas-Arkansas border. Goodson was known for many things: the multimillion-dollar fees he'd collected as a class-action lawyer; his long history of giving and raising money for Democratic political candidates and, more recently, a few Republicans; and the public disclosure in January 2011 of more than $99,000 worth of jewelry, trips, coats, and gadgets he had given the previous year to Courtney Henry, a married appellate court judge who, after her midyear election to the Arkansas Supreme Court, was divorced by her husband, freeing her to quietly marry Goodson a year later.

Certainly a divisive figure in the minds of many, Goodson was taking the lead in yet another controversy—this time on behalf of the accused, not the accuser. The UA System Board of Trustees had decided that the court-savvy Goodson, not Board Chair Jane Rogers, would testify and respond to the committee's questions. Rogers, the only woman in years to serve on the ten-member board, sat nearby and observed.

"Do you solemnly swear and affirm that the testimony you are about to give is the truth, the whole truth, and nothing but the truth?" asked Hammer.

"I do," Goodson answered.

"Go ahead and share what's on your heart and mind, sir."

Goodson began by establishing his *bona fides* as a representative of the University of Arkansas. His father was a UA graduate. His two sisters were graduates. His wife was a graduate. He was a graduate. And within a few months, his daughter would be a UA graduate.

"As a member of the Board of Trustees, I would like to thank the ladies and gentlemen of Legislative Audit and this legislative committee for their actions in this matter.... We have accepted every single recommendation that Mr. Norman and his folks made. We're in the process of implementing every recommendation that Mr.

Norman made. And as a result of that, the University of Arkansas Fayetteville campus is a better institution.

"I came today to let y'all know firsthand that we've heard you loud and clear." With that short acknowledgment, Goodson the lawyer began to redirect the topic of conversation.

"What concerns me is that over the past year that we've been dealing with this matter is, all of the good that's going on at the Fayetteville campus has been overshadowed. As you walk across that campus, you see students that are energized, that are happy to be there. It's a great place of learning. It's got numerous construction projects that are underway.

"You may like Dave Gearhart," he said, stressing the verb. "You may *not* like Dave Gearhart. But these items in this matter"—meaning the campus climate he had just described, not the audits or accounting that were the committee's topics of the moment—"have been moving in a progressive state under his watch. I don't think it would be fair not to recognize his efforts and the good things that are going on at the Fayetteville campus.

"He could win a few more football games next year," Goodson added. "But that concludes my remarks. I sincerely appreciate you allowing me to speak today."

"Are you still willing to take questions?" Hammer asked, to clarify and possibly to get more specific answers regarding the board's response to the deficits and audits.

"Yes, that's what I said I'd do."

"OK," Hammer noted.

As Hammer was preparing to invite Choate and Sharp to the witness table, a committee member spoke up to steer the morning's proceedings in a different direction from what the committee co-chairs had planned.

"Mr. Chairman!" a voice yelled.

"Senator Sample?" Hammer was acknowledging the call of Senator Bill Sample. Sample had not previously involved himself publicly in the committee's review of the Advancement audits, possibly to avoid the appearance of a conflict of interest: his pest-control business had a contract with UA.

"Yes, Mr. Chairman. My question is for Mr. Norman," referring to Roger Norman, the legislative auditor seated nearby. "Mr. Norman, did you receive a copy of the prosecuting attorney's report?"

"Yes, sir," Norman replied. "We received that yesterday afternoon."

"Have you read it?" Sample continued.

"I read it last night. Yes, sir."

"Do you agree that the four questions forwarded to the prosecuting attorney were thoroughly investigated?"

"I was not involved in the investigation of the prosecuting attorney," Norman responded, recognizing the leading nature of Sample's question. "But based upon the comments in the letter, it appears he requested assistance of the FBI and other individuals. And from the contents of the letter, it looks like a thorough investigation."

"Were there any criminal charges made?"

"No, sir," Norman answered. "The letter says that Mr. Bercaw did not see anything criminal to file charges—"

"Did the prosecuting attorney find any intentional intent to mislead the auditors or anyone else?" Sample said, cutting off Norman before he could explain that the prosecutor recommended sending the issue of Gearhart's possible perjury to the county attorney in Pulaski County.

Hesitatingly, Norman replied. "That's what his letter states. That he did not."

"Mr. Chairman, I move that we accept this report as reviewed," Sample declared.

"Seconded!" Senator Linda Chesterfield quickly chimed in.

Hammer, the hearing's presiding officer, paused. Like most everyone else in the room, he expected the committee would spend the next several hours hearing testimony from Choate, Sharp, Goodson,

Gearhart, and others about the audits and prosecutor's findings; that was the plan. Only after completing the Q&A did he and most everyone else expect the committee to vote on whether or not to accept—to "close," in legislative parlance—the audit reports that were initially presented to the committee in September.

"We have a motion, it's seconded," Hammer announced. "Do we have any discussion to the motion?"

Representative Nate Bell spoke up.

"Mr. Chairman, in the previous meeting I requested that Audit forward to the prosecuting attorney my concerns related to Mr. Pederson's false representation to our auditors via his letter. I will go back to page A6 of the report where he signed a statement saying we have no knowledge of any allegations of fraud or suspected fraud affecting the entity received in communications with employees, former employees, analysts, regulators, or others that was signed at the exit conference on October 25th—"

"Point of order!" interrupted Sample. "He's not talking about the motion!"

Bell tried to respond. "Mr. Chair, my statement directly relates to the motion—"

Again, Sample interrupted with another parliamentary point of order.

"Representative Bell, hold a minute, please," Hammer instructed. "Senator Sample, I heard your point of order. Representative Bell, would you restate? And it has to be to the motion, please."

Bell, appearing frustrated and flustered by his fellow Republican's interruptions, continued. "Mr. Chair, the motion is based on the basis that no fraud occurred. There is legal evidence that fraud occurred. And I would appreciate the opportunity by the members of this committee to be heard!"

Senator Bryan King spoke up. "Mr. Chairman, we've had people come down here to testify about this matter who've had serious consequences—they've lost their job. They need to be heard before this report is accepted. I think it's doing an injustice to those people, and I think that we need to hear all sides of the story. I think to close this report at this time would be an injustice…to those who have suffered personally. I would ask for a 'no' vote on this motion."

Representative John Walker, one of the legislators who on September 13th had pushed to have additional testimony, asked for clarification: if Sample's motion passed and the report were closed, would that preclude Choate and Sharp from testifying? Would it keep committee members from asking questions of Goodson, Pederson, Gearhart, and me?

"It is my position as chair," Hammer explained, "that if you want to continue to discuss this… if you want to have a discussion with the people who came down here, and if you've any other questions, we need to defeat this motion so that we can go on and have the discussion."

"We haven't even heard the testimony!" added Representative Justin Harris. "Why would we approve this if we haven't even heard the testimony?"

Things were getting heated. Chesterfield, a Democrat who seconded Sample's motion, tried to assuage concerns. "There is nothing that would preclude this body from hearing anything it wishes to hear," she assured her colleagues. "There's nothing about this motion that would preclude that from happening."

At that point Hammer tried to flex in public the muscle that committee chairs usually exercise behind the scenes in order to persuade colleagues. "If we leave here and everything the committee wants to ask is limited or not asked, then all we've done is just left a cloud hanging over the university. I'd just as soon let the storm pass through myself if there's one coming. We'd just have a good, honest, thorough discussion about it.

"We have folks who have come down here at their own expense, on their own dime," Hammer continued. "The university's come down here, I guess at the expense of the university. And so I think we owe it to them—an honest forum in order to have discussion. So

I would appreciate that you vote the motion down."

Sample, continuing his fight, challenged his committee leader and colleagues.

"Members, we are wasting taxpayer dollars," he argued. "We asked the prosecuting attorney to do a job. He involved the FBI in his investigation. He came back with these results. Let's accept them and move on."

One final time, Hammer clarified that a "yes" vote would accept as complete the findings in the audit reports. "Any questions about the vote we are about to take? Seeing none, all in favor of the motion to file the report say 'aye.'"

Members voiced their votes, with Sample by far the loudest, drawing laughter.

"Any opposed?" Hammer asked. Opponents offered their "nays."

"I rule that the 'nays' have it," using the prerogative of the chair to interpret the outcome of voice votes. Sample, like many in the room, didn't agree with that interpretation and demanded a roll call of members. Norman, in his role as senior staff associate, then read off members' names one by one. Most everyone in the room silently kept score as each legislator offered his or her vote. Once the roll call was over, the results were obvious before they were formally announced. Moving his microphone aside, Hammer turned to Norman and whispered a remark that an audio recording of the hearing captured.

"I want to say, 'If there's no objection from the members, we're going to let them come and speak,'" intending to fulfill the assurances Chesterfield had offered. Norman acknowledged Hammer with a "Yeah" and, back on microphone, he announced the results.

"I have a vote of 21 to file and 13 no's." Sample had prevailed.

"The motion passes," Hammer declared. After a brief huddle with his co-chair, Bryan King, he continued. "Once a report has been filed, traditionally that concludes the conversation of it. It is the chair's desire that, subject to no objection, that we would go ahead and...give everybody an opportunity to speak. That would be the chair's intent.

"It is the chair's desire, subject to no objection, that we would let anybody who wanted to come and make a comment," he repeated, hoping that members would respect him, both as committee chair and as a colleague, and grant him that courtesy. It was a procedural request to allow testimony and discussion while adhering to the outcome that Sample's motion achieved. Under legislative rules, Hammer's request could be blocked if just one member objected. And one did.

"I object!" shouted Sample. Laughter followed, until those in the room realized Sample was serious.

Hammer paused, staring at Sample then looking down at his desk. Twenty seconds later, he conceded.

"Any other business?" he asked. "Any other business to come before this committee?"

King spoke up. "Mr. Chair, are we going to allow those people who have traveled up here to come speak before the committee or are we ending the committee meeting?"

"As much as it discomforts me, I'm going to adjourn the committee meeting." With that, Hammer, appearing frustrated and betrayed by several colleagues, rapped his gavel to close the hearing.

Free of protocol constraints, the room took on a chaotic buzz. Reporters chased the principals for explanation and reaction. Many in attendance, including legislators, were puzzled by the adjournment. Others chuckled at the parliamentary maneuvering that prevented Choate from speaking in the only forum available to him under his gag agreement with UA. The vote and Sample's objection precluded members from asking Gearhart, Pederson, Schook, me, and possibly others any questions in response to the disclosures and disputes offered on September 13th—the primary reason this hearing was scheduled.

The moves also kept trustee Goodson from having to answer questions under oath about the board's oversight of UA—i.e., its own handling, debate, and actions related to the Advancement deficit; its knowledge of Pederson and Schook's unorthodox accounting practices; the diversion of the Tyson donation in a manner that temporarily minimized, on paper, the size of Advancement's shortfall; and Gearhart's and Wyrick's involvement in withholding documents sought by reporters.

Sample, victorious and momentarily the center of attention, smiled broadly. Still seated at his desk, he looked toward Chesterfield, sitting in one of the two rows separating him from the observers' gallery, and conspicuously gave her a wink.

Amid the cacophony that filled the room, Hammer remained at his committee chair's seat, gathering his papers and likely anticipating the questions that the news media would soon ask him. Moments later, a member of the committee sidled up to him to reassure him. Though the hearing was over, Hammer's microphone remained on. The ambient noise in the room was too loud for anyone to notice the conversation over the public address system, but the committee's audio recording of the hearing—standard practice—remained active. It captured a telling exchange between the discouraged committee chair and an unidentified legislator.

First noting that he had voted with Hammer to block Sample's effort, the legislator shared his take on how the day's developments would play out.

"This makes it worse!" the lawmaker said. "There are going to be more conspiracy theories than the Kennedy assassination over this!"

"What else could I have done?" a dejected Hammer asked.

"Nothing," his colleague responded. "You did the right thing. Because the other people are going to have to answer. I mean, I think there's going to be a big outcry because this was obviously orchestrated. You did the right thing.

"There will be enough pressure that they'll bring them back at some point," the legislator continued. "I never thought that there was any stealing or fraud. I think they just didn't want you to know where they were spending—"

At that point Hammer's microphone was shut off, ending the recording—but not before capturing enough of the unidentified legislator's intent to interpret his assessment of the day's events. He didn't necessarily disagree with Gearhart's oft-repeated statement that neither Choate nor Sharp was guilty of "malfeasance, misappropriation or personal inurement"—Gearhart's careful and narrow definition of fraud, which he had proffered to justify his decision to reassign, not terminate, his two former close associates. Rather, the legislator felt that the university's attempts to conceal information and block testimony—on this day and over the past year since the Advancement deficit broke— was to avoid public scrutiny of how UA used its Foundation funds, particularly as they might relate to the travel and lifestyle that Gearhart and others enjoyed at the expense of donors' generosity. Along with the threat of legal consequences related to non-existent accounts receivable, perjury, and withholding public records, Gearhart and UA officials had legitimate reasons to worry about how public disclosure of perceived extravagances would hurt their relationships with legislators, benefactors, alumni, and taxpayers. Foolishly, they and their loyalists within the Legislative Auditing Committee thought that suppressing any more testimony under oath would protect the university from further fallout.

Chapter 16

GEARHARTGATE

After John Goodson had delivered his reassurances on behalf of the UA System Board of Trustees, he walked over to where Choate was seated in the public gallery. As Choate rose, Goodson extended his hand, lingering long enough for news photographers to capture the moment. "Thank you for your good work. We appreciate your service," Goodson said, according to Choate. "Thank you," Choate responded unenthusiastically, recognizing the awkwardness of the moment: clasping Goodson's palm with one hand while, in the other, holding a notebook whose cover photo depicted human bodies lying underneath a yellow school bus that bore UA's logo—Choate's metaphor for the treatment he felt he had received as Gearhart's fall guy.

Choate had prepared a lengthy statement that had been distributed to the committee early that morning—and was soon shared with UA officials by at least one committee member in advance of the hearing. Choate's statement included new details about his conversations with Gearhart, Pederson, and Schook about the deficit and Sharp's mismanagement. It also included dates and quotes regarding the professional and financial pressures Gearhart put on him to be quiet. Choate's statement also addressed mistakes in the audits that he said were based on misleading information provided by UA officials.

But Sample's parliamentary move squelched the opportunity. Choate recognized the strategy behind the move, later saying that UA officials "obviously had been working the politicians to pull that ploy to keep me from testifying." Feeling a combination of frustration, anger, and disgust, Choate again rose from his seat, grabbed his briefcase, and packed it with the notebook featuring the UA bus.

"I think I'm about done with this," he told *Arkansas Times* reporter Benji Hardy as they stood together in the hearing room. "People here aren't interested in the facts." Hardy quoted Choate further:

> "[Auditors] relied on some work done by one of the three people I can't disparage....It's just flat out in error. And I can prove it. I can prove it up there," he corrected himself, gesturing to the witness stand in front of the emptying committee room. "I can't prove it standing here."

That didn't matter to Senator Linda Chesterfield, who had seconded Sample's motion that effectively blocked any testimony other than Goodson's. "We don't have to hear both sides of the case... We're not a court," she explained to Hardy. Sample himself avoided explaining his motion and objections to the media until a few days later when he argued to Nic Horton of *The Arkansas Project*, a political blog, that House Co-chair Hammer, not he, should bear the blame for Choate's inability to address the committee.

Before Choate exited the hearing room, Senate Co-chair King caught up with him and apologized for the committee's actions. With reporters and onlookers present, King told them that he had read Choate's testimony and that he felt that it needed to be made public. King told the reporters that unlike Choate's gag agreement with UA, nothing prohibited him from giving them Choate's prepared remarks, which he did. Although Choate was precluded from elaborating on his planned testimony, at least his main points would be made public.

Standing apart from that scene, Julie Choate was in tears. "I don't understand what happened," she said to Marcia and me as Choate and King spoke. "Does this mean it's all over?"

"Believe me, this will backfire," I reassured her. "The media blowback will make the board and the committee look like they're all in cahoots."

"But so what?" Julie said. "What difference will that make if they're not going to do anything?" It was a good question, one I couldn't answer.

The four of us returned to the hotel where Marcia and I had left our car. A few minutes later, after exchanging regretful goodbyes, Brad and Julie began their drive back to Texas. We headed north to Fayetteville.

Media blowback did indeed occur, along with less vociferous outrage among members of the Arkansas General Assembly. In the weeks following the hearing, UA officials as well as their perceived accomplices on the Auditing Committee took plenty of heat for what Representative John Walker labeled Choate's "pre-ordained" silencing. When Max Brantley of *Arkansas Times* asked Walker if he felt the actions at the hearing were "a product of pressure" applied by UA, the veteran legislator didn't mince words: "I have absolutely no doubt about that....There are sacred cows in the state that you cannot touch. One of them is [UA] Fayetteville." As Brantley reported:

> The decision...deprived the committee of hearing all sides about the intent of those involved at UA, particularly management by Chancellor David Gearhart. "I had a number of questions to raise but was precluded from raising them," Walker said...."[N]obody could inquire to the extent of whether bad motivation was the cause of termination of Diamond and Choate....In this situation, we saw actual intent to conceal information. That's an ethical issue. It's of interest to the public."

Editorial writer Paul Greenberg of the *Democrat-Gazette* poked the university's trustees, "whose clearest response to Friday's hearing was to change the subject: from the university's all too clear failings to the achievements of its faculty and students."

> They weren't the subject of this hearing. But they can be used to distract the public's attention from what ought to be bothering the state's educators and taxpayers....Friday's hearing wasn't the first whitewash attempted in this long-running scandal. This one may have worked. For now.

Columnist John Brummett, also of the *Democrat-Gazette*, didn't accept the argument that Sample's motion and objection to discussion was "orchestrated," as Walker and others believed.

> I don't have anything particularly supportive to say about certain leading officials of the University of Arkansas in Fayetteville. I deplore the pattern of overspending in the school's fundraising office, not to mention the hesitance of responsible administrative parties to own up to it.
>
> But I am fairly certain that nobody strong-armed anybody to whitewash anything....The back story is that [trustee John Goodson], trained in settling matters, had gone to Senate President Pro Tem Michael Lamoureux to ask what the university might do to begin to move beyond this audit brouhaha. Lamoureux said the best thing would be for someone with the UA to act humbly, an apparent inability of Fayetteville officials. Goodson said he knew how to do that.

Brummett then summarized Sample's motion and the reasons the legislator had offered, followed by Senator Linda Chesterfield's profession that testimony and questioning could take place even after the committee "closed" the audit report. Brummett faulted what he described as a "huffy" and "out of sorts" committee chair, Kim Hammer, for unnecessarily shutting down the hearing; citing Chesterfield, Brummett related that Hammer could have considered other parliamentary counter-moves to keep the issue alive. But ultimately, Brummett wrote, it wasn't UA's strong-arming of committee members that kept Choate and Sharp from testifying. Rather, "legislators simply made a mess. Not as big a mess as the Fayetteville flagship campus made of its chronically overspending fundraising operation. But a mess nonetheless."

UA spokesman Mark Rushing denied to reporters that UA officials lobbied the committee to accept the audit report. (If Rushing was telling the truth, the lack of any lobbying was a radical departure from UA's typical approach to its legislative strategy.) Meanwhile, when a reporter asked Goodson if trustees had been lobbying to influence the hearing's outcome, the trial lawyer gave a qualified answer: "*I* wasn't."

John Deering, the *Democrat-Gazette's* award-winning editorial cartoonist, captured the essence of the hearing in a cartoon a couple of days later. His drawing depicted a 19th century American clipper ship, the "U of A Fayetteville" sailing on rough seas. The flag atop its main mast read, "Don't Ask, Don't Tell."

I remained disappointed and frustrated by Bercaw's report, particularly its section on UA's handling of public records requests. Along with citing the wrong paragraph of the *Democrat-Gazette's* FOIA—the one that applied to the budget document that Gearhart told Reynolds to "get rid of"—he made no attempt to address the complementary matter of Wyrick's mishandling of the newspaper's July 22nd records request. I went back and reviewed what I had turned over to Bercaw and Hatcher as evidence: 155 pages of documents that revealed how and perhaps why Wyrick acted as he had. Along with financial and organizational records that directly pertained to the public records request, I had provided email exchanges with UA and System lawyers about the FOIAs in question and about Gearhart's attitude toward complying with the July 22nd request. I also provided the "problem" video of Wyrick's June 20th staff meeting, which was among the "electronic records" covered by the FOIA but which Wyrick failed to turn over.

Through those documents and my interviews with prosecutors,

I thought I had clearly established for them a pattern of behavior, something that began on January 14th when Gearhart told Reynolds to "get rid of" the budget document and stop creating them. It's important to note that the document was never turned over to reporters until the following November, despite several follow-up FOIAs for budget records submitted in the nine months following the first request. Prosecutors had found no criminality because, they said, the budget document was eventually turned over to the media in a subsequent request. That was a strange rationalization; the document's relevance to the public interest was in January, when reporters were asking about Advancement's financial condition at the time. By the time it was turned over, its only value was that it proved, for the first time, that the document actually existed. How and why did the meticulous Reynolds, who had not provided it in response to other FOIAs in January, February, March and beyond, forget or lose track of it until prosecutors asked her, in late October, whether or not she did indeed "get rid of it"?

I decided to search for answers myself. With the audits accepted and the prosecutor's report filed, the materials Bercaw and Hatcher gathered during their investigation were now accessible to the public. The day of the legislative hearing, Bill Bowden of the *Democrat-Gazette* took a look at the files; two days later, his newspaper published a lengthy story based on the interview notes, focusing primarily on what Sharp, Choate, and Gearhart had said about each other. Many other important aspects of the investigation were left unreported.

On December 16th I submitted a FOIA request of my own, this one to District Prosecutor John Threet, asking for copies of his office's files from the investigation. I was invited to visit the Washington County Courthouse to view the records at the office itself to determine which ones I actually wanted copies of. When I arrived, I was led to a small room where a couple of interns from UA's law school were working. I was allowed to use a small table as I worked through several boxes of documents—a few thousand pages, at least—that Bercaw and Hatcher had accumulated during the course of their investigation. Hours later, when a clerk asked if there was anything I wanted copied, I was like a kid at a dessert buffet: "One of everything, please."

The contents were remarkable—and troubling. Among Bercaw's and Hatcher's notes were quotes from UA System Internal Audit Director Jacob Flournoy, candidly stating that Pederson and Schook "should have told Legislative Audit about [the] deficit and [the] reversed entry" that camouflaged the practice of booking non-existent accounts receivables. "There were reserves to cover [the] deficit," the notes cited him as saying, yet UA didn't use them for the very purposes for which they existed.

Along with the interviews regarding the deficit, the prosecutors' records included their notes from their interviews with me. They had listened to the recording of the September 13th Legislative Auditing Committee hearing, apparently comparing it with the more detailed accounts of the January 14th meeting with Gearhart that I provided to them. Their notes also made reference to the conference call the lawyers and I had on July 29th to discuss Gearhart's FOIA objections; Wyrick's delay in responding to that FOIA and his withholding of the June 20th video as well as budget and reorganization material that had been covered by the FOIA; and the shredding of payment authorization forms after the request for audits was announced. In addition, their notes included other items that I had shared that were not yet public but were relevant to any investigation of UA's compliance with Arkansas' public records law. They included the March 2013 instructions I received to stop sharing FOIA requests with Gloria Sutherland, Gearhart's executive assistant and the person who maintained his files (including many of the emails that Gearhart sent and received) and those of his executive committee. Based on prosecutors Bercaw and Hatcher's own records, clearly they had heard me share these points; I was anxious to see what their notes contained about how the others they interviewed had responded.

According to their records, Gearhart met with Bercaw and Hatcher on November 20th. The notes said he was accompanied by UA lawyer Scott Varady and by Marshall Ney, a lawyer with the Mitchell-Williams law firm that was the chancellor's personal legal counsel. Gearhart's statements included many factual errors regarding Advancement operations dating back to his days as the division's vice chancellor, such as claiming that someone else, not he, had promoted Joy Sharp to the budget director's position. He also said that when he was head of Advancement before Choate's arrival, Sharp didn't have budget management authority; instead, she was "more of a bill payer." Bercaw quoted Gearhart as saying that Sharp "didn't have [the] competence for making budget decisions"; that she was "apt to get confused from time to time when she worked for me"; and that he "wouldn't give Joy authority to make spending decisions." He made this claim, distancing himself from any responsibility for her promotion and performance despite an avalanche of financial and human resources records that contradicted those statements.

During his interview, he reiterated his reasons for not firing Sharp—"a loyal employee," he noted—and said that he asked for (and apparently received) the UA System Board of Trustees' permission, in November of 2012, to let both Sharp and Choate stay on the UA payroll through the end of the fiscal year on June 30, 2013. He also told prosecutors that the Board of Trustees "wanted to fire Pederson and Schook." If that was true, Gearhart obviously persuaded the governing board to change its mind.

As I sorted through the prosecutors' notes, I was most interested in how Gearhart would explain what transpired at the January 14th meeting. He disavowed having a close relationship with me and said that while I "made some good decisions," he thought I "wanted to spin things with the media." He also said I wanted to "create documents to explain things to the media." According to the notes, he told prosecutors that "Diamond came into the meeting talking about creating docs and was supportive of Choate." Gearhart said he "never gave a directive to destroy documents" but said "we were not going to create documents for the media." It was "not [a] discussion of FOIA," he said.

Gearhart went on to say that I didn't like him "to have contact with the media," an argument that contradicted the scores of email requests I possessed, in which I had asked him and his scheduler to consider interviews and media events. Additionally, Gearhart claimed that I "was providing info under the table" to the news media and that "a short time would elapse between a discussion [with Diamond] and the *Democrat-Gazette* asking for a FOIA." Gearhart and Wyrick had made similar claims at their August news conference following my termination. In doing so, they were accusing me of unethical behavior, something that, if it were true, would be a violation of all professional standards as well as my moral obligations to UA. In my own defense, I had provided prosecutors with emails, documents, dates, and times that disproved Gearhart's and Wyrick's assertions[1].

Following up on Gearhart's allegations, one of the prosecutors asked Gearhart about something I had mentioned during my own interview with them. In January, Gearhart had asked me to give reporter Chris Bahn's phone number to Don Pederson; he had said he wanted Pederson's staff to cross-reference the number with those of UA's deans and fundraisers to see if they could determine who might be leaking information to Bahn about the controversial gift tax idea. According to the investigators' notes, Gearhart said he "decided not to pull phone records." Based on his phrasing, he apparently didn't deny to prosecutors that he had made the request.

Denise Reynolds was also interviewed. According to Hatcher's notes, the session lasted two hours. Reynolds was critical of Sharp,

1 By the way, I invite any reporter, columnist, or blogger to "out" me if I ever leaked university information to you at any time prior to my termination on August 23rd. As I have stated all along, I openly and publicly provided reporters, legislators, and prosecutors relevant information about the audits, FOIA responses, and my reassignment and firing from UA only after I received my termination notice.

stating that Sharp began "stonewalling" her when Reynolds sought information. "Joy wouldn't give answers," despite Reynolds' asking her "about ten times." Reynolds explained that the decision to clean out storage units was to reduce storage costs, creating an annual savings of $3,600. She said the February "housecleaning" I had referred to at the September 13th legislative hearing was intended to "prevent ID theft" by disposing of old documents that included Social Security numbers and driver's license numbers. Responding to questions about shredding payment authorization forms (the documents that auditors said they were not given), Reynolds did not dispute giving Renea Dillard and others instructions to do so, assuming that the prosecutors' notes were accurate. Instead, Reynolds pointed out that UA was "not required to keep forms since they"—i.e., UA—"don't create [the] record." Rather, the UA Foundation does. (This was a point of contention between the university, auditors and prosecutors: in its written response to auditors, UA argued against the recommendation that it maintain copies of payment authorization forms as part of its new system of checks and balances, saying that it would create an unnecessary duplication of files. But there was another, unstated objection: maintaining its own copy of a payment authorization form would create a public record of whatever expense the private Foundation covered on UA's behalf. Such a record would be subject to FOIA requests and, depending on the nature of the expense, could be interpreted as extravagant or frivolous.)

Asked about the January 14th meeting, Reynolds was even more emphatic about what did and did not occur. She called the meeting "tense" because FOIA was the topic. (In his own interview, Gearhart said FOIA was not a topic at the meeting, according to prosecutors' notes.) She was also highly critical and accusatory of me personally and professionally. She said I was "vocal and confrontational" at the January 14th meeting and that the FOIA discussion that afternoon "went on for 42 minutes"—a curious claim, because that was exactly the same length of time that I was told my "woodshed" meeting with

Gearhart on January 24th had lasted. "Gearhart didn't say to get rid of it or anything like that," she reportedly told them. She said that Gearhart simply said not to create any more documents for reporters.

Remarkably, when one of the prosecutors asked Reynolds about the nature of the document Gearhart was holding during the disputed event, she said she didn't remember what the paper was. Reynolds told prosecutors that she would check her files and the meeting agenda to determine the nature of the document. Several days later, she produced it—the budget report for the month of December 2012. Only then—ten months after that budget document was first FOIA'd—did UA give it to reporters who had originally asked for it.

Continuing to sort through Bercaw's and Hatcher's notes, I found the ones from their interview with Kris Macechko, the Advancement division's former director of Constituent Services. Though no longer an employee, she had been accompanied by a university attorney for the interview, as had all of the individuals who met with the prosecutors except for Renea Dillard and me. Macechko had little to say about the January 14th meeting, according to the notes. She spoke of the gift tax discussion, which she had brought up as the first item on the meeting agenda. She reportedly said that "Diamond felt that more information was needed," referring to our explanation of what we would do now that the gift tax was off the table, while "Gearhart felt that all that was necessary had been given." She was correct; that was the extent of the exchange before we moved on to Reynolds and the agenda items regarding the budget.

Nothing in Bercaw's notes indicated what, if anything, Macechko might have said about the budget document. There was nothing noted about what Gearhart said or didn't say or that the meeting ended abruptly. However, two remarks of hers are cited later in the interview: One is that she "decided to retire after January 14th because of the ugliness between Gearhart and Diamond." The "ugliness" hadn't been on my part, she had told me.

In fact, her action months earlier supported that point. Shortly after hearing about my January 24th "woodshed" meeting with Gearhart, Macechko sent me the following brief email: "REMEMBER, you are doing a great job!!! [Husband] Mike and I appreciate your efforts more than you will ever know."

The other point she made to prosecutors was that Gearhart "told her on February 12th that Wyrick was being hired as the new vice chancellor." The next week, the 62-year-old Macechko surprised all of us by announcing she intended to retire in June.

In October, in the days following her interview at the prosecutor's office, the now-retired Macechko related her experience to several friends in Fayetteville. She told them that in addition to Bercaw, Hatcher, and one of UA's lawyers, another person sat in on the meeting: Robert Cessario, an FBI agent. Macechko recounted to friends how she had shared information about Advancement's history and inner workings covering the 22 years that she was affiliated with the division. She had also anticipated a question that addressed the possibility of perjury at the Legislative Auditing hearing: Did Gearhart say to "get rid of" the budget document Reynolds distributed in January? Being Gearhart's longtime associate and friend, she was reluctant but ready to answer truthfully, "Yes." But, as she explained to her friends, she wasn't given the opportunity.

"They never asked me!" she volunteered to me four months later, during a chance encounter at a neighborhood supermarket. The story she shared with me that day was virtually the same as the one that had circulated in Fayetteville in October. Her account was also consistent with what I found in the prosecutors' notes.

Graham Stewart, the associate vice chancellor for Alumni Affairs, was accompanied by UA attorney Bill Kincaid when prosecutors interviewed him in early November. At the time, Stewart was quietly awaiting word on whether he would be selected for a similar position at Vanderbilt University, where he was confident his new boss would never refer to him as "Brother Honky," as Wyrick had. He told the prosecutors that in the course of discussion about the gift tax idea, I brought up "responding to the press" about it. Stewart, according to Bercaw's notes, said that Gearhart later "got irritated and slammed hands down, [saying] Why do we have these documents. Get rid of them. I don't want to have any more meetings. Gearhart walked out. Not upset with Denise. Upset at John. Upset in general....Sensed frustration and not a directive."

Stewart also acknowledged the distribution of Reynolds' budget report, according to the notes, but they include no reference to any confrontation between Gearhart and me, just that Gearhart was angry about the presence of FOIA-able documents.

Bruce Pontious was interviewed by phone a month after he had abruptly left Arkansas to return to his native Ohio. Whether it was Pontious' lack of concern for his future employment or because no university lawyer was present to watch him, he was direct and forthcoming. According to Bercaw's notes, Pontious recalled the January 14th meeting this way:

> Reynolds presented a spreadsheet as a budget document that reflected [revenues and expenses through the end of December]. Gearhart wasn't in a good mood. Went into a tirade. Why do you still have these documents? [It represented] Reconciliation of budget. Didn't want information in writing. Pushed it back away and said get rid of them. Went into a tirade and said Brad fucked up. [Pontious was] shocked. [Gearhart] called the meeting to an end.

If Bercaw and Hatcher kept score about whether or not Gearhart said to "get rid of" the budget document, the results of the six interviews were three "Yes-he-dids" (Pontious, Stewart, and me), two "No-he-didn'ts" (Gearhart and Reynolds) and a "No-question-no-answer" (Macechko).

In graduate school we learned that if you want to understand perspective and intent, pay attention to your subjects' working papers. I found a revealing example of that as I foraged through the half-dozen reams of documents that I received from the District Prosecutor's office. Included was a marked-up copy of the report Bercaw had drafted after conducting his investigation. The handwritten edits reflected changes that it appeared he wanted a clerical assistant to make. A few of the modifications seemed to reflect suggestions that his colleague, Mieka Hatcher, sent to him in a separate email.

A couple of the revisions toned down some of the editorializing in the report. One example was the deletion of this sentence referring to Choate's duplicate reimbursement: "We were surprised that there was only one instance of a duplicate payment found in light of the breakdown in internal controls within the Advancement division."

Others were more substantive. Two dealt with Sharp's management and handling of finances. One sentence in both the draft and final versions stated that "the auditors indicated that most of the deficit came from unfunded hiring." The rest of the sentence was deleted from the final report; it read, "and Ms. Sharp was not telling anyone that the positions were unfunded when they were approved." Another change pertained to Sharp's redirection of the $1.3 million Tyson funds to an undedicated account with a large deficit. The final account read, "When we asked Ms. Sharp why she put the incorrect code on the transmittal form, *she stated it was a mistake*" (italics mine). The italicized phrase was added to the final version. But the original language, had it not been deleted prior to the report's public release, likely would have raised eyebrows and questions. It stated:

> [T]he only explanation that [Sharp] gave was that she had a lot of the Foundation Payment Authorization Forms on her desk and she typed in the wrong code. We found that puzzling since the correct code was in front of her on the face of the check. Ms. Sharp kept saying that she made a mistake.

There was another substantive change that was particularly relevant to me and to my claims about the January 14th meeting with Gearhart. It appeared on page 11 of Bercaw's draft report. If it had remained in the final version of the report, it would have had a dramatic effect on perceptions of Gearhart's credibility and truthfulness when, in September, he testified under oath at the Auditing Committee hearing. The report's language, made public on December 12th, stated:

> During the meeting, Chancellor Gearhart was holding a document that was provided to him by Mrs. Reynolds. We were able to identify that the document he was holding as a budget activity report for December 2012. Mr. Diamond referred to it as a budget update.

However, the draft version of that paragraph, which existed the day before the report's release, included an additional sentence—a statement that changed the paragraph's content from descriptive to incriminating: "Apparently Chancellor Gearhart asked why documents were being created and to get rid of it." Why that sentence was deleted, and at whose request, was never explained, even after the draft report's existence became public. But based on the prosecutors' interviews with six of the ten January 14th attendees, it appears Bercaw had concluded that Gearhart had indeed made the statement.

Meanwhile, media criticism of the Auditing Committee's decision to "close" its review of the Advancement deficit helped prompt several state lawmakers to action. Representative Mark Lowery successfully persuaded another legislative panel, the Joint Committee on Performance Review, to hold a hearing in January that would allow Choate, Sharp, and others, including me, to testify on issues related to the university's finances and management. In addition, 14 legislators from the Auditing Committee sent a joint letter to Bercaw's boss, District Prosecutor John Threet, seeking a thorough investigation of a question unanswered in Bercaw's findings: whether CFO Don Pederson lied to state auditors when he signed an exit conference affidavit stating that he knew of no allegations or suspicions of fraud related to the university's finances, despite his knowledge of the Schook memo.

Also that week, the *Democrat-Gazette's* Hammersly finally reached Pontious and Stewart, both of whom told her that Gearhart did indeed say to "get rid of" Reynolds' budget document, publicly confirming what they and I had told prosecutors. Those revelations and requests, combined with the Auditing Committee's truncated December 13th session and new calls for investigations and hearings, sparked deeper coverage and unsettling headlines that underscored the seriousness of the scandal:

"2 Quote Gearhart: 'Get Rid Of' Papers"

"Prosecutor to Review Claim UA Official Told Lie on Deficit"

"Panel Readies Subpoenas for UA Deficit Witnesses"

Max Brantley of *Arkansas Times* provided a pre-Christmas observation of the drama that he was now calling "Gearhartgate":

> Gearhart, who swore under oath that he never ordered the destruction of documents, now faces at least three eyewitnesses who quote Gearhart as saying at a Jan. 14 staff meeting to get rid of budget documents. Others, one an eyewitness and another reporting contemporaneous statements by multiple eyewitnesses, buttress the accounts at variance with Gearhart's....You can be innocent of a crime and guilty of dishonesty. Indictment or no indictment, such a verdict on UA actions in Gearhartgate — past and present — continue to appear justified.

Steve Barnes, a popular and respected TV host and syndicated commentator, also offered his take on UA's scandal as 2013 was coming to a close:

> What began as a fiscal fiasco—and not a small one, but millions of dollars in overspending—steadily has expanded to involve not merely lax supervision and accounting incompetence, but allegations of improper document shredding, subordination of the state Freedom of Information Act and an overall calculated absence of candor with the public, the press and the General Assembly....A handful of dismissals and reassignments in the development and communications bureaus have not satisfied the skeptical and, indeed, have whetted appetites for a fuller assessment of the university's administrative hierarchy. If the mistakes began in the Advancement department,

> they now extend to the highest office on campus, and a steadily hardening consensus in the state's political and business community (they are all but one and the same) is that Chancellor David Gearhart's job is in peril. Whispers to that effect in mid-summer have risen to murmurs audible across a crowded room, and when such was mentioned to a senior official of Gov. Beebe's administration this week, his only response was to nod matter-of-factly.

Barnes also pointed out that Gearhart wasn't the only one under fire:

> The university trustees are under pressure as well, grappling with a dilemma rather larger than securing suitable Razorback seats for big donors. Embarrassed early this year by the unprecedented resignation of a fellow trustee — poultry magnate John Tyson, reportedly angry over the disposition of a family contribution to the Advancement fund — their agenda now includes a tempest grown to a storm.

Meanwhile, the Joint Legislative Performance Review Committee had set a date for its own hearing on UA's management: Tuesday, January 7, 2014, in Little Rock, back in Room A of the Big MAC Building—the same venue but a different audience, one whose members said they were committed to learning the truth.

Chapter 17

REMOVING THE GAG

The lineup was set for the January 7th hearing. The Joint Committee on Performance Review—"JPR," as legislators called it—had asked seven current and former UA officials to testify: Choate, Sharp, Gearhart, Pederson, Schook, System President Bobbitt, and me. Others were told that they might be asked to testify during the course of the hearing, though none were. Given trustee John Goodson's offer to answer questions at the December 13th hearing, it was surprising that neither he nor any other member of the ten-person board was included in the list of scheduled witnesses. Their absence became even more conspicuous when it was announced that Bobbitt wouldn't be attending; he was delayed because of travel complications. That meant that no one higher than Gearhart on the university's governance hierarchy would have to answer for whatever role they played in enabling the UA scandal to escalate.

The UA hearing was expected to last a few hours at best. Unlike what occurs in the U.S. Congress, individual committee members would not spend hours prepping with staff to develop questions and identify weaknesses. They'd be on their own to demonstrate whether or not they had done their homework before participating. Some of them proved to have done a more thorough job than others.

Like the Joint Legislative Auditing Committee, JPR was large: a total of 30 House and Senate members. There was some overlap of the two committees, including Representative Kim Hammer, the House Chair of the Auditing Committee, and Senator Keith Ingram, the Senate Minority Leader. Representative Terry Rice was JPR's House Chair; Jane English was his Senate counterpart. Rice was the designated presider for the January 7th hearing.

A few weeks earlier, after JPR had decided to hold a hearing, Rice had contacted Choate in Austin. The committee chair wanted to make sure that the still-silenced witness would be willing to return to Little Rock. Choate wasn't so sure, he told him. He and Julie were bitter about what had happened on December 13th. They had made the seven-hour drive from Austin to Little Rock at their own expense, only to be preempted from testifying. Choate wasn't willing to be treated that way again. *Fool me once….*

Rice assured Choate that he'd be allowed to speak. And to make sure that Choate felt he could do so without violating his gag agreement with UA, Rice said he would subpoena Choate to appear, compelling him to speak even if the university objected. He also said the committee would arrange to reimburse Choate for his travel and lodging. These were unusual inducements for a state legislative hearing. But this would be no ordinary session.

Rice gaveled the hearing to order shortly after one p.m. After clarifying the committee's role and purpose for the benefit of newcomers to its work, he addressed the reasoning behind the committee's decision to take up the Advancement matter.

"I believe it is important for the U of A institution, the legislature, and the citizens of Arkansas to have the freedom to speak," he stated, "[and] to have open and honest answers to questions concerning the management of Advancement division funds of the U of A and related matters." To accomplish that, he asked his colleagues to approve a motion to subpoena the already present Choate "in order to have full and open testimony."

When the votes to issue the subpoena were cast, all but one committee member supported it. Moments later, Captain Lindsey Williams of the Arkansas State Police strode to the rear of the hearing room where Choate was waiting. Photographers scampered to capture the image. Once the task was completed, Rice called me and the other scheduled witnesses to take our designated places at the long table in the well of the hearing room. Sharp was seated to my left as we faced the committee; Choate, Gearhart, Pederson, and Schook were to my right. Rice announced that Bobbitt was unable to attend because of travel but did not explain why no other System official or trustee would be testifying.

With all of us in place, Rice repeated the once-unprecedented step that the Auditing Committee adopted for its September 13th hearing. "Do you solemnly swear and affirm that the testimony you are about to give is the truth, the whole truth, and nothing but the truth?" he asked all of us after we stood and raised our right hands. One at a time, each of us affirmed the oath.

"Any criminal investigation into this matter has been and is being appropriately performed by the prosecuting attorney," Rice began. "The prosecuting attorney must determine whether a crime has been committed or whether he can prove beyond a reasonable doubt that the crime was committed. He does not make determinations beyond that duty.

"It's possible for an act to be wrong even though it does not meet the elements of a crime or cannot be proven beyond a reasonable doubt," Rice continued. "This committee is charged by law with the duty to conduct investigations into specific problem areas of the administration of state government. While committee questions may be similar to those raised during a criminal investigation, this committee is not raising them for the purpose of determining whether a crime has been committed. We are here to address whether a problem exists in the administration of this state agency."

Brad Choate was one key to understanding whether a problem did, in fact, exist. Rice gave the erstwhile UA executive his first opportunity to share what he knew since signing the gag agreement with UA eleven months earlier.

"Thank you, Chairman Rice and Chairperson English," Choate began. "And my thanks to the entire committee for presenting an opportunity for me to speak today—and for providing the people of Arkansas an opportunity to hopefully, finally, hear the truth about the budget deficit and the administration's handling of the situation. Given the actions the university orchestrated at the Joint Auditing Committee, I also appreciate you providing me with a subpoena today. As you know, I came here today and was here last month of my own free will. I am here today of my own free will but understand the subpoena will provide extra protection should the university decide to attempt further efforts to stifle me as a result of the agreement we signed.

"Thanks to Senator Bryan King, the statement I had originally planned to make was made public in spite of the efforts of the university and a few elected officials. That ploy was simply the latest to try to keep the truth from being shared and to control what information is made public. I understand you have a copy of the statement I had planned to make in your packets today. Therefore, I intend to only address a few very key points today and then take any questions you may have for me.

"I have never mismanaged or ignored the responsibilities entrusted to me by my employers over my 32-year career in higher education," Choate declared. "Prior to this situation, the teams I have led have never—not once!—gone over budget. And I would argue that even in this case we didn't go over what we believed was our budget; we worked with the numbers we were given and did not exceed that budget. As it turns out, and as the audit has shown, we were given bad numbers as a result of poor financial staffing at the top of the organization and the university's own highly questionable accounting practices. Folks, I didn't wake up stupid or lazy one day. We built a top-notch program for the University of Arkansas that produced outstanding results. Unfortunately, the financial affairs staff and procedures we relied upon let us all down.

"There are, in my view, three key issues. I plan to address them today. They are first, [Why] this budget deficit occur[ed], second, the actions of Dave Gearhart, Don Pederson, and Jean Schook once the deficit was discovered, and third, the destruction and withholding of information that could have helped inform the situation.

"Let me begin by trying to correct the way this issue has been branded. By controlling information released to the media, the university has been successful so far in branding this situation 'a failure of University Advancement.' This is not a University Advancement failure; this is a failure of the university's Finance and Administration division.

"University Advancement had great success—pound-for-pound, arguably as good as any of our peer institutions across the United States. We had three straight years of raising more than $100 million dollars, something the University of Arkansas had never done before. We launched the university's first integrated marketing campaign, which contributed significantly to enrollment increases and raised the university's national reputation and ranking in *US News and World Report*, *Forbes*, and other publications. We grew our membership in our alumni association and launched some great alumni engagement programs. We organized a number of prestigious events that showcased the university, our alumni, and the state of Arkansas in positive ways. And we were good stewards of the philanthropic gifts bestowed upon the university by generous and supportive donors.

"The men and women who make up University Advancement are hard working professionals," Choate stated. "It is a disservice to them and the many generous benefactors to inaccurately call this fiasco a 'failure of University Advancement.'" To underscore his point, Choate offered an analogy. "When a pilot takes off in his or her plane, that pilot trusts that the plane's maintenance team has the engine in proper working condition," he said. "But if the engine blows up and the plane goes down, do we call that 'pilot error'? Of course not! We don't blame the pilot or crew for mechanical failures that others were charged with monitoring and correcting.

"We do not have a case of 'pilot error' here," Choate continued. "The financial systems and financial people we counted on failed us, and our plane went down. But Dave Gearhart and Don Pederson, with the help of Jean Schook, decided to cry 'pilot error'. That simply is not accurate. As the audit showed, the actions of a few people at the top of the Financial Affairs organization and highly questionable accounting practices, along with errors by Joy Sharp, led to the budget deficit."

Choate then described the part that Sharp, two seats away, played as his and Gearhart's longtime budget director. "Joy made mistakes and played a central role in creating the deficit," he noted, agreeing with the auditors' finding. "But Joy is not a bad person. She loves the university. She was very loyal to Dave Gearhart before and after I joined the university, and I think she was loyal to me. She did not want to hurt anyone or anything. This situation is a tragedy for many people, and Joy is certainly one of them.

"Before I arrived, when Dave Gearhart was vice chancellor for Advancement, he and Joy had offices in separate buildings," Choate explained. "Just before I arrived at the University in July of 2008, I made arrangements for Joy's office to be moved from University House to my office in the Administration Building because I wanted immediate access to my budget person. When Joy's office door was open and my door was open, we could literally see each other. Don [Pederson], Dave Gearhart, and everyone else I talked with told me Joy was very talented and experienced and maybe the most valuable person on the team. Unfortunately, Joy was in a position where she ultimately would fail. However, no one knew that was the case until July 2012.

"When the interviews conducted by the Washington County prosecutor's office were made public, I noticed that Dave Gearhart told them that when he was vice chancellor, Joy did not have budget responsibilities," Choate related. "According to what Dave told the prosecutor, Joy's job for him was to simply write checks. That description of her role is another falsehood. Joy and I talked about that when we were in this room last month. She can confirm for you today that her job did not change when I took over for Dave. She was Dave's budget director."

Choate then turned to the discovery of Advancement's deficit. "In June of 2012, just a few days prior to the discovery of the budget shortfall, Joy asked me to approve a new position in her area of responsibility to assist her. When I asked her if we had sufficient funds to add the position, she assured me that we did. I wasn't accepting budget information blindly; for years, every Monday afternoon, Joy gave me and the rest of Advancement's leadership team weekly budget status reports. She had shown me and the associate vice chancellors financial reports that indicated our finances were in sound shape. To accuse me of not providing proper management oversight is simply ludicrous and untrue," Choate stated. He wanted the committee and public to believe him: he had indeed been watching the numbers. Except that, unbeknownst to him, the numbers were wrong.

"In July and August of 2012, as the magnitude of the problem began to emerge, Dave became very concerned that there might have to be an audit," Choate continued. "I said to Dave on at least three occasions, 'If we need an audit, let's have an audit!' Dave's response to me was to say, 'Brad, an audit will make you look very bad'. I did not argue with him. But I frankly thought an audit would be helpful to understanding and resolving the overall problem. I was willing to live with the consequences of an audit if it showed that I was indeed at fault.

"After one of these exchanges, I went back to the office and asked Denise Reynolds, who had taken over as our budget person, 'Why do these guys not want an audit?' I knew Dave did not want to have to tell Don Bobbitt and the Board of Trustees about what we had discovered because it would then become public. But there seemed to be more to the issue.

"Denise, who reported to Don Pederson then and now, told me the reason why Don and Jean Schook did not want an audit," he related. "She said it was because an audit would show serious issues with financial practices throughout the university. The last thing Don Pederson and Jean Schook wanted was to have auditors looking into this situation. That conversation took place in Denise's office. Dave, Don, and Jean kept saying an audit would not tell us anything we did not already know. I suppose that was actually true—for them. However, the rest of us were unaware of the questionable accounting practices that directly led to the deficit."

Choate then addressed the Schook memos. There were two, not one, he pointed out: the first one that he, Schook, and Reynolds drafted on October 4th as part of the initial investigation into the Advancement deficit; and the second, damning one that Pederson had given him on October 19th, which was later presented to trustees and auditors. The first one, he explained, "was the result of the initial work the three of us had conducted to determine how and what led to the division's deficit and the Foundation's action. In Jean's words, Joy had been 'masking' the real condition of the division's finances. She and Denise both said—on that day and on multiple other occasions—that there was no way I would have been able to realize what [Sharp] was doing. They also said that her misrepresentation of finances appeared to go back to the time when Dave Gearhart was in charge of Advancement and that he wouldn't have been able to spot what was going on, either." To make his point, he quoted directly from the first Schook memo: "'It is clear the information provided to Dave Gearhart when he was [vice chancellor] and subsequently

Brad Choate was inaccurate.' End of quote.

"When Jean told me there was no way Dave nor I could have known the true condition of the division's finances, I thought Dave would be happy because it showed he and I both were misled," Choate testified. "But instead, Dave panicked when his own financial people told him the problem began when he was the division's vice chancellor.

Choate said he waited more than two weeks for CFO Pederson to respond to him about the memo that he, Reynolds, and Schook had prepared. Choate said he did not know that it was being "reworked with input from Don Pederson" to include "unsubstantiated and inaccurate accusations" that had never been raised with Choate.

"In it, [Schook] said she interviewed, 'key personnel' in Advancement," Choate stated. "[She] said, quote: 'Advancement staff were unable to explain the circumstances that led to the deficit balances, were not aware of the magnitude of the deficits in both the University and Foundation accounts, and could not propose curative steps to achieve a sound financial position.'

"In fact, Jean Schook did not interview any of the associate vice chancellors on my staff," he pointed out. "They don't get any more 'key' than the people who worked with Joy and me on budget and operational matters! Since Jean did not interview any of Advancement's associate vice chancellors, I remain unclear about who the 'key' personnel would be that she referenced.

"I was stunned by the memo, and contacted Dave to discuss it," Choate continued. "He didn't want to discuss the accuracy of the Schook memo. Instead, he said he had spoken with my direct reports, and they had confirmed elements of what the Schook memo said. In fact, that was another false statement. He did not have those conversations. You can ask the associate vice chancellors yourselves. I view Dave's response as the first indication that a false narrative was being created to rationalize placing the blame on me rather than on the university's own lack of checks and balances to ensure proper financial management and support of its various units."

Choate said he was confident that Pederson and Gearhart influenced the modifications to the original Schook memo. "But why would they do this?" he asked rhetorically. "Because by pointing the finger at me—by accusing me of being inattentive and neglectful in my duties—they hoped to deflect attention away from serious, systemic problems that would raise questions about the university's inadequate financial management controls and, as the audit revealed, its questionable accounting practices."

To underscore his belief that he had been "thrown under a bus" as a scapegoat, Choate told the committee about an October 22, 2012 email he had received from Pederson, days after Choate saw the revised, accusatory Schook memo for the first time. Attempting to document to Choate that he had been neglectful in the past, Pederson had forwarded to him a series of emails from 2009 in which he had asked Choate to transfer funds from Advancement's UA Foundation-held accounts to UA's own accounts. Citing those emails, Pederson accused Choate of never following through on those transactions.

Upon receiving the old emails, Choate didn't think they were accurate, so he checked his own email files. He discovered that Pederson had apparently edited the email thread; it didn't include parts that showed Choate had instructed Sharp to make the transaction, nor did it include Sharp's response or Pederson's own email thanking Choate and Sharp for their "quick and positive response."

"Those emails, which Don had copies of, documented and proved I instructed Joy Sharp to make the requested transfers," Choate argued. "So when I received Don's October 22, 2012 email with those key exchanges edited out, I confronted him about it. I wanted to look him in the eye when he realized he had been caught trying to manipulate the facts. When I pointed out to Don that he did not include the email from Joy or his response to her, he said he did not do so because Joy never made the transfer. I asked why he didn't let me know she had not made the transfer. He said it was because he didn't follow up to see if she actually made the transfer. I pointed out to him that was the exact situation I was in with Joy.

"The fact that Don chose not to include Joy's email and his response is indicative of his desire to place blame rather than find facts," Choate asserted. "I also think it substantiates a conspiratorial atmosphere on the part of Dave Gearhart, Don Pederson, and Jean Schook…to redirect attention from their own culpability in failing to catch and remedy the systemic flaws in the university's method of checks and balances. What other conclusion can one draw? If this were simply a matter of Joy Sharp misrepresenting and overspending Advancement resources, the logical and prudent response would have been to remove her from budget responsibility, investigate the matter, and remedy the matter in a transparent and accountable manner.

"But that didn't happen," he continued. "Instead, we got months of convoluted attempts to blame two individuals and conceal information that auditors and the public could have used to draw their own conclusions. That's what happens when people have something to hide. That's what happens when leaders panic."

After months of having to hold his tongue, Choate wanted to make sure his audience of lawmakers and taxpayers understood what happened in Advancement, and why.

"We were making personnel and budget decisions based on the information Joy provided at our Monday afternoon leadership meetings and other meetings," he emphasized. "We did not know that the spreadsheets and financial information that we reviewed were inaccurate. That was compounded by the fact that the university itself did not have a system of checks and balances at the CFO level that would have detected the budget problems. There were other things I wasn't told but should have been: I did not know that the university's chief financial officer and the university's treasurer were quietly booking millions in a non-existent 'receivable' at the close of the fiscal year and then removing them just as quietly. For whatever reason, they concealed that action from me. And they made that questionable booking two years in a row, as the auditors discovered. It would be good to know who else besides the university's CFO and Treasurer knew about the appearance and disappearance of those accounts receivable," he added, suspecting that one possibility was his former boss, seated to his right.

Continuing, Choate turned to Gearhart's decision on November 6, 2012 to reassign him for the remaining eight months of the fiscal year. "He told me the Board of Trustees met in executive session, discussed the Advancement budget, and that the Board wanted me fired. He said, and I quote, 'I couldn't save you'.... Did I like that? No. Did I think Dave was looking out for me in his conversations with the Board? At the time, yes. But two weeks later, on November 20th, Dave sent me an email saying he had been told I was blaming Don Pederson for what Dave referred to as my, quote, 'demise.' He then wrote, 'If I continue to hear these reports I will be forced to remove you from this building and assign you space elsewhere. The other alternative is to dismiss you immediately for cause.' As you can see, he was giving me serious career and financial reasons—threats, actually—not to share what I had learned about what had occurred and why it happened."

By this point Choate had been speaking for close to a half-hour. He had one more point he wanted to make, not knowing whether the Q&A session that was expected to occur later would bring up his closing observation.

"Finally, I want to say a few words about what the Legislative Auditing Committee was told at its meeting in September," he stated. "At great risk to his future employment possibilities, John Diamond told you the truth. He did so to help this university, this state, and to try to protect his co-workers—at great risk to himself. Mr. Diamond lost his job for those same reasons—he tried to keep the university in line with Freedom of Information Act laws and tried to be honest with the public. And Dave shot the messenger.

"Representative Kim Hammer asked John about the January 14th meeting that included my former staff reports and the chancellor," Choate recalled. "I was in my office that day, and within 60 seconds of that meeting ending, two of the attendees at that meeting—Laura Villines and Denise Reynolds—came back to the office with a shocked look on their faces. Obviously, something significant had occurred. They told me and Stephanie McGuire, who was a secretary in our office at the time, that Dave had just pitched a major fit. That he had used very foul language with reference to me, that he had pushed a stack of budget sheets Denise had prepared back at her and told her to, quote, 'get rid of these and stop putting budget information on paper.' Later that night another witness, Bruce Pontious, told me the same story. The next day yet another witness, Graham Stewart, told me the same story. A few days later, John Diamond confirmed the story when I asked him about it. And a few days after that another witness, Kris Macechko, told me the same story.

"All of them were in that meeting," Choate continued. "None of them said anything about John or anyone else somehow provoking Dave's behavior. Some of the witnesses at that meeting also shared those accounts with other colleagues on campus. There is no doubt whatsoever what occurred. And then Dave cancelled the weekly meetings of that leadership group altogether, even though he was the acting leader of the division and the division had major financial issues that needed to be resolved.

"Today I'm sure some attendees in that meeting would feel awkward about reliving that meeting. Prior to these witnesses being interviewed by the prosecutor, university lawyers—along with Dave Gearhart's own personal lawyer—brought witnesses in one by one on September 24th to find out what they knew about the January 14th meeting. Some of them may have developed what I would call 'convenient amnesia.' That's understandable. They need to protect their jobs because they either still work there, or they just don't have an appetite for such confrontation. When Denise Reynolds and

Laura Villines told Stephanie and me about Dave's outburst—just minutes after it had occurred—I remember Denise Reynolds asking me, 'How am I supposed to deal with budgets if I can't create spreadsheets?' It was a rhetorical question but a legitimate one.

"There's a matter of perjury here. I certainly hope the Pulaski County Prosecutor doesn't 'punt' on this issue. What really happened at that meeting is pretty well known because so many people were in the room and those people told lots of others. The university has tried to dismiss this by splitting hairs and playing semantic games, but the truth is pretty obvious. It will be interesting to see if power politics trumps the truth in this case."

Having made his points, Choate issued a final appeal to the committee. "If the members of this committee, the other members of the Legislature, the Board of Trustees, and the media will not step up and deal with the truth of this situation, who will? Who will protect hard-working employees at the university who dare stand up to superiors who do not want to follow the law?

"As surprising as the deficit was, the truly disturbing result of all of this has been the creation of an atmosphere of hostility, secrecy, and cover-up," he concluded. "If this body and the Board of Trustees do not want to address those issues and the people responsible, then that is their and your choice. After today, I feel like I have done my duty to report the truth."

Chapter 18

NO ACCOUNTABILITY

The star witness had spoken. Choate's testimony was even more revealing than many observers expected—damning not just to Gearhart but also to Pederson, Schook, and UA's system of fiscal checks and balances.

The committee chairs had decided to allow opening statements from all invitees before engaging in questions. Unlike Choate, Sharp's opening statement would be brief—a short but confusing *mea culpa.*

"I just wanted to say it was totally human error on my part," she opened. "There was no fraud or intention of fraud. All expenses were used for the university only, none for personal gain at all. I did not stay on top of the revenues that were projected and that I was using to cover the expenses. One reason was I was just overworked in what I was doing, and that's one of the reasons why I asked for additional staff to help me. Until 2012, I was able to cover the final budget with balances, so the worksheets we were working with would have showed the projected income I was working with, that would be coming in to cover the deficit—the expenses we would have for the division. Thank you."

If anyone expected Sharp to reveal any new information in this, her first public comment on the controversy, they were disappointed. Her brief statement was remarkable only in that it parroted the very phrasing that Gearhart had been using since word of the deficit broke more than a year earlier: *No fraud or intention of fraud. All expenses were for legitimate university business. No personal gain.*

When Gearhart's turn to speak arrived, he stayed focused on his talking points. "The most important message that I want to deliver today is that we have embraced and are actively implementing new practices gleaned from the campus level internal review," he said. "The two extensive audits—independent audits—and the detailed investigation performed by the Washington County prosecutor's office with the assistance of the Federal Bureau of Investigation have basically said to us that much of what's been alleged here today is just not accurate. I want you to know that we take the deficit in the Advancement division and the constructive recommendations we have received very seriously, and we are working very hard to prevent any similar occurrence in the future.

"I also want you to know that this has been a very humbling experience for me and the university staff involved in the situation," he continued. "I am not here to make excuses. I am here to say that I am sorry that it happened. I take full responsibility for the operation of the university. As I have said before, the proverbial buck stops here. And I embrace that overall responsibility."

And as quickly as he embraced it, he let it go.

"The Advancement division failed to maintain and monitor its budget," he declared. "The simple truth is that Mr. Choate failed to carry out his duties and responsibilities as vice chancellor by ignoring his duty to manage and supervise budgetary matters. Mr. Choate was paid to manage and control all aspects of the operation of the Advancement division, including its financial wellbeing. But he did not do this. Having been in that very same position for ten years before I became chancellor, I believe I am in a unique position to tell you that no justifiable explanation exists for lacking the basic knowledge and control of the budget that resulted in the accumulation of a four million dollar deficit.

"Now, the facts in this case have been confirmed by external auditors," Gearhart continued. "They have been confirmed by the prosecuting attorney. They have been confirmed by the Federal Bureau of Investigation. And they also determined that absolutely no theft, no fraud, or no misappropriation of funds occurred. The prosecuting attorney also found no wrongdoing with regard to the issues referred by legislative audit. Nor did they substantiate any of Mr. Diamond's claims."

Gearhart's spin of "facts" was dizzying. The FBI had provided no such confirmation of anything. Its only involvement was to allow an agent to help Bercaw and Hatcher understand UA's complicated and unconventional accounting practices. Gearhart also exaggerated Bercaw's findings, stretching the prosecutor's statement of no criminality into a false, self-exonerating declaration of "no wrongdoing."

"For the past fifteen years I have dedicated all of my heart, all of my soul, and all of my energy to the University of Arkansas," the chancellor continued. "And I am committed to leading it forward for the benefit of our students and the people of the State of Arkansas. As part of that effort—and with humility—I recognize that there are many lessons to be learned from the events and issues surrounding the advancement deficit. And I want you to know that I am committed to incorporating the lessons we have learned to make the university stronger and better. I welcome input from members of the committee as we move forward in the future."

Schook and Pederson were invited to offer opening statements of their own but declined. They had not helped themselves at the September 13th hearing with their defense of their performance as UA's financial chiefs when they defended their limited responsibilities for oversight of divisional budgets, the booking of non-existent "accounts receivable" to balance end-of-year budgets, and the failure to disclose to state auditors the details of Advancement's recently discovered financial mismanagement. They would wait until the Q&A to speak.

My own prepared remarks expounded on the much-briefer statement I presented to the Auditing Committee on September 13th. Back then, I had kept my opening comments relatively short, expecting that I could elaborate once committee members asked questions. But that didn't occur because the committee chair decided that the possibility of perjury and illegal activity raised that day might be better addressed at a second meeting. I decided to make sure I had the opportunity to publicly finish sharing what I knew.

"My prepared remarks today will focus on issues relating to the university's handling of public documents requested under the Freedom of Information Act," I stated. "I'll provide you with the context in which key actions related to FOIA occurred. I'll share with you documentable examples of the university's willful disregard for the letter and spirit of FOIA. And I will explain to you why I believe citizens of Arkansas deserve further investigation into the possibility of perjury and of efforts to subvert the state's Freedom of Information Act, which as you know is a criminal offense in our state."

I began by walking the committee through the FOIA process: how I worked with Scott Varady and Bill Kincaid to determine what the reporter wanted and who might have the records being sought; how we would prepare and distribute the written notification to those who might have those records; how we would review what we received in response to the notice; and how we would confirm the clarity and accuracy of the records with the proper university officials. Only then would I pass along the documents to the reporter, blind-copying or forwarding the response to Gearhart, Pederson, Varady, and possibly other members of the legal staff for their records.

"This approach ensured that we demonstrated due diligence in responding to FOIA requests," I explained. "This protocol worked well during my first two years as associate vice chancellor. I recall no complaints from university officials. But that began to change shortly after the issues with the Advancement division's spending became known. Let me address that now.

"The first news report about the Advancement situation came on December 3, 2012, a few weeks after Chancellor Gearhart had reassigned Brad Choate and Joy Sharp. The university received numerous FOIA requests over the next several weeks seeking budget information and other documentation regarding the situation. That's what people in the news business do.

"It was an intense period for the administration," I continued. "Chancellor Gearhart had taken over as the acting head of the Advancement division. Denise Reynolds, a member of Don Pederson's staff, had taken over administrative responsibility for the Advancement division's budget. The three associate vice chancellors in the division—Bruce Pontious, Graham Stewart, and I—were desperately in need of regular, accurate budget updates for the current fiscal year. We depended on our weekly meetings with the rest of the Advancement leadership team to gain that information.

"With this as the context, it was during this period where the university's adherence to the Freedom of Information Act started to weaken, and the university's senior leadership's irritation with the media noticeably started to grow. Allow me to explain." I told the committee about the two detailed FOIA requests for budget documents I received in early January and how I had shared those requests with Gearhart, Pederson, Denise Reynolds, and Varady. I retold the story of the January 14th Advancement meeting where, shortly after the meeting began, Gearhart angrily told us to "get rid of" Reynolds's budget document and directed her and the rest of us not to create any more of them. I repeated the story about how Gearhart launched into a tirade about Choate before storming out of the meeting.

"On Tuesday, January 15th—the day after the meeting I just described—university attorney Bill Kincaid and I met with

Chancellor Gearhart and Don Pederson to discuss the outstanding FOIA requests and review responsive documents," I related. "The budget document was not in the financial documents we received from Don Pederson or Denise Reynolds. Consequently, the FOIA response we provided simply said that the breakdown of the current FY13 budget did not exist in a printable form.

"The chancellor's conduct at the January 14th meeting is relevant to understanding key issues before you. Not just because of his denial and the possibility of perjury, but because it initiated a new environment within the division and in other parts of campus, whereby the chancellor's and other leaders' preoccupation with FOIAs and the news media influenced and interfered with our work."

I offered an example. "A few days after the January 14th meeting, we received new FOIA requests from the media about the Advancement situation. Per standard operating procedure, I shared the FOIA request with the Chancellor, Don Pederson, Denise Reynolds, and the university's lawyers. On January 23rd, I received the following email about the FOIAs from Don Pederson:

> 'John, this is really getting to be harassment in my mind. I think we all feel, provost, chancellor, Dr. Bobbitt and me, that we need to end this dialogue. They are obviously trying to find something that damages the UA and the chancellor and there is nothing there, as you well know. I have spoken to the chancellor and legal counsel. Below is what we believe should be the response to Lisa Hammersly. I do not plan on responding to any further inquiries. I have spent way too much time on this matter, as have you.'

"And then Don provided the following message for me to send to the reporter:

> 'Lisa: While I appreciate your continued questions, we believe we have answered your numerous inquiries multiple times, the same questions over and over again, and we have spent hours and hours trying to explain every aspect of this issue. We can continue to explain it to you, but we cannot understand it for you. Your questions

as well as continued FOIA requests for the same information, to which we have previously responded, borders on the absurd and frankly, harassment. We have no further comment.'

"As the university's chief PR advisor, I hate the phrase 'no comment'," I told the committee. "It's the verbal equivalent of holding a trench coat over your head as you leave the courthouse. Fair or not, it suggests guilt. And for a university whose strategic plan is titled 'Transparency and Accountability for the People of Arkansas', Don's response suggested neither."

I shared what happened after that—my response to Pederson in which I cautioned about the dangers of a blanket refusal to respond to any questions whatsoever, even when it was in our own best interest to help reporters understand the materials they possessed or received through a FOIA. I told the committee about how Gearhart called me to his office the following day and said that System President Bobbitt and the trustees told him to "shut John Diamond up." I told the committee that immediately after Gearhart asked for the Advancement audits, we adopted the stance that no one from UA could respond to questions about Advancement's finances "in order to protect the integrity of the auditors' investigation.

"But of course invoking that statement could not excuse us from responding to FOIA requests," I explained. "The law doesn't allow that. Over the next several months, there were multiple FOIA requests for records and budget updates related to Advancement. In several instances, I was told updated budget information had not yet been assembled. And I believed it because my fellow associate vice chancellors and I were not receiving the budget information ourselves.

"It wasn't until July 29th, during a tense meeting of our Advancement leadership team, that we discovered that monthly budget documents—public documents—had indeed been prepared. But neither our new vice chancellor [Chris Wyrick] nor our budget director had been sharing them with the three associate vice chancellors—the very people who were supposed to run the day-to-day operation of the lion's share of the division. Furthermore, we were kept in the dark about the additional millions of dollars that were quietly being transferred to Advancement so that the new vice chancellor could publicly claim he successfully balanced the FY13 budget after three months on the job.

"The lack of financial information we received from our own vice chancellor and budget director was, I believe, a residual effect of the January 14th meeting," I stated. "It changed behavior, and not for the better. For example, Denise Reynolds sent me and one other associate vice chancellor, Bruce Pontious, an email on February 6th regarding a budget matter. It began with the statement, 'Please delete after reading.' Bruce and I understood why she opened her email that way. Though later, when the media asked her about it, she said she couldn't recall why she wrote that. It was within this environment that we were trying to maintain respectful, professional relations with the news media—and abide by the law. A culture of 'delete and destroy' came to exist, and not just in Advancement."

I then described in detail what I labeled "the tipping point" on the university's efforts to subvert the state's public records laws: the July 29th meeting in Gearhart's conference room about the *Democrat-Gazette's* lengthy FOIA request dealing with Advancement's past and current years' budgets and Wyrick's reorganization plan. I told the committee how Gearhart made it clear to Varady, Kincaid, and me that he was angry about the breadth and nature of the FOIA, and how he once again said the newspaper was "out to get" him. I shared how, after we left Gearhart's conference room, Varady, Kincaid, and I immediately contacted Fred Harrison, the university system's chief legal counsel, to relate what we had just been told. I told the committee how Harrison had assured us he would contact Gearhart to "set him straight" on our obligations to respond to the FOIA.

I explained the set of events that followed that assurance: Gearhart's instructions to have Wyrick, not any of us, gather the records that the newspaper had FOIA'd; Wyrick's justification for not fulfilling the request because Gearhart was "preoccupied with" the anticipated release of the Advancement audits; Wyrick's four-week delay in completing that assignment; and Wyrick's instruction to me to give the *Democrat-Gazette* just a single, one-page document and tell its reporters that it represented the totality of "responsive" (i.e., public) documents the newspaper had FOIA'd.

"I knew this was far from a complete record," I explained. "For example, there was a large budget notebook for FY14 that was kept in Denise Reynolds' office. Chris had told the Advancement leadership staff to go in and look at our section of the book but not to copy it or take it out of the office. Furthermore, he wanted us to sign something or send him and Denise an email to confirm that we reviewed the notebook. That notebook was clearly 'responsive' to the FOIA, but he did not provide it.

I offered another example. "Chris himself maintained a large notebook of materials related to his reorganization plan. He didn't allow any of us to look at it but would bring it to our weekly leadership meetings and hold it up and fan the pages, making a point to show us all the yellow highlights he had added. That information was 'responsive' to the FOIA but was not provided.

"There were four copies of a video of the June 20th staff meeting Chris had had us make when he announced the reorganization plans," I continued. "Under the law, videos are considered electronic documents—the kind sought in the July 22nd FOIA. Those videos were not provided in response to the FOIA. Nor was the non-searchable link to the YouTube video of the June 20th meeting that Chris had an employee create so that he could share the video that evening with the chancellor.

"And there were countless email exchanges dealing with these topics between and among individuals, including the chancellor, Chris, and Don Pederson, that were specifically asked for by name or title," I explained. "But none of these was provided as responsive to the July

22nd FOIA. I know they existed because I was cc'd or blind-copied on many of them. I gave the Washington County prosecutor's office over one hundred pages of potentially 'responsive' documents related just to the July 22nd FOIA alone. In Arkansas, knowingly and negligently violating a FOIA request is a criminal offense."

Then, I reminded the committee of the details of my termination on August 23rd and the revelations I shared with the Legislative Audit Committee in Little Rock three weeks after that. "As you know, the Washington County prosecutor issued a report last month in which he said he would not pursue criminal charges in the matters referred to his office," I said. "I'm not going to criticize the prosecutors' work. However, I do want to point out some important points as they pertain to my testimony under oath on September 13th.

"I testified that the Chancellor said on January 14th to 'get rid of' documents. He swore he did not say that. Two others besides me independently told the prosecutor that the Chancellor did say that. That's three of the six people the prosecutor interviewed. That's already enough to at least show probable cause.

"The prosecutor said the January 14th budget document that we were told to get rid of was eventually transmitted to the newspaper and therefore the university complied with the FOIA," I related. "But what the report did not say was that it was turned over 10 months after it was FOIA'd, well after it could have shed light on the true financial condition of Advancement. The timeliness of that budget document and its relevance to the public interest was important in January, not in November, when it was finally given.

"I testified that documents referred to in the audit as unavailable to auditors were shredded before and immediately after the audit request was submitted. The prosecutor's notes show that some payment authorizations that were not available to auditors were indeed among the documents that Advancement staff said Denise Reynolds told them to shred.

"I testified that despite the university's claims, neither Jean Schook nor the Chancellor interviewed me or the rest of the Advancement leadership team as part of the investigation that led to the October 19, 2012 Schook report. Ironically, the only time the Advancement leadership team's input was sought came nearly a year later, on September 24, 2013. That's when at least five of the individuals present for the January 14th meeting were called in, one by one, to be de-briefed by university lawyers and the chancellor's personal lawyer, all just a few weeks prior to their interviews with the Washington County prosecutors.

"A credibility gap exists, and it's damaging to the university and the state. Just 20 months ago, UA was receiving widespread national praise for the integrity with which it handled the Petrino situation," I said, referring to the firing of football coach Bobby Petrino. "The only way to restore that kind of public trust and the university's accountability is for some entity—a district or special prosecutor, with or without the help of a grand jury—to put all relevant witnesses under oath to get to the truth. That includes the university's lawyers—all of them good people who know a great deal about what has happened. I respectfully ask that this committee use whatever authority it has to make sure the tuition payers, taxpayers, students, employees, alumni, and donors all learn the truth."

After we all had been given a chance to make opening statements, Representative Rice, the co-chair presiding at the hearing, checked the queue of legislators who wanted to question the witnesses. Looking at the list, he knew it would be a long afternoon.

Early on, it became evident that, to the committee, Sharp was a sympathetic figure, perhaps a victim of lapses of attention and responsibility by the highly paid UA officials—current and former—seated alongside her. Rightly or not, the five of us each minimized the role and responsibility that we felt Joy should take for what Gearhart had labeled a "colossal fiscal crisis." The misdirection of the Tyson check. The unjustified movement of funds from one account to another. The fabricated budget reports she had provided that bore little resemblance to what she knew was Advancement's true financial condition. Her failure to ever tell Choate about the end-of-year bookings of millions in "accounts receivable" that allowed him to believe, for two years, that his division's budget was staying within total resources that UA and the private UA Foundation had allocated to it.

Sharp received the same treatment from the questioners on the legislative committee. They directed few inquiries to her, apparently rewarding her eager willingness to shoulder the blame without excuses or elaboration. No one asked her to detail the tactics that allowed her to escape detection until the UA Foundation froze the accounts she controlled. No one asked her about any conversations she might have had with Gearhart, Schook, Pederson, or Choate about the annual shortfalls that prompted Schook to perform million-dollar patches each July—actions that state auditors highlighted as inappropriate in their findings. It didn't get much more pressing than this:

"Somewhere down the line somebody dropped the ball," Senator Bobby Pierce stated to Sharp. "And you said a while ago, 'I think I dropped the ball.'"

"Yes, I did," Sharp answered.

"So you started all this mess, is that what you're saying?" Pierce asked.

"Yes, I am," she responded.

"I appreciate you saying that," Piece replied. "Do you have a degree in accounting, yes or no?"

"No, I do not."

"But you're overseeing how many millions of dollars?"

"Approximately ten million," Sharp answered.

"Without a degree in accounting."

"Yes, sir."

"Of all the people I feel sorry for, I feel sorry for Ms. Sharp," Representative Kim Hammer volunteered when it was his turn to ask questions. "Because everyone seems to want to throw her under the bus. But yet for as vital an organization as Advancement is, nobody was keeping a better eye on it. What appears to be happening is that we all want to dump it on Ms. Sharp."

The topic that committee members most frequently raised as each addressed witnesses dealt with UA's accounting practices. Since the audits' release back in September and the legislative hearing that followed a few days later, there had been plenty of head scratching and criticism of the university's defense of posting nonexistent accounts receivable—i.e., money purportedly owed to it. The UA Foundation, supposedly the university's debtor, disputed the point to auditors. As everyone knew by now, the Foundation actually had been advancing funds to the university until June 2012, when the Foundation finally said, *Enough!* No one could name any other university that booked faux revenues at the end of the year to balance the books, much less drop those same numbers from the balance sheet once the new fiscal year began.

Representative Bruce Westerman, the House Majority Leader and a former Razorback football player, wanted to tackle the issue. "We've heard some dramatic testimony today under oath, testimony that conflicts," he began. "One of the things that's a center of controversy is the booking of non-existent accounts receivable. Can you elaborate on that, Dr. Gearhart?"

The chancellor responded with a non-answer, simply saying that the university has agreed to change its ways and that no auditor previously had ever told them not to do it. It was left to Schook, the treasurer, to actually respond.

"The booking of an accounts receivable was a practice, a standard closing accrual adjustment that we believed was required under our interpretation of the authoritative literature for financial reporting for our institution," the CPA explained in a measured, clinical manner. "It had been a practice that had been reviewed, as the chancellor said, for many, many years with our annual financial statement audits. Never had a question been raised about that particular practice or that particular closing adjustment by any of our external auditors."

"OK," Westerman responded. "So by booking these accounts receivable, could that cover up the fact that there's a deficit?"

"First of all, let me say that there's an idea that centrally—within Financial Affairs—that these entries were created without the knowledge of the affected divisions or units on campus. That's simply not so." Schook wasn't answering Westerman's question; it would have required her to acknowledge that the practice could indeed cover up a deficit, just as it had for Advancement in the two prior years.

"These entries were made in concert with discussions with the budget officers," she continued. "In the case of the division of Advancement during this time, our conversations were with Joy Sharp. And she was involved—and in fact declared that the receivable was accurate and that deposits would be made in July that would bring forward the reimbursements that we believed were due."

That was a most revealing statement. Schook, the university's treasurer, had taken at face value Sharp's assurance, two years in a row, that Advancement was owed millions by the UA Foundation and that the division would be paid shortly. The treasurer—and those above her—never checked to make sure those outstanding payments actually existed and were ever received. Nor did Pederson, the university's chief financial officer who spoke and met with Choate several times a week, ever mention or question the status of Advancement's finances or Schook's discussions with Sharp. It's easy to understand that Schook and Pederson would have assumed Sharp was telling the truth—and that she had shared with Choate the need for the additional end-of-year funds before asking Schook for them. But by admitting that, Schook and Pederson would be guilty of the same offense as what had cost Choate his job: trusting Sharp.

"So how did the deficit develop if there were accounts receivable available to cover those deficits?" Westerman asked. "And who knew that there were deficits there? Or was this just a surprise to someone when this four million dollars in deficits appeared?"

Schook didn't answer. Instead, she turned and looked at Gearhart, who pulled his microphone toward him.

"Let me see if I can answer that," he began to explain. "What happened was, there wasn't enough money on the Foundation side to satisfy that debt. It is the first time that had ever happened. It had never happened on my watch. It had never happened on Bud Edwards' watch, the vice chancellor before me. All I can say is that it was a shock to us as it was, I think, to Mr. Choate and Ms. Sharp, that there wasn't enough funding there to cover what was on the university side. Frankly, it's hard for me to understand why that is the case, having managed that budget for ten years. I knew where every penny was. And I knew precisely what we had spent."

Again, a non-answer. No one wanted to admit that they, like Choate, had relied on Sharp's word.

Representative Randy Alexander, himself a former UA administrator, followed up with Schook.

"If you're transferring money from a Foundation account to a university account at the end of the year, there'd be no reason to do that if there's money already in the university account to finish the year in the black." His point was that the Foundation funds for the year would have already been distributed to Advancement so they could be used in that budget year. The 'reimbursement' Sharp and Schook had been talking about was actually a matter of Advancement receiving an early payment on the upcoming year's disbursement—like a child getting a large advance on her allowance. It should have been obvious to Schook and Pederson that by booking fully six months' allocation of Foundation funds in non-existent receivables at the very end of the fiscal year, something was wrong; Advancement clearly wasn't operating within the budget that Gearhart and they, the senior financial officers, had set for that division. "Where were the institutional checks and balances?" Choate had asked rhetorically in his own defense. Committee members were starting to pursue that question themselves.

"Does Mr. Pederson monitor the monthly financials comparing actual and budgeted revenues and expenditures?" asked Representative Jon Eubanks.

"No, sir," Pederson himself responded. "I monitor the institution as a whole." That, too, was a remarkable admission for someone whose job was to minimize the university's financial risk and vulnerability.

"So nobody monitors the individual units as to their financial wellbeing as far as they are staying within their budget?" Eubanks continued. "I know that revenues and expenditures can fluctuate during the course of a year—you might be down one month and up the next—but nobody was monitoring anything?"

Gearhart saw where the questioning was leading and spoke up. "I can't say nobody was, sir. I would say that the responsibility is on the executive who is in charge of the area"—in this case, Choate.

"And nobody within the university monitors them to make sure that—"

"Yes," Gearhart interrupted, keeping Eubanks from finishing his question or point. "But you have to go back to what I said earlier—that this unit is unique in the way it is budgeted. There are not any other units to my knowledge in the university that are funded the way Advancement is funded. It's complicated."

"I don't think it makes any difference where the money is coming from," Eubanks responded, "other than you know how much it is and how much is available."

When Representative Mark Lowery's turn to speak came, he wanted to pursue the dispute over the affidavit Pederson signed in which the CFO disavowed any knowledge of suspicions or allegations involving UA's finances.

"Ms. Schook," he said to the treasurer, "in the memo that you sent to Mr. Pederson dated October 19th, you reference that you believe that there may be some issues of conflicts of interest and a number of other allegations and concerns that you had. To date, I don't believe you have been asked specifically to give us what were the issues that you saw that would lead you to say that there were... 'likely conflicts of interest, misdirection of funds, and risk of fraud.' You saw something that actually rose to that level. Could you give us more information to let us know what were the specific instances?"

"Yes, sir," Schook replied. She listed several reasons: the fact that Choate had given Sharp his login credentials so that she could access the university's financial system as Choate; Sharp's use of her sister to provide the second level of approval necessary for some of Sharp's online transactions; and the inability of Choate and Sharp to provide her with financial records—"Not one single document," Schook emphasized. Her explanation certainly underscored the serious possibility of fraud, just as her October 19th memo to Pederson had.

"OK," Lowery said. "Let me follow up on that with Mr. Pederson. I know you're aware of this question being asked. That this memo was sent to you on October 19th with these very generalized concerns. With no specifics. However, on October 25th auditors asked you whether there had been any kind of communication to you about potential problems or fraud. Your letter of October 25th to the auditors said, 'We have no knowledge of any allegations of fraud or suspected fraud affecting the entity received in communications with employees, former employees, analysts, regulators, or others.' And I'm sure Ms. Schook would be included in that group. Is that letter, then, a false statement?"

"No, sir," Pederson answered. "I did not make a false statement. I believe I correctly certified that there was no suspected or actual fraud. I answered the question based on my knowledge and experience and the information provided by Ms. Schook. I never read any single sentence or phrase in her review, in isolation, [and] I read all of her narrative. I talked with her about it that intervening week. Now a week sounds like a short period of time, but we had a number of meetings during that week in which I gathered additional information. We had no suspicion of fraud. Of course, the prosecutors have now validated that conclusion." Pederson did not share what additional information he received during that week that removed any possibility of actual or suspected fraud, nor did he acknowledge the narrow scope prosecutors applied as they investigated Sharp's actions a year later.

"But would you not agree that there's a difference between suspicion and an allegation?" Lowery responded. "You specifically said, 'We have no allegations.' Ms. Schook, in her letter of October 19th, actually made—*presented to you*—allegations."

"I'm sorry to disagree with you," Pederson replied. "She presented the risk of things happening. Certainly, that was ambiguous enough that we had a lot of discussion about it and concluded that there was no evidence to lead us to believe there was any fraud that occurred [or] that the possibility of fraud was really present." A judgment made despite Schook's declaration moments earlier that she had received "not one single document" related to Advancement's finances as she assessed Sharp's and Choate's behavior as managers.

Lowery did not accept Pederson's justification. "The only thing we have to go by is the record, which shows that as of October 19th there was a likelihood of allegations. That communication seems to have been ignored in your October 25th statement."

"There are likelihoods of all kinds of frauds that can occur in any complex system," Pederson countered. "That's not the question that the management representation letter asks about."

Lowery gave up, believing he had made his point. Pederson seemed to be making a distinction that didn't exist. There had indeed been correspondence. It had not been investigated. Neither Schook nor anyone questioned Pontious, Stewart, or me, the three people within the division who, with the exception of the vice chancellor himself, had the most direct and regular interaction with Joy Sharp on budget matters. In the light of Gearhart's earlier warning to Choate—"an audit would make you look very bad"—advising a state auditor of the Schook memo's existence could have made more that just Choate look bad.

Representative Nate Bell took over the questioning. "Mr. Pederson, most of our hearing today has been centered on the management practices that y'all have in the division of Advancement....For us to exercise our oversight function effectively via audits, we have to depend on open communications with the people that our auditors deal with. Would you not agree that to exercise that function, it's critical that we receive honest, forthright answers and open communication from the people who are being audited?"

"Yes, sir, I would agree with that," Pederson answered.

"Ms. Schook testified that you had received her letter and that you had knowledge of it on the 19th. What actions did you take as a follow up to receiving that letter?"

"During that following week, I had a number of discussions with the chancellor about the impact and consequences of that letter," Pederson said. It was the first time that anyone had mentioned Gearhart's influence in the context of why Pederson and Schook didn't disclose Schook's conclusions to state auditors. "I had discussions with Ms. Schook to make sure I understood everything she was saying in the report—the *memorandum*," correcting himself to avoid labeling it as a "report," a careful distinction that Gearhart had emphasized months earlier; it would have been much more difficult to justify placing a "report" in someone's personnel file or withholding a "report" under the state's public records law. "There were a number of discussions where I wanted to make sure I understood completely what was being concluded in that report." Again he failed to offer any information that would explain why he dismissed Schook's accusation of fraud.

Bell pursued the issue. "The following week you met with our legislative auditors for your exit interview for your normal audit on an unrelated topic," he said. "Would you care to give us a real short synopsis on your discussions with our auditors at that exit interview?"

Pederson knew Bell wanted to discuss the affidavit—i.e., the "representation letter"—the CFO signed. "I don't recall there being a specific discussion with the auditor about any subpart of it," Pederson offered. "I may be forgetting about it. I don't recall."

"I want to take you to a couple of key points in that letter and what you stated by signing that letter," Bell explained. "The letter states, 'We have no knowledge of any allegation of fraud or suspected fraud affecting the entity involving management or employees who have significant roles in internal control or others where fraud could have a material affect on financial statements.' We're essentially here today because we had some financial statements that weren't exactly kosher. That letter goes further to say, 'We have no knowledge of allegations of fraud or suspected fraud affecting the entity received in communications from employees, former employees, analysts, regulators, or others.'

"There are seven specific references in [Schook's report] expressing concerns about the accuracy and veracity of the division's accounting records. Statements used such as 'likelihood of conflict of interest violations,' 'intentional efforts to disguise,' 'misdirection of funds,' 'risk of fraudulent activity,' 'deliberate efforts to disguise'....I'm just a farmer and a small business owner. I'm not an attorney. But I think any reasonable person making a read of that would have to assume that there's at least suspected fraud or an allegation of it here. How can you square your representation to our auditors as being forthright, honest with no attempt to mislead, with your knowledge that was kept from our legislative auditors at that time?"

"Sir, very good questions," Pederson replied. "I understand your perspective based on your discussions at the earlier hearing. Number seven"—the statement about knowledge or suspicions of fraud—"is a black and white question. I did not believe at the time I signed the management representation letter that there was, one, fraud, or that there was suspected fraud by Ms. Schook or any other person at the university related to the Advancement division."

Bell's disbelief was evident. "So you don't think there was any misrepresentation? You know, one of the definitions of fraud in *Black's Law Dictionary* is 'misrepresentation or intent to mislead.' There's been a lot of misconception here that fraud always involves missing money. That's clearly not the case by any unbiased legal standard. There's at least an allegation that someone was misled here and that it materially affected financial statements. That's a key point in [Schook's memo]! Are you sitting here today and saying that at that time you had no knowledge that there was a financial statement that was improperly drafted or presented?"

"I believe the financial statements were materially correct, sir," Pederson responded, not addressing Bell's broader point about the nature of fraud.

"Do you believe that your statements to our audit team were completely forthcoming and truthful to the best of your knowledge?" Bell asked. "And that you made no effort to conceal or withhold any information that would be useful to our auditors?"

"Sir, I perhaps can't address that full question," Pederson replied. "But I believe I answered those questions truthfully."

"And you believe you were completely forthcoming in your statements?"

Pederson's circular answer sounded like a line straight out of *Alice in Wonderland:* "I was no more or no less forthcoming than answering the questions truthfully."

As the afternoon passed along, patterns emerged. The Joint Performance Review committee members weren't buying the university's justification of its financial management practices. Pederson was unconvincing as he defended signing the affidavit attesting that he knew of no suggestions of fraud. Gearhart was turning almost every question he was asked into an opportunity to state that a deficit never occurred when he had been vice chancellor, a relatively minor point given the more serious issues auditors and lawmakers had with

UA. For his part, Choate was forced to reiterate his point that the university's lax system of checks and balances, not his management style, allowed the Advancement deficit to occur. Meanwhile, Sharp was allowed to sit at the witness table and, for the most part, simply observe the proceedings.

Another pattern that emerged was the apparent lack of interest among committee members in the matters I had raised on September 13th. For the first few hours there had been just passing references to the possibility of perjury, document shredding, and withholding of documents from auditors and the news media. From my perspective, the committee needed to address those issues as well. After all, "JPR" was the committee of the General Assembly with explicit authority to conduct investigations into "specific problem areas" of state funded agencies. And in Fayetteville, they had a problem.

Representative Mark Lowery was one of the few members who wanted to delve into those issues. Lowery was a professor at the University of Central Arkansas—a public university that was not affiliated with UA or the UA System. Earlier in the hearing, when questioning Gearhart about the nonexistent accounts receivable, Lowery described UA's practice as "a bookkeeping trick" and offered a sharp riposte: "I hope to God that this isn't the way we're teaching accounting at the University of Arkansas!" Now he wanted to talk about Gearhart himself.

"The statement you gave us—your prepared statement—said that the Washington County prosecutor's office investigation showed that 'all' of the allegations—every one of the allegations—are not accurate. Is that your statement?" Lowery asked the chancellor.

"I'm not sure I recall exactly what I said, sir, and what it was relative to," Gearhart responded.

"That's what I wrote down—'All investigations, including the FBI, the Washington County prosecutor, every one of them show that the allegations that have been made publicly are not accurate,'" Lowery recited.

"I would say to you that all of those agencies did indicate that I did not perjure—let me step back," Gearhart responded, catching himself on his wording. "The prosecutor did indicate that I did not perjure myself and has since told us that and has made that information available to the media. He also indicated there was no theft, there was no private inurement, or anything like that. Does that answer your question?"

"Actually, it doesn't," Lowery answered. "Because isn't it an accurate representation of [Washington County Deputy Prosecutor Bercaw's] letter that some of the issues were not under their jurisdiction, like issues of perjury? That's why the Pulaski County prosecuting attorney has been asked to look into perjury."

"Actually, he has told us verbally that he looked at that issue and has informed the media to that effect," Gearhart asserted. "What the prosecutor will do here in Pulaski County, I don't know. He hasn't made a determination yet. But I can tell you that he did say he looked at that issue."

In December, Bercaw had told the General Assembly and the public, in his report, that his office lacked the authority to review the possibility of perjury since the statements at the September 13th hearing took place in another county. But here Gearhart was stating that he or his staff had been told something different in an oral conversation. If true, it was a possible reflection of UA's relationship and influence with the prosecutor's office. Or it might have been just another of Gearhart's misstatements under oath. When UA first made that point in December, the *Democrat-Gazette's* Lisa Hammersly sought to confirm it with Bercaw's boss, District Prosecutor John Threet. Deputy Mieka Hatcher responded in a three-sentence answer that was less definitive than what Gearhart had just reported to the legislative committee. Hatcher wrote:

> The substantive issues of the alleged perjury charge were part and parcel of the [Freedom of Information Act] review. The investigation did not reveal any evidence of perjury. However the jurisdiction

with the controlling authority is Pulaski County.

However, the question of perjury at the September 13th hearing did not pertain to whether or not Reynolds' budget document had been FOIA'd; it was whether or not Gearhart said anything at the meeting that prompted anyone to dispose of documents and not to create any more of them.

"The chancellor just gave testimony that the prosecutor said there was no perjury," Representative Justin Harris said, directing his comment to me. "There was none of that. Do you have something to say to that?"

"I respectfully disagree with that assertion," I answered. "I think if you look at the prosecutor's report you'll find that the prosecutor was silent on a lot of the issues that were brought before him. He narrowly defined the scope of what he looked at. I can give you a couple of examples. One of the things in the report that was not mentioned was the fact that there were multiple people who did say that the chancellor used the phrase 'get rid of' documents, and in the same tone that I described. In the penultimate draft—the next to last draft—of the prosecutor's report, there is a line in there that says, 'Apparently Chancellor Gearhart got angry and said to get rid of documents.'

"I FOIA'd those documents. I went down to see them myself because I wondered why it was not addressed in his report. And there's a hand-drawn line through that sentence done by a higher-up within the prosecutor's office. It's that office's right, of course, before they issue a report. But whoever drafted the report—based on the facts that were presented—concluded that the chancellor did say that. And if you look at the notes from the interviews, the two other associate vice chancellors as well as me said the same thing."

I offered other examples of discrepancies and oversights. "The prosecutor's report was completely silent on the issue of [FOIA violations] related to July 29th. The prosecutor did ask me extensively about that but did not bring in anybody else to ask them about that, despite the fact that he had ample evidence that [violations] existed. I don't know why he didn't do that. Another issue: there was an error that I brought to the attention of the Legislative Audit Committee on December 13th. The prosecutor said that the budget document that was discussed at the January 14th meeting was not subject to an outstanding FOIA at that time. He cited a section saying that the FOIA was asking for documents between January 1st, 2012 and July 30th, 2012. But in the next paragraph of the FOIA it specifically asked for the status of the budget for FY13. So the prosecutor didn't address that question at all. There were other things there, but I do not believe the university got a clean bill of health or was vindicated on some of the very serious charges that I presented and others have presented, including members of the Legislative Audit staff."

As the hearing wore on, Representative Charlotte Douglas delved into my termination on August 23rd. "Mr. Gearhart, why was he fired?"

"He was fired for a number of reasons," he answered. "I'm not sure we need to go into all of them, but let me make few points to you if I could. We lost faith in Mr. Diamond. His argumentative nature, his inability to take any direction—not just from me but from the senior leadership of the university, our provost. His failure to respond to requests from deans and others. His failure to answer telephone calls. He was invited to come to his supervisor's office, which is Mr. Wyrick, who is here today, and he was told that the university had lost faith in him, but we did not want to hurt him, we did not want to do anything to embarrass him. And we would give him plenty of time to find a job. He went ballistic at that meeting. He said to his direct supervisor that 'you're management style is laughable' and proceeded to denigrate someone who had been hired and placed into that position. Now all I can say to you is if I told my boss, the president of the university, that his management style was laughable, I don't think I'd last very long in the organization. Mr. Diamond did not have a right to employment. We had lost faith in him as an executive of the institution. And we told him that. And I told him on many occasions before that particular session that we were unhappy.

"The thing that is interesting to me is that, leading up until he was dismissed, he really wasn't that unhappy with me, because he asked me to be a reference for him," he continued. "He had asked me to talk with a number of people, and he also had applied for multiple jobs. So he was unhappy, he wanted to leave the university, and we gave him that opportunity with his head up. And he didn't take it."

Douglas gave me an opportunity to respond.

"I think there's a slight amount of truth in the chancellor's statement," I answered. "And a lot of fabrication. Personnel issues are not the matter. The issues that were problems for me—with the chancellor and later with Chris Wyrick—were the issues I related to you earlier in my statement. They centered on what I saw as a deliberate attempt to interfere with the legal obligations of the university to respond to issues of great public interest involving one of the biggest public institutions in the state. An eight hundred million dollar operation. I thought we were on very thin ice about some of the arguments being made to place, in Brad's and Joy's personnel files, a document that the university itself realized [was] a public document—the Schook memo—and that's why they did not want to go to court with the *Democrat-Gazette*. It dealt with the chancellor's behavior, as I talked about before, pertaining to the media: trying to get me to send letters—very disparaging and untrue letters. A variety of things like that.

"The tipping point was the situation with Chris Wyrick," I continued, "when he clearly violated the Freedom of Information Act—knowingly violated the Freedom of Information Act, in my opinion. The lawyers for the university understood my point. It was much easier to move me out than it was to deal with the reality. And of course, the other issue that came up, as I mentioned earlier, were issues involving Chris Wyrick and derogatory things—some of which have been in the paper—that he said about religion, race, and gender issues that others witnessed. I expressed that, as I thought I should, to the chancellor's chief of staff just a few weeks before I was terminated. I think the combination of those two things—me objecting to what I saw as violations of the law and my objections to what I thought were objectionable and inappropriate and threatening behavior. Instead of dealing with the problems, it was easier to get rid of me."

Following up, Representative Nate Steel noted that in the months following the January 14th meeting, I had listed Gearhart as a reference when I was a finalist for vice presidencies at the University of Arizona and the University of Iowa. "Is that true? Did you ask for reference for either one of those two schools?"

"Yes, I did. That's certainly common in higher ed. If you're looking to go somewhere else, you usually use your boss or your CEO."

"I understand that would be common," Steel replied, "but it seems that if the culture was such that you've been testifying to today and in the last couple of meetings, it seems like the last thing you would want is a recommendation from the chancellor of that university. If something were to unravel, even after you got the job, that would reflect very poorly on you, would it not?"

"I think it's a reflection that our relationship was nowhere near as bad as he just presented," I answered. "In fact, I've got email where we talk about—we go back and forth—about my interest in those two positions. The issue for me was, I wanted to get out when things were getting bad, particularly after the incidents with Mr. Wyrick and the behavior he demonstrated once he started working in April as vice chancellor. That was understandable. I wasn't alone in that, and I'll let others speak for themselves. If things were as bad as the chancellor just made them out to be, and if he were as dissatisfied or so upset with me, I would not be using him or some of the people he referred to as my references. And I think my colleagues at the university would attest to that."

Douglas had more questions for the chancellor.

"Mr. Gearhart, you're still under oath," she prefaced. "I know you've been accused of asking that documents be shredded or—not really being shredded but, 'Please don't bring these back to me, don't generate these documents so they cannot be FOIA-able'—could you respond to that?"

"Yes, certainly. My response is, all of that was reviewed by the prosecutor. In this country, we have a judicial system, a system where you allow the prosecutor to look into those kinds of issues. He spent several months looking into the issues. He interviewed several people. And he did not find that I asked for the destruction of documents."

Douglas stopped him there. "I have found today that you have referred back to what the prosecutor has found. But when we directly ask you for information—for you to make a statement—I prefer that you make that statement based on the truth that you know, instead of what the prosecutor has found. So, if you don't mind, make that statement. I have asked you to respond, please, to that."

"I'd be happy to do that," Gearhart replied. "Would you state the question again?"

"Would you please respond to the question I asked about documents? You have been accused of asking that the documents either not be—either they be shredded, they be done away with, they not be put together, or they be manipulated in any way so that the newspapers—so that they could not be FOIA-able."

"I did not," he responded.

"So you are saying that the accusations of those three or four people, saying that in their presence you did not ask—"

Gearhart cut Douglas off before she could get to the heart of her question, one she had not yet articulated as directly as it could have been.

"First of all, what Mr. Diamond has said to you today is not accurate. If you look at the statement that was made by the head of the alumni association, Graham Stewart, he said the words 'get rid of them' may have been used, but that I at no time made a directive that anyone took as serious at that meeting. And that is in the report, that is in the documents that were released by Mr. Bercaw. Secondly, the other person that he's saying today— that I asked for the destruction of documents—made the same statement to our attorneys. There are five other people at that meeting that will tell you that the entire conversation was built around Mr. Diamond wanting to create documents. And I said to Mr. Diamond that we had no obligation to create documents for the media. The law does not require that, and we have no obligation to do that. And he is suggesting that when I told him that that I was asking for the destruction of documents. And that simply is not true.

"And as a matter of fact, the document he is referring to was not subject to the FOIA as determined by the prosecutor," Gearhart said, his voice rising. "And the document he was referring to was never destroyed and was subsequently released to the newspapers and to the other folks! So all I can say to you is that I'm going to rely on what the prosecutor said, and I would hope that the committee would rely on what the prosecutor said."

Rice, the committee chair, interrupted to say that the committee was running out of time. Before moving on to another member's questions, he asked me if I'd like to respond to Gearhart's assertions.

"Thank you," I said. "I've read those documents. The question that I said at the beginning, back in September, and what all of us have talked about since January 14th, was the chancellor angrily said, 'Get rid of those and don't create any more.' He's been very careful not to use that phrase, and I think it's important. You can ask him directly: Did you say 'Get rid of that' or anything very close to that? If you look at the prosecutor's notes, you'll find that Bruce Pontious and Graham Stewart both said that he did. Nobody thought he was joking. He was in no mood to joke. You don't sit through a meeting with the CEO of an organization who drops an F-bomb in a meeting like that. That doesn't happen unless the person was in the state of mind that we talked about. The other thing that I think is important to note here is that the chancellor has said, as part of a narrative he has been working on with other people, he said I was disruptive in the meeting. As I told you, if you look at the agenda, which I believe may be in your files, the second item on the agenda was the budget. We never got to me! It was a very short meeting. We had plenty of time after the chancellor stormed out of the meeting for us to get together and process this.

"As Brad said, people came down to his office immediately. I noticed that Denise Reynolds told the prosecutor that, at the chancellor's meeting, I rambled on for 42 minutes. Well, she heard that somewhere, and it didn't happen at that meeting, even though she was there. She was referring to a meeting—a one-on-one meeting I had with the chancellor on January 24th, the meeting where I said 'I'm trying to help you.' Because both he and Judy Schwab told me that meeting lasted 42 minutes."

"So maybe I could rephrase my question to Mr. Gearhart," Douglas said, seeking the chair's indulgence. "Did you request the destruction or removal of any documents?"

"I did not ask for any documents to be destroyed that were subject to FOIA," a nuanced answer. "I get rid of documents all the time. Everybody that I know gets rid of documents. But if they are subject to FOIA, we absolutely do not get rid of them. And that is what I think the prosecutor found. Mr. Diamond can claim otherwise all day. But he has no basis on which to make those claims."

As the hearing approached the five-hour mark, fatigue had set in among the committee. About two-thirds of the members had vacated their desks, watching or listening elsewhere or had simply left the building. Interest levels seemed to be waning. Keith Ingram, the Senate's minority leader and a member of the committee, restored their attention.

"Dr. Gearhart, you're the most outstanding fundraiser the university has ever had," Ingram stated. "I guess you'd agree with me that confidence in fundraising is paramount to the donor."

Gearhart paused before responding. "When you say 'confidence,' what do you mean?"

"That money is going to be used for its intended purpose. It's not wasted."

"Yes, certainly."

"Well," Ingram continued, "this has taken a toll on everybody—the legislature, everybody at your table, the Advancement division, you. These series of events that have taken place? To me, any one single event would not be of a major nature. But when taken in context—and I'm just going to try very quickly to summarize what we're dealing with—when the shortfall was discovered, we found out that there were accounting practices that led to concealing the deficit. We found a coincidence that as soon as Ms. Sharp left, documents started to be shredded. We received reports from former employees of the division not to create any more FOIA-able documents. There began a blaming of employees in the Advancement division that were either hired by yourself or promoted by yourself. Reassignments have taken place. There has been pressure to retire, dismiss, or negotiate settlements with employees with non-disclosure clauses. There was a misapplication of a major donor's contribution to a restricted fund to an un-restricted account. Subsequently that major donor, who was on the Board of Trustees, resigned from the university board.

"Chancellor, you picked a fight with the statewide newspaper," Ingram noted pointedly. "I mean, you sent the letter that promoted a fight with the *Democrat-Gazette*. So, the one constant in this issue has been you, Chancellor.

"I guess my only question is this," the Senator stated. "With all of this combined, do you think that you have the confidence to lead with all the things that have gone on?"

"Yes, sir, I do," Gearhart replied.

"That's my question, Mr. Chair," Ingram said, in conclusion.

"Would you permit me the opportunity to respond to your accusations?" Gearhart asked?

"I didn't make any 'accusations'," Ingram answered. "I just stated everything succinctly. There's been so much thrown at this committee today and at Audit. I was just trying to put it in a context of what we're dealing with. Right, wrong, or indifferent, there have been so many things that have come out of this, that this has led to a major hearing that none of us in this room wanted to take part in, I assure you."

"I certainly agree it's been an embarrassment," Gearhart acknowledged. "I certainly agree that it's been too bad for all the people involved. But I really must take exception to the comments you made. And I'd be delighted to go through each one of them. I think you made some statements that are just simply inaccurate. And I think we can show you that."

"Well, whether it is or isn't, Chancellor, it's all of these things in one pile. As I said in my statement, any one of these things wouldn't even be noticed. It's the cumulative effect of all of these. We have a series where you have stated in front of this committee that you were trying to take care of Mr. Choate, you were trying to take care of Mr. Diamond—in my business, if somebody makes a major blunder, I cut them off immediately! I don't carry them! I'll say this, Chancellor, that's the difference between somebody in private ownership spending our dollars versus somebody that's raising money that's spending somebody else's dollar…All of this cumulatively has been devastating to the public relations of the University of Arkansas."

It was nearing six o'clock. Rice, the committee chair, brought the hearing to a close with some final thoughts. Thanking those who remained for the entire five hours, he reminded the committee of the reason why the hearing was held: to get the truth and have it discussed openly, something that wasn't permitted at the truncated December 13th Auditing Committee meeting. Rice expressed dismay about how the scandal had affected the lives and behavior of so many individuals affiliated with UA.

"It's the people that it hurts," Rice stated, "the people who have lost their job and their families. There are employees now that I feel are more on-guard of anything that they say, even if it needs to be said. It's sad, to me. And that's not throwing an accusation at anybody. I think the best thing the university could do is to try to go on from here and let people know that they're going to try to do the right thing for the right reason. People need to be able to speak up.

"I feel like the board of trustees hopefully understands the magnitude of this," Rice continued. "It's been discussed here today that we've all gotten a little bit tarnished...We all need to do a better job. The people of Arkansas deserve open and honest answers."

I agreed, and thought that as a result of this hearing, the Board of Trustees—the citizen organization responsible under law for ensuring the prudent and honest management of the UA System—would finally realize how poorly they and the public had been served by UA's paid leaders. I also thought that the hearings would prompt the board to take the necessary corrective actions to restore public trust and integrity. But once again, I overestimated those leaders' commitment to transparency and accountability.

Chapter 19

END OF AN ERROR

It was now all over except for the waiting. During the previous 14 months, UA had experienced one aborted lawsuit, two audits, three legislative hearings, a four-point prosecutorial investigation, and the unforeseen departures of five top officials within the Advancement division. Two more possible criminal offenses remained unresolved—perjury at the first legislative hearing, which had been referred to prosecutors in Pulaski County, and Pederson's failure to disclose to state auditors his awareness of Advancement's financial and management troubles during his exit conference with them. But other than those questions, the only force keeping the university from bringing accountability to the Advancement scandal was the UA System Board of Trustees, the nine men and one woman who were legally responsible for the University of Arkansas' leadership, performance, and transparency.

At issue was the future of Dave Gearhart and Don Pederson—and maybe Jean Schook and Chris Wyrick. Through their decisions and behavior, those four persons had contributed in damaging ways to the evolution of the scandal. The question of the moment was,

To what degree—if any—would the public's trustees hold those UA officials accountable for the series of embarrassments enveloping Arkansas' flagship university?

The media as well as others within and outside higher ed expected the UA System board to answer that question when it met in Little Rock on January 23rd and 24th. *Democrat-Gazette* columnist John Brummett had offered that trustees, as well as many legislators and members of the public, were ready to "move on" and put the scandal behind them:

> What seems inevitable—right or wrong, fair or foul—is that Gearhart will reap great and deserved praise for the undisputed fact that the university is doing spectacularly well (Advancement spending and football excepted), then submit his resignation over the deficit failing in the greater interest of the school's continued well-being. Loose ends of various investigations either will be tied up or left permanently loose.

Arkansas Times' Max Brantley offered his own thoughts on where things were headed:

> The investigation of financial foul-ups and the degree of openness at the University of Arkansas under Chancellor David Gearhart's leadership is pretty well at an end at the legislature, despite some grumbling. There are at least some on the board who are unhappy about the UA handling of the matter. And there are some stout supporters of Gearhart (they probably outnumber stout critics). The expectation is that current Chair Jane Rogers is working to produce a Board vote of confidence for Gearhart.

Brantley also noted claims that some trustees appeared to believe that the recent scrutiny of UA's handling of Advancement was much ado about nothing. Brantley encouraged readers to let their opinions be known.

> Some of [Gearhart's] supporters on the board profess to wonder what all the fuss is about. They say nobody has called them to express any concern about what's going on at UA....[There's] no need

> for Gearhart's review to be considered by the Board in a vacuum. Anybody with a thought on the UA situation—its handling of financial matters, its firing of the university spokesman John Diamond, its accountability—should get in touch with UA Board members. Pro or con.

In Fayetteville, university staffers were working to make sure Gearhart was on as solid a footing as possible when trustees took up his future. Gearhart's close friend and longtime *Democrat-Gazette* columnist Mike Masterson wrote two commentaries about Gearhart in the days between the final legislative hearing and the trustees meeting. One of Masterson's columns criticized members of the General Assembly for their "ugly legislative pile-on" during the recent UA hearing. He also tried to reinforce a relatively minor point in the audits that Gearhart insisted on professing *ad nauseam* since the joint audit report was issued in September: Advancement had an end-of-year surplus when he left the division in 2008 to become UA's chancellor. Masterson's follow-up commentary, entitled "Gearhart's Enviable Results," praised all of the good things Gearhart had done for UA as chancellor. None of Masterson's water carrying surprised me; during my days at UA, Gearhart asked me to prepare talking points regarding the university's handling of the Advancement deficit for Masterson because the columnist "wanted to help."

To aid in Gearhart's defense, UA also issued a news release announcing that it had exceeded its fundraising benchmark for the first six months of the current fiscal year. (A large percentage of the final amount included software and other in-kind contributions that would not have been included in previous years' calculation of giving totals, according to an Advancement employee with knowledge of that year's donations.) The statement signaled to trustees that under Gearhart, UA continued to attract donor support despite the Advancement debacle. It also helped plant the seed that UA might lose access to valued donors if or when Gearhart departed.

Leading up to the board meeting, news stories continued to assess the most recent of the three legislative hearings and what it might portend for Gearhart's future. Representative Terry Rice, the Performance Review Committee's co-chair, believed that his committee's January 7th hearing had served a useful purpose. He described it in vivid terms to the *Democrat-Gazette's* Lisa Hammersly: "Sometimes when you have a wound, you have to pick off the scab to heal. I think we did that." Representative Mark Lowery also thought the latest session was valuable, adding that some of the testimony would justify further legislative review. "I was surprised by the chancellor's response," Lowery told Hammersly, "in that he admitted Choate was told to destroy a document—a document that could have been used to show his only work product during that time period, something that could have justified the expense—because no one had FOIA'd it yet....It stretches the imagination. It shows a total lack of willingness to be transparent."

But a committee colleague of Lowery's, Senator Jonathan Dismang, was not inclined to have the General Assembly continue its involvement. His response to the hearings reflected the *look forward, not back* motif that trustee John Goodson offered to lawmakers in December. "Yes, [the Advancement issue] was troubling to begin with," Dismang told reporter Hammersly. "But [UA has] accepted the audit findings. They're making the changes, and they're moving forward differently....I'm confident this won't arise again."

Another influential committee member, Senator Keith Ingram, remained concerned about what the hearings had revealed but told Hammersly that he thought the time had come for trustees, not legislators, to act. Ingram had been the lawmaker who, at the January 7th hearing, rattled off a list of bad decisions and behaviors that had occurred on Gearhart's watch. He had also questioned whether Gearhart thought he still had the public's "confidence to lead with all of the things that have gone on." Gearhart had answered that he did. However, at this point, it was the board's confidence, not the public's, that would decide the chancellor's fate. It was unknown if the two groups shared the same sentiments.

A week before the board meeting, I learned from a UA employee that Chris Wyrick's executive assistant, Laura Villines, was taking a new position within the Advancement division as a manager within one of the Development office's small units. I hadn't spoken with Laura since August and didn't know whether her relationship with Wyrick had improved since then. However, the position she was taking over was, in my estimation, lower in pay, stature, influence, and responsibility than the one she was leaving. In fact, she was part of Advancement's senior leadership team and, as she had immediately shared with Choate, had been present a year earlier when Gearhart told Reynolds to "get rid of it." I wasn't sure whether she was changing jobs of her own volition or if Wyrick had made the decision for her.

Knowing the signigicant pay differential between Villines' current job and the one she was moving to, I checked with someone with knowledge of campus payroll data to see if Laura would be taking a cut in pay. I learned just the opposite: she was awarded a $2,500 pay increase, her second raise in seven months. UA records showed that with her increase, Villines' annual salary would be $14,500 higher than her new supervisor's. I looked further into UA's salary records and was amazed to learn that at least 18 employees working within Chris Wyrick's Advancement division had received pay increases of 10 percent or more during the prior seven months. Those pay raises occurred despite the fact that UA leaders had just required their academic colleges and other campus units to pick up more than $500,000 in Advancement-related salaries in order to help Wyrick balance the division's budget and reduce its $3.2 million deficit.

I found other payroll matters even more disconcerting. Following the September 13th legislative hearing at which I disclosed Gearhart's January 14th outburst over budget documents, my concerns about document shredding, and UA's non-compliance with Arkansas' public records law, a couple of the key players in the scandal had received a second round of pay increases beyond the ones they had been given in July. In October, Denise Reynolds was given a 20 percent raise on top of the 2.75 percent raise she had received three months earlier. The raise was made retroactive to July 1st, an unconventional adjustment. Additionally, Scott Varady, UA's legal counsel and a person I had previously confided in about my FOIA concerns, received a 27.5 percent raise in November after receiving a three percent raise in July. Normally, out-of-cycle raises in an employee's base pay are granted only when there is a significant and documented increase in job responsibilities as part of a promotion or because an employee has received a formal, written offer of employment elsewhere. The size and timing of the increases were conspicuous, as neither exception appeared to apply; both Reynolds and Varady were performing the same jobs as they had been when they received their July raises. I shared the information with *Arkansas Times*' Max Brantley, who at this point was writing about UA management issues almost daily.

Around the same time, I sent individual email messages to several members of the board of trustees, in which I included my January 7th testimony. "If you have not already done so, I respectfully ask you to read it," I requested, before continuing my message:

> I have been surprised and disappointed that no one from the UA System office or board of trustees has contacted me to discuss the concerns I expressed about UA obstruction of FOIA compliance. It is especially disconcerting given that I had reported my concerns to UA's legal counsel and had multiple discussions about those concerns with [those] university attorneys. I remain willing to discuss the FOIA matter should you wish. Thank you in advance for reading my testimony.

The board began its two-day session in Little Rock on Thursday, January 23rd on the campus of the University of Arkansas for Medical Sciences. Usually the first day is consumed with committee work, and the meeting of greatest public interest that day involved the trustees' own audit committee. Originally, that four-member committee was supposed to consider the recommendations of state and UA System auditors on September 13th immediately after the first legislative hearing. But that discussion was postponed when the Joint Legislative Auditing Committee voted to continue its own review in light of my testimony that day. With the audits now accepted and filed away somewhere within the State Capitol complex, it was time for trustees to reflect on the joint report's findings.

According to the *Democrat-Gazette*, the committee spent just seven minutes discussing the Advancement audits before voting to accept them as originally presented. Reporter Bill Bowden captured one trustee's positive assessment of how the lemons of scandal had been turned into lemonade:

> "For some people this has been a very painful experience," committee member John Goodson of Texarkana told about 70 people attending the meeting...."But I view it as a beneficial experience for two reasons. We accepted today new budgetary policies that we're looking at, new guidelines. And then I think, maybe more importantly, it has brought to light all the good things that have happened on that campus," he said. "Exactly how fortunate we are to be a part of such a prosperous university as the University of Arkansas."

The news report noted that UA's chief financial officer, Don Pederson, had agreed to the auditors' 16 recommendations, including that his office "monitor and resolve significant deficit spending issues monthly or quarterly rather than waiting until year end." Reading that sentence, I doubted that any other university CFO in America had to be given such a basic instruction.

Later that day, the full board of trustees went into executive session to discuss personnel matters. Bowden reported that the closed-door session lasted three hours before adjourning for the day. Jane Rogers, the chair of the board, announced that the executive session would resume the following morning.

Of the board's ten members, Sam Hilburn was the only trustee who did not attend the meeting, due to recent surgery. As a close friend of Gearhart's, Hilburn wanted to be on record in support of the chancellor. He sent a letter to Rogers, which in part said:

> I regret that I cannot [attend], but I want to express my hope that the board cease any attempts to scrutinize Chancellor Gearhart regarding the Legislative Audit. For the board to pursue this investigation is divisive and damaging to the university....[T]here has yet to be evidence uncovered of any illegality on the part of the chancellor. We all know what happened. It is a shame that it happened. But, we should not cannot [sic] condone the further vilification of the Chancellor as a scapegoat. To continue on this path only serves to perpetuate the biased agenda of outsiders who seek to undermine the university.

Nobody other than board members themselves knows exactly how persuasive Hilburn's appeal was with his fellow trustees. All that is publicly known is that when board members emerged from Friday morning's half-hour-long executive session, Chair Jane Rogers had a statement she wanted to read:

> As trustees, we take very seriously our responsibility to ensure the financial health, stability, and accountability of all of the institutions in the University of Arkansas System. I know my colleagues understand and share many of the concerns that have been raised regarding the deficit in the Advancement division at the University of Arkansas, Fayetteville. On behalf of the board, I want to express my thanks to all of the auditors, law enforcement officials, legislators, news media, and others who have looked into this issue and provided valuable insight on what happened and how to keep something similar from happening again.
>
> I also appreciate that Chancellor Gearhart has taken responsibility for the problems surrounding the deficit and for implementing the changes necessary to ensure the fiscal health of the division and improve the accountability of the university as a whole. As we've said,

> the board will continue to monitor the progress of implementing all of the recommendations from the audit report. And, as we've shown in passing the new board policies, our board is committed to financial accountability and freedom of information.
>
> I recognize that this has been a difficult episode for the university, and I pledge that the university can and will do a better job in the future. At the same time, I recognize the many wonderful accomplishments that have occurred across the campus, and I am proud that the overall financial and academic health of the institution is outstanding and continues on an upward course under Chancellor Gearhart's leadership. With that in mind, as chair of the board, I'd like to reiterate my full support of the chancellor in his effort to move the university forward in a positive direction for our students, faculty, staff, and our state.

It didn't require any insider knowledge to recognize that Rogers' declaration of support, expressed in the first-person *I* and not the collective *We*, was a negotiated testimonial. There would be no reason for not sharing it as the consensus of all trustees unless one or more trustees objected, during the closed-doors executive sessions, to being included in such a proclamation. Why else would Rogers' prepared remarks be presented to the public as one person's opinion?

Trustee John Goodson wanted to make it more than just Rogers' position on Gearhart. Usually when board members make predetermined motions under parliamentary procedure, the language is scripted out for them in advance. However, given the unstructured way Goodson expressed himself, he gave the impression that it might not have been part of an agreed-upon plan. "I would like to consider the comments you made this morning as a resolution of support for Chancellor Gearhart," Goodson said to Rogers, "and I make a motion that reflects that." The board then voted and approved it unanimously.

It may seem a stretch to suggest that Goodson's motion may have caught some of his board colleagues off-guard and that he intended for it to do so. The trial lawyer was known to possess a bag of tricks, and it may have been that he intended his awkwardly-phrased motion to force Gearhart's detractors on the board to rally 'round Chair Rogers as a show of loyalty to their leader. The savvy Goodson understood that individual trustees were highly unlikely to object in public to being associated with Rogers' statement, even if they had done so during the executive session. One or more "no" votes would expose a division among a board that prided itself in always speaking with one voice. Adopting Rogers' personal statement to become the board's public position would keep peace among the trustee family without jeopardizing any conditions or concessions the group might have agreed to behind closed doors.

Whether Rogers' statement about Gearhart and Goodson's subsequent responses were orchestrated or organic, one thing was certain: the handling of that particular board action was far different from the carefully stage-managed manner with which the trustees normally acted in public session. Other business related to the Advancement scandal, quickly disposed of in the moments following the vote on Rogers' statement, demonstrated the usual degrees of structure and pre-consideration with which the board performed its work.

Take, for example, the board's acceptance, without further discussion, of its audit committee's report from the previous day's meeting. Or the adoption of a new board policy providing "guidelines for the handling of and responses to public records requests under FOIA by the System, campuses, divisions, and units." ("Diamond's Law," as an attorney friend of mine called it in an attempt at gallows humor.) Or another new policy adopted that day that established a "University Code of Ethical Conduct," the introduction of which states that employees must demonstrate "conduct that is beyond reproach and integrity of the highest caliber; honesty and fairness; and accountability, transparency, and commitment to compliance." (*How different the past fifteen months would have been had those standards and principles been enforced,* I thought.) Or consider the board's revised policy on financial reporting and accounting, designed to make clear to UA and its sister institutions that they were not permitted to engage in any alternative interpretations of generally accepted accounting practices. Or take another example: a policy establishing similar controls and oversight responsibilities for budgets, directed at Pederson and other campus-level CFOs. All five of those new policies, adopted on the same day as passage of the Gearhart statement, followed the normal conventions of board deliberations.

After trustees concluded their two-day meeting and adjourned, it was evident that incongruence existed between the new policies they felt were necessary and the level of responsibility that UA's man at the helm bore for the scandal that occurred on his watch. The buck stopped somewhere, and based on the board's actions and inactions, the "where" seemed to be at the feet of Brad Choate. At least that was the message trustees sent to the public. Gearhart, it would seem, was a faultless victim of his trusted subordinates' own ineptitude.

Or perhaps the board had an unusually low standard for what it considered as acceptable performance. A possible reflection of that can be found in an email exchange between Jane Rogers and Trustee Clifford Gibson a couple of days before the board meeting in Little Rock. The topic was my January 21st email to several trustees offering to speak to them about UA's mishandling of FOIA requests. Rogers wrote:

> Seems to me that the issue he is speaking about is the same issue that went to the prosecutor....If the prosecutor sees no problems, I believe it is out of our hands.

Based on Rogers' response, it would appear that the governing board's chair had defined the System's measure of acceptable leadership and management as anything short of an indictment or actual prosecution. *Time to move on, folks. Nothing more to see (or learn) here.*

As much as the board, System President Bobbitt, and many others hoped the trustees' actions at the January 24, 2014 meeting would bring "Gearhartgate" to a close, it didn't. References to the scandal that started in 2012 with Joy Sharp's confession of her "terrible mistake" would continue to appear in news stories and in conversation. A week after the board meeting, the *Democrat-Gazette's* Bill Bowden reported that UA was transferring another $5 million in university reserves to Wyrick's Advancement division to fund it for the remainder of the fiscal year. Bowden also reported that starting in July, UA would provide an additional $2.3 million annually to that division to help cover its operating costs. Had Gearhart and CFO Pederson taken that same corrective action 15 months earlier in response to Jean Schook's now-infamous memo, they and other UA officials probably could have avoided the secrecy, misrepresentation, trauma, and drama that consumed them in the year that followed. But they had not.

Just as the board appeared to have settled the question of Gearhart's future, Washington County Deputy Prosecutor David Bercaw seemed to perform the same action regarding Pederson. On April 29, 2014, Bercaw announced he had concluded that Pederson committed no crime when, in his exit conference with state auditors, he failed to tell them about the existence and findings of Jean Schook's memo. Bercaw told the *Democrat-Gazette* that it was not illegal to withhold information about a *risk* of fraud, which Pederson had claimed was all that he had gathered from reading and discussing Schook's report. Bercaw's conclusion about Pederson's possible criminality would have been different, he explained, had Pederson withheld knowledge of *accusations* of fraud, which is how auditors and at least 14 members of the Legislative Auditing Committee had interpreted Schook's written findings. A couple of state lawmakers involved in the legislative hearings criticized Bercaw's limited scope but were helpless to do anything more about it.

On May 16th, less than three weeks after receiving Bercaw's exoneration, UA announced that Pederson was going to retire. By June 30th, he was gone. The prosecutor's willingness to accept

Pederson's declared interpretation of the Schook memo and the speed with which all of these related reactions occurred gave me the impression that some off-line discussions had influenced the outcomes. District attorneys and the affected parties in an investigation frequently negotiate mutually acceptable remedies to bring closure and resolve cases, a longtime prosecutor reminded me.

Meanwhile, Pulaski County Prosecutor Larry Jegley announced in June that he would not pursue perjury charges involving Gearhart's sworn denial that he told Reynolds to destroy any budget documents. In a brief letter to Legislative Audit Director Roger Norman, Jegley explained his decision:

> While there may be differing versions of the events and discussions concerning matters at issue, none rise to meet the standards meriting further action under Ark 5-53-103 [the state's perjury statue]. We now consider this matter closed.

The law Jegley cited reads, "A person commits perjury if in any official proceeding he or she makes a false material statement, knowing it to be false, under an oath required or authorized by law." Jegley apparently concluded that Gearhart's September 13th declaration under oath ("I categorically deny that we have ever said to anyone to destroy documents. That is not true.") differed in intent and effect from the "Get rid of it" statement that three witnesses reported to Washington County prosecutors. The fact that no one from Jegley's office interviewed any of the three who confirmed the "Get rid of it" declaration may have made it easier to come to that conclusion.

With the two remaining questions now put to rest, the general consensus was that the UA scandal was history. ("The cliché is now applicable: the fat lady has sung on this mess," wrote Max Brantley on his blog.) But I am of the opinion that the real conclusion occurred six months later. In January of 2015, Chancellor G. David Gearhart announced he would be retiring in July. The 62-year-old leader said he wanted to spend more quality time with his grandchildren.

State media reacted to the announcement with reflections on

Gearhart's decades of leadership and service to UA. Record-high student enrollment. Increased levels of research funding. Tremendous growth in the number and quality of campus facilities. And of course unprecedented success in raising money. The accolades that accompanied the stories about his tenure as a chancellor and vice chancellor were well deserved. The only qualifiers in the coverage of his announcement were the inescapable references to his role in the Advancement scandal.

Many people, myself included, had believed that Gearhart's early retirement was inevitable. The long and unnecessarily drawn-out attention over Advancement, FOIAs, and UA-related hearings had become his albatross. As news reports and legislators had revealed, Gearhart had been clearly and directly involved—not in matters that led to Advancement's deficit *per se* but in decisions and actions that resulted in a much bigger and broader university crisis. The resulting scandal was a consequence of multiple judgment and performance failures, and as Senator Keith Ingram pointed out to Gearhart at the final legislative hearing, the one constant in all of them was the chancellor.

To the casual observer, it might have appeared that UA System trustees had, at their January 24, 2014, meeting, absolved Gearhart of responsibility for the scandal, even while they adopted a series of policy changes in response to it at the same meeting. That might have been the impression that Gearhart's supporters on the board wanted to convey when the chancellor received what only he himself declared as a "vote of confidence." But in fact, the board vote on Chair Jane Rogers' statement expressed "support," not "confidence." The words are not synonymous: I can support a person's efforts and still lack confidence in their ability to do the job. The invocation of *support* instead of *confidence* may have been deliberate, reflecting the politics and outcome of the board's executive sessions prior to its public vote on Gearhart. Gearhart himself would recognize that; the chancellor had demonstrated great skill at parsing words during the course of the scandal.

I, for one, do not believe that Gearhart's decision to resign in 2015 was solely his own. Given all that had occurred on his watch regarding the conduct of his top deputies, past and present, it is conceivable, if not likely, that Bobbitt and some trustees felt that in order to change the conversation about UA, they needed to change its leadership. That action, along with the policy changes that trustees adopted following the audits and hearings, would symbolically put the ugliness of the scandal in the past.

However, it wasn't going to happen publicly when the board gathered on January 23, 2014 to discuss Gearhart's future. He had too much influence with a majority of the trustees to be turned out of office at that time. It was more likely that in exchange for an expression of support, Gearhart would agree to announce his retirement at or within a mutually agreed-upon period of time. The fact that he made his announcement nearly a year to the day of the board's executive session on his fate probably was no coincidence.

It didn't have to end that way. Had he sought the audits immediately after receiving Shook's October 2012 report rather than wait months until publicly pressured to do so, he could have gotten the thorough answers that were necessary to identify the problem. He could have publicly announced what had occurred and the disciplinary and remedial steps that were necessary to correct things. He could have humbly and responsibly reported to all stakeholders that things had been mismanaged—both in Advancement and in Pederson's own Finance & Administration division—and accepted full responsibility as UA's chief executive officer, promising to take all proper actions to ensure that such oversights and mistakes never occur again.

By responding in this manner in 2012, Gearhart could have showcased a true and sincere commitment to his promise, first offered in his early days as chancellor, of transparency and accountability to the people of Arkansas, even in times when the results might prove embarrassing. It would have been temporary pain, like ripping off a Band-Aid. It would have been an opportunity to display character:

"Judge us not just on the mistakes we make but on the manner and integrity with which we respond to those mistakes."

Sure, Gearhart would have taken a few rhetorical hits in the media and at the State Capitol. However, he would have weathered them—and earned far more numerous accolades—because he had "done the right thing and got caught doing it." Gearhart would have continued on as chancellor through the conclusion of the capital campaign, which was always his plan. He could have then retired at age 68, widely renowned as one of the most successful and transformative higher education leaders the South had ever seen.

But Gearhart chose a different approach. Consequently, any review of his remarkable legacy as UA's chancellor will always note his involvement in the scandal—an avoidable one that he helped create as a result of his decisions. Right or wrong, he blamed Choate for not watching Sharp closely enough. He kept both of them on the payroll while simultaneously accepting Schook's extraordinary, detailed declaration of their mismanagement and policy violations. He protected his right-hand man, CFO Don Pederson, even in the face of incriminating administrative failures. He insulated Chris Wyrick, his handpicked choice to replace Choate, from any repercussions for the policy violations, FOIA issues, and outrageous behavior he demonstrated after becoming vice chancellor. Gearhart also said things in public and under oath that distorted the truth, compounding the embarrassment to UA and to the governing board that oversees it. With such a string of errors on Gearhart's performance record, the board would have been irresponsible had it allowed their chancellor anything more than a face-saving way out. Which seems to be what occurred.

That said, the UA System Board itself failed to perform at the level the public expects. It abrogated its oversight role by reportedly deferring to Gearhart's appeals to keep Choate and Sharp on the payroll and to keep Pederson and Schook on the job. Furthermore, trustees failed to assert their roles as public stewards when they allowed the scandal to first smolder, then sizzle, and then smolder some more, exerting no apparent desire to consider the possibility that Gearhart's version of the facts might be wrong and self-serving. To be sure, governing boards should not micromanage; however, they have to be willing to intervene when the conduct and performance of their senior administrators seriously threaten the institution's reputation, funding, and credibility. That occurred as a result of the UA scandal; the board, System President Bobbitt, and Gearhart all behaved as though public accountability was something that should be practiced and enforced in private, if at all.

There is an adage that a lawyer who represents himself has a fool for a client. Early on, before the scandal became a scandal, the generally consultative Gearhart personally took charge of the Advancement deficit situation, possibly motivated by uncertainty about how far back his loyal and trusted former aide, Joy Sharp, had been mismanaging the books. In the process, Gearhart chose to limit the voices and perspectives he was willing to consider. Eventually, his circle of advisers narrowed to vulnerable stakeholders such as Pederson and Wyrick, both of whom had their own reputations at risk. Gearhart's fall from grace—at least in the eyes of some—reminds me of a tragic character who becomes afflicted with "Hubris Syndrome." Lord David Owen (a physician, researcher, and British politician) and Duke University Professor Jonathan Davidson have written about this condition. In the May 2009 edition of the Oxford University scholarly journal, *Brain: A Journal of Neurology*, they described certain behavior among successful, entrenched, and powerful leaders:

> Charisma, charm, the ability to inspire, persuasiveness, breadth of vision, willingness to take risks, grandiose aspirations and bold self-confidence—these qualities are often associated with successful leadership. Yet there is another side to this profile, for these very same qualities can be marked by impetuosity, a refusal to listen to or take advice....A common thread tying these elements together is hubris, or exaggerated pride, overwhelming self-confidence and

> contempt for others....How may we usefully think about a leader who hubristically abuses power, damaging the lives of others?

As researchers Owen and Davidson point out, powerful and effective leaders—like Gearhart—can develop such a high level of confidence in the infallibility of their own judgment that they dismiss and demean advice or opinions offered by others, even from those who are fully committed to helping the leader achieve success. In dealing with the perceived threat posed by the Advancement deficit, Gearhart acted in ways that were risky, self-destructive, and at times arrogant. Over time he limited the perspectives he was exposed to, and in some situations chose not to consult with aides whose advice might cause him to consider other possibilities and options that he didn't want to entertain. Hiring Chris Wyrick as Choate's replacement contributed to that cloistered environment. Wyrick rightly wanted to please the boss as a member of "Team Gearhart" and to have a closer, more intimate relationship with the chancellor than he had with his former boss, Athletics Director Jeff Long. But Wyrick put his own ego and desires ahead of his obligations to the university and its stakeholders. So much of the damage inflicted on Gearhart and UA came as a consequence of a single decision: Wyrick's failure to comply with the letter and spirit of FOIA law when, in July of 2013, the *Democrat-Gazette* asked for print and electronic records related to Wyrick's June 20th reorganization presentation to his Advancement staff. Other than revealing Wyrick's temper and impulsiveness, the contents of those materials were of little interest to the media and public. However, they *became* of greater interest only because of Wyrick's unjustifiable delays and incomplete response to the FOIA request. Those acts, along with the behind-the-scenes drama related to them, created a second layer of scandal.

"We have high standards and a national reputation," Jeff Long declared the night he fired football coach Bobby Petrino. "Our expectations of our employees can be no less than what we expect of our students. No individual can be bigger than the team, the Razorback football program, or the University of Arkansas." For a time, the trustees and Gearhart himself behaved in ways that suggested there might be an exception or two to Long's statement.

True, Dave Gearhart performed remarkable, transformational acts on behalf of the University of Arkansas. However, his insular, panic-fueled handling of the Advancement deficit broadened it into a university-wide scandal that damaged his institution and irreparably tarnished his legacy. As Gearhart, Pederson, and others at UA showed, good people in public life can and do make mistakes in judgment and behavior. The test of their mettle is revealed in how they choose to respond to those mistakes: by owning up to them, by concealing them, or by pointing a finger and blaming others. For leaders of public institutions, only the first of the three options is acceptable.

EPILOGUE

In December of 2014, following seven months in an interim post with the University of Wisconsin System, I moved home to Maine with Marcia to finish this book and to launch a consultancy business focused on higher education communications and advocacy. Several other central characters in this book also experienced life changes:

Brad and Julie Choate retired and are living in Georgetown, Texas.

Bruce Pontious became the managing partner of Caritas Unlimited, a philanthropy consultancy business based in Columbus, Ohio.

Graham Stewart became associate vice chancellor for Alumni Relations at Vanderbilt University in Nashville, Tennessee.

Joy Sharp retired from UA after her reassignment ended on June 30, 2013. She later accepted a position with a financial management firm in Northwest Arkansas.

Don Pederson retired from UA on June 30, 2014. Tim O'Donnell, a financial management expert with 22 years of professional experience, was named Pederson's interim successor.

G. David Gearhart was scheduled to retire from UA on July 31, 2015. A national search for Gearhart's successor was underway at the time of this writing.

Meanwhile, Chris Wyrick, Jean Schook, and Denise Reynolds remained employed by UA.

ACKNOWLEDGMENTS

I have many people to acknowledge for their support, encouragement, and in many instances love during the worst days of the scandal and through the recovery and writing periods that followed. I'll start where I began: in Maine. Thanks to the following individuals and families who offered encouragement from immediately after I was fired in August 2013 through to our eventual move back to Maine in December 2014: Tracy Bigney, Joe and Ellen Carr, Monique Hashey, Steve and Kathy Hewins, Jeff Kirlin, the Lammerts, Peggy Leonard, John Lisnik, Jeff and Tammy Mills, Barbara Owen, Harold Pachios, Diana Richardson, Todd Saucier, Gayla Shaw, Gary Striar and Cathy Durand, Elizabeth Sutherland, Donna Thornton, Ellen Toole, Jake Ward, Kelley Wiltbank, Mark Woodward, Becky Wyke, and the Yardleys. In addition, many thanks to these non-Mainers: Scott Farrell, Jimmy Gownley, John and Kathy Halstead, and Randy and Mary Ann Presson.

My thanks also to our amazing friends and extended family in Northwest Arkansas. I am grateful to the Bishops, Kate Evertsen, James and Stacy Keenan, Mike and Debbie Mohler, Barbara Lupton, Luz Morlet, Paul and Kristin Rossi, Megan Sturgeon, the Thomases, Maria Vasquez, Paul Warren, Lydia Worden, James and Sofia Vawter, Chrissy and Mark Wilburn, Kathleen and Patrick

Wolf, and Mike and Sylvia Wulf. Five people who helped me keep things in perspective were my favorite men in black, the current and former priests of St. Joseph Catholic Church in Fayetteville: Fr. John Antony, Fr. Les Farley, Fr. Ravi Gudipalli, Fr. Larry Heimsoth, and Fr. Shawn Wesley. A double-dose of thanks and love to two very special families: the Busteeds and the McClintons.

I met and worked with many wonderful faculty, staff, and students through my work at the University of Arkansas. Thanks to all of you who made the effort to stay in touch. Furthermore, I am grateful to have met scores of donors, alumni, and UA friends during our time with the university. While I knew some better than others, I am grateful that I got to know passionate alumni/ae such as Heather Nelson, Steve Nipper, John Reap, and Stephanie Streett, and dedicated benefactors such as Lewis and Donna Epley, the Hembree family, and Julian and Nana Stewart. You are all examples of what we loved about being part of the Razorback family.

Thanks to the presidents and chancellors I worked for and learned from during my years in higher ed administration: Fred Hutchinson, Peter Hoff, Joseph Westphal, Terry MacTaggart, Rich Pattenaude, and Ray Cross. I'm also grateful to Jane Friedman, my publishing consultant; Andrea Cumbo-Floyd, my senior editor; Jane Littlefield, my editor; Presson Design Associates; design consultant Devon McNerney; and Sutherland Weston Marketing Communications for the help they provided from the start of this project through its publication and promotion. Special thanks to Larry LaRochelle and Sara Wright for providing me with such an inspirational location to work on the book.

Most important of all, thanks to my wonderful family for supporting us so lovingly. Understandably, our experience in Arkansas deeply affected Heather, Johnny, and Sarah. No children like to see their father and mother involved in such a situation. The kids were always there for us. The same goes for the rest of the family: the LaRochelles, Diamonds, Bournivals, Burridges, Crookers, Josephs,

Littlefields, and O'Dares.

But the top honor goes to my wife, Marcia. She had to maintain her energy and enthusiasm for her work as a school principal while coping with the stress of my termination, the hearings, and life after Arkansas. She was an incredible resource throughout the months it took us to research and write this book. Marcia reviewed thousands of documents and fact-checked and proofed everything. Many times she challenged me to provide stronger evidence of my assertions. Through that work, she had to relive some of the most unpleasant experiences of her life. Fortunately, Marcia's passion for the truth is unsurpassed. This book would not be possible without her. That's why I dedicate it to her.

Photo courtesy of Jeff Kirlin

John Diamond spent 22 years as a senior communications leader for universities in Maine, Arkansas and Wisconsin. A former journalism professor at the University of Maine, Diamond was a panelist on *MediaWatch*, a weekly television program on Maine PBS that critiqued media coverage of current events. He also co-produced *Inside Augusta with John Diamond*, a documentary series on the inner workings of state government for which he won a national journalism award. Before moving into higher education, Diamond served eight years in the Maine Legislature, including four years as House Majority Leader. Recipient of a national award for crisis communications, Diamond owns a consulting firm specializing in higher education communications and advocacy. He and his wife Marcia live on the Maine coast, which allows them to indulge their passions for the Red Sox and seafood.

CPSIA information can be obtained
at www.ICGtesting.com
Printed in the USA
LVOW04s1329190116
471346LV00022B/668/P